Endorsement for The City Rebooted

Cities are beginning to recover from and transform following the shock of COVID-19. Singapore is no exception. A casual survey of our Central Business District (CBD) with its much lower traffic volumes, less crowded trains and fewer people in shops attest to this. Yet the suburban malls are as crowded as before as working from home becomes rooted. This book provides an impressive survey and thoughtful insights into how cities will reshape post COVID using the case of Singapore. Ideas like transient social capital, poly centricity and the evolving role of the CBD are being extensively studied. This book will provide both policymakers and researchers an authoritative road map with evidence from Singapore as a living urban laboratory.

Khoo Teng Chye
Director and Practice Professor, NUS Cities
College of Design and Engineering
National University of Singapore

How can cities build back better following the trauma of the COVID pandemic? Beyond the imperatives of recovery, regeneration, and resilience, how might this moment be seized upon as an opportunity to rethink and even reimagine the city? In *The City Rebooted*, an interdisciplinary team of scholars tackle these timely questions from a range of perspectives and vantage points, capitalizing on the singular status of Singapore as a breeding place and proving ground for innovative solutions.

Jamie Peck
Professor, Canada Research Chair in Urban &
Regional Political Economy
Professor of Geography
University of British Columbia

This collection of essays, edited by Prof. Chan Heng Chee and Dr Harvey Neo, offers a refreshing and forward-looking exploratio of urban resilience and transformation in the wake of unprecedented challenges. It is a comprehensive and critical review of Singapore's urban evolution vis-à-vis other cities worldwide, through crisis management and city planning. What sets this book apart is its ability to seamlessly blend academic rigor with practical relevance. It is an essential read for architects, planners, urban enthusiasts, policymakers and anyone interested in the dynamic interplay of urbanism, technology and human interaction. As we continue to grapple with the aftermath of a global crisis, this book provides a roadmap to create cities that are not just resilient but also socially vibrant and inclusive.

Angelene Chan
Chairman
DP Architects

The essays in this excellent book provide well-written, scholarly and highly stimulating guides to possible urban futures for Singapore in the uncertain wake of the COVID pandemic. There is a central focus on how cities are being transformed by changes to the global economy, by the experience of working from home and by broader changes to the nature of work, especially for younger people. The book demonstrates emphatically, however, that human contact and place-making to cultivate urban 'magic' remain vital in a digital world of unparalleled connectivity because of their importance in strengthening resilience and new forms of social capital.

Stephen Hamnett
Emeritus Professor of Urban and Regional Planning
University of South Australia, Adelaide

When the COVID-19 pandemic hit, it gave urban thinkers a valuable opportunity to rethink the city for the better. Our needs are changing, and cities must change with them. In this excellent collection of essays, Chan Heng Chee, Harvey Neo, and their co-authors frame their discussion through the city-state of Singapore — the microcosm and apogee of the modern city. This is an important book, approaching one of the most important questions of our age: how can cities use the digital for the sustainable development needed for the future?

Carlo Ratti
Professor & Director of the Senseable City Lab
Massachusetts Institute of Technology (MIT)
Curator of the Venice Architecture Biennale 2025.

THE CITY REBOOTED

Networks, Connectivity and Place Identities in Singapore

Chan Heng Chee • Harvey Neo *Editors*
Lee Kuan Yew Centre for Innovative Cities
Singapore University of Technology and Design

THE CITY REBOOTED

Networks, Connectivity and Place Identities in Singapore

NEW JERSEY · LONDON · SINGAPORE · BEIJING · SHANGHAI · HONG KONG · TAIPEI · CHENNAI · TOKYO

Published by

World Scientific Publishing Co. Pte. Ltd.
5 Toh Tuck Link, Singapore 596224
USA office: 27 Warren Street, Suite 401-402, Hackensack, NJ 07601
UK office: 57 Shelton Street, Covent Garden, London WC2H 9HE

British Library Cataloguing-in-Publication Data
A catalogue record for this book is available from the British Library.

THE CITY REBOOTED
Networks, Connectivity and Place Identities in Singapore

Copyright © 2024 by World Scientific Publishing Co. Pte. Ltd.

All rights reserved. This book, or parts thereof, may not be reproduced in any form or by any means, electronic or mechanical, including photocopying, recording or any information storage and retrieval system now known or to be invented, without written permission from the publisher.

For photocopying of material in this volume, please pay a copying fee through the Copyright Clearance Center, Inc., 222 Rosewood Drive, Danvers, MA 01923, USA. In this case permission to photocopy is not required from the publisher.

ISBN 978-981-12-8783-1 (hardcover)
ISBN 978-981-12-8784-8 (ebook for institutions)
ISBN 978-981-12-8785-5 (ebook for individuals)

For any available supplementary material, please visit
https://www.worldscientific.com/worldscibooks/10.1142/13719#t=suppl

Desk Editor: Claire Lum

Typeset by Stallion Press
Email: enquiries@stallionpress.com

Printed in Singapore

© 2024 World Scientific Publishing Company
https://doi.org/10.1142/9789811287848_fmatter

Preface

In mid-2019, when co-editor (then Chair of the Lee Kuan Yew Centre for Innovative Cities) Professor Chan Heng Chee first rallied researchers at the centre to work on this collection of essays, COVID-19 was still a largely unknown entity. The premise of the book, as she first pitched to the contributors, was deceptively simple: "In your view, what are some of the most compelling urban challenges we would likely face in the near future and how might we address them?"

While the catalyst of the book was COVID-19, it is not about the pandemic per se, as we very quickly realised. Through the initial sharing of responses to Professor Chan's question, it was obvious the pandemic was not viewed as a paradigmatic shift in how we understand cities. Indeed, the pandemic merely agitates us to address perennial (e.g., decentralisation of urban cores and revitalising the city centre) and nascent (work-life balance, digitisation of social economy) urban challenges with a greater sense of urgency. These are discussions which will resonate beyond Singapore, the empirical focus of the book.

Such a consensus on how we might view the pandemic is all the more remarkable given the fact that the contributors hail from more than half a dozen countries (China, India, Mexico, Singapore, Slovenia, Sri Lanka, Sweden, and the United Kingdom) and represent just as many social science disciplines (anthropology, geography, urban planning, architecture, environmental psychology, urban studies, political science, data analytics, public policy, and organisational studies).

Yet, these differences precisely enable us to make collective sense of the visceral and grounded experience of living through the most trying times of the pandemic together. More importantly, with each additional disciplinary gaze, we gain nuanced knowledge on how to make better cities. A process which sprung from a collective passion, interest, and curiosity to understand an unprecedented crisis became an unexpected lesson on how to conduct serious interdisciplinary research, with unceasing discussions and debates where everyone brought something unique to work towards a common vision. From figuring out a way to measure a concept as amorphous as polycentricity to a relook on how to reclaim and recreate the magic of the city that was amalgamated from an opiniated team of authors (sociologist, geographer and anthropologist), the outcomes are, in our opinion, invigorating and insightful. That is how we do interdisciplinary work.

The book had benefitted from the generous sharing of data by Gojek and the Land Transport Authority of Singapore, and their support is duly acknowledged. Emma Goh has provided invaluable editorial assistance for the project and Serena Lin has been outstanding in attending to each and every administrative matter relating to the project. We thank them both.

Professor Cheong Koon Hean, Chair of Lee Kuan Yew Centre for Innovative Cities, has also participated in many of our contributors' discussions and the insights she shared are much appreciated.

Last but not least, on behalf of my fellow contributors, I put on record our heartfelt gratitude to my co-editor, Professor Chan Heng Chee. She has been indefatigable in shepherding this project to completion. Her attention to detail and her ability to deftly crack the occasional whip on straying or lost sheep are requisite skills all aspiring editors should have. Above all, throughout the entire process, she was an abundance of grace, good humour, and all-round inspired learning. This journey has been an utter joy because of her.

Harvey Neo

Lee Kuan Yew Centre for Innovative Cities
Singapore University of Technology and Design
October 2023

© 2024 World Scientific Publishing Company
https://doi.org/10.1142/9789811287848_fmatter

Notes on Contributors

Chan Heng Chee is Professor and Founding Chair of the Lee Kuan Yew Centre for Innovative Cities, Singapore University of Technology and Design. A political scientist by training, her long career spans both academia (as Director of Institute of Policy Studies and Head of the Political Science Department in the National University of Singapore) and public service (as Singapore's Ambassador to the United States of America and Permanent Representative to the United Nations). Her research interests include international politics, Sino-American relations, urban policy, and urban inequality.

Felicity HH Chan is a Fellow at the Lee Kuan Yew Centre for Innovative Cities and teaches urban planning in the MSc in the Urban Science, Policy, and Planning Programme at the Singapore University of Technology and Design. She enjoys researching urban issues from a socio-spatial angle, and loves experiencing cities by walking. Felicity is the author of *Tensions in Diversity: Spaces for Collective Life in Los Angeles*, published by the University of Toronto Press in 2022.

Samuel Chng is a Senior Research Fellow and heads the Urban Psychology Lab at the Lee Kuan Yew Centre for Innovative Cities at the Singapore University of Technology and Design. He is an applied social psychologist, and his research focuses on human behaviour and decisions in cities across a range of areas including sustainability, mobility, and well-being.

Yunkyung Choi is a Research Fellow at the Lee Kuan Yew Centre for Innovative Cities. She received her PhD (City and Regional

Planning) from the Georgia Institute of Technology. She adopts interdisciplinary approaches to explore the complex interaction between the built environment and urban transportation system, and how this impacts the resilience of cities.

Emma Goh is formerly a Research Assistant at the Lee Kuan Yew Centre for Innovative Cities, Singapore University of Technology and Design. She is presently pursuing her Masters in Urban Planning at the University of California, Berkeley.

Fredrik Hansson is formerly a Research Fellow at the Lee Kuan Yew Centre for Innovative Cities, Singapore University of Technology and Design. He obtained his PhD in Econometrics from Uppsala University, and his dissertation investigates the socio-economic implications of unequal residential living conditions. His broader research interests include urban economic modelling, housing and rental policy/regulation and health economics.

Nazim Ibrahim is a Research Fellow at the Meta Design Lab, Singapore University of Technology and Design. His current research explores frameworks in creating generative and parametric design environments as well as data visualisation for design decision making.

Dinithi Jayasekara is a Research Fellow at the Lee Kuan Yew Centre for Innovative Cities, Singapore University of Technology and Design, and holds a PhD in Economics from Nanyang Technological University, Singapore. She explores economic behaviours of individuals by blending techniques from experimental economics with insights from psychology. Her research interests include applied econometrics, economic growth, long-run development, and behavioural economics.

Sam Conrad Joyce is an Associate Professor and Head of the Meta Design Lab at the Singapore University of Design and Technology, that focuses on applying data, machine learning, and analytics to better understand and design the city. He is interested in visualising novel and under-considered aspects of urbanism and applying generative design to respond to these issues.

Bayi Li is a PhD candidate at the Delft University of Technology. His research focuses on computational social science — integrating diverse approaches such as agent-based modelling, geographic information systems (GIS), and urban planning, to address intractable urban problems. He is presently investigating the complexities of urban stratification through the lens of micro-modelling.

Rafael Martinez is a Research Fellow at the Lee Kuan Yew Centre for Innovative Cities, Singapore University of Design and Technology. He holds a PhD in Anthropology (National University of Singapore, 2018). His research focuses on mainland and insular megacities in Southeast Asia where he looks at informal landscapes and the connection between urban mobilities and temporary social identities.

Špela Močnik is a Research Fellow in inclusive ageing at the University of Southampton, where she researches on public health issues, social determinants of health, as well as inclusive and healthy ageing. She obtained her PhD in Sociology from the University of Sussex on the evolving theory of critical cosmopolitanism.

Harvey Neo is a Professorial Fellow at the Lee Kuan Yew Centre for Innovative Cities, Singapore University of Design and Technology, where he heads the Cities and Urban Science Programme and Urban Environmental Sustainability Programme. His research interests include nature-society issues, urban developmental politics as well as food and animal geographies.

Sara Ann Nicholas is formerly a Research Assistant at the Lee Kuan Yew Centre for Innovative Cities. She is presently with the Urban Redevelopment Authority of Singapore.

Winston Yap is a PhD candidate at the Urban Analytics Lab, National University of Singapore. His research specialises in applying a systems approach to urban planning and design, utilising open data, software, and urban complexity theory.

ps://doi.org/10.1142/9789811287848_fmatter

Contents

Preface	ix
Notes on Contributors	xi
List of Figures	xvii
List of Tables	xxv

Introduction — 1

Post Disaster Cities: Reboot, Rethink or Reconfigure? — 3
Chan Heng Chee & Špela Močnik

The New Economic Trends of Singapore City — 33

Is the City Centre Hollowing Out? — 35
Sara Ann Nicholas & Winston Yap

The Digital Economy Takes Over — 65
Dinithi Jayasekara & Fredrik Hansson

The Future of Office — 105

The Spatial Antifragile Nature of Work in the Age of New Normal — 107
Sam Conrad Joyce

Future of Work is Hybrid, but How? — 129
Sam Conrad Joyce & Nazim Ibrahim

The Future of Polycentres — 161

Polycentricity in a City State? Regional Centres as Singapore's Exceptional Socio-Spatial Development Project — 163
Harvey Neo & Li Bayi

The Emerging Socio-Spatial Implications of Cloud Kitchens and Cloud Stores — 185
Samuel Chng

Sustaining the Magic of the City — 211

Through the Looking Glass Everyday Urbanism in a Pandemic City 2020–2022 — 213
Felicity HH Chan, Yunkyung Choi, Emma En-Ya Goh, Bayi Li

The Magic of Modernity — 242
Chan Heng Chee, Winston Yap & Sara Ann Nicholas

Cultivating Magic: The Discreet Charm of the City Centre — 275
Rafael Martinez, Sara Ann Nicholas & Špela Močnik

Epilogue — 309
Index — 315

© 2024 World Scientific Publishing Company
https://doi.org/10.1142/9789811287848_fmatter

List of Figures

Figure 2.1	Singapore's City Centre	37
Figure 2.2	Point Pattern Distribution of Office, Retail, and Shop House Transactions	41
Figure 2.3	Density and Proximity of Transactions (200m Raster Grid)	42
Figure 2.3.1	Transaction Count Aggregation	42
Figure 2.3.2	K-Nearest Neighbour (KNN-30) Weighted Distance to Nearest Transaction	42
Figure 2.4	A Theoretical Monocentric Bid-Rent Curve as specified by Von Thünen	43
Figure 2.5	Singapore's City Centre's Bid-Rent Curve	44
Figure 2.6	Vacancy Rates in the City Centre from 2019 to Q1 2021	46
Figure 2.7	Median Rental in the City Centre from 2019 to April 2021	47
Figure 2.8	The Upper Plot Shows Office Rental Rate Across Different Planning Areas. The Lower Plot Displays the Overall Central Area Office Rental Rate — Increase (Green) and Decrease (Orange)	48
Figure 2.9	Transacted Office Space in the City Centre from 2019–June 1, 2021	50
Figure 2.10	Concentration of Employed Residents Aged 15 Years and over in Different Industries in the City Centre in 2020	51
Figure 3.1	Scope of the Digital Economy	67

Figure 3.2	Marginal Income Tax Rates in Sweden and Singapore in 2022	78
Figure 3.3	Supply of Gig Talent by Country	80
Figure 4.1	Office Features and Their Digital Counterparts	109
Figure 4.2	A Summary of Office Typology During Different Eras	111
Figure 4.3	The Evolution of the Three Main Workspaces	117
Figure 4.4	Spatial Temporal Relationships of the Office in the City	118
Figure 4.5	Sankey Diagram Showing Current Work Situation During Survey on the Left and Desired Situation on the Right	121
Figure 4.6	Distribution of Work Type by Age Group, with Situation at Time of Survey Above and Ideal Situation Reported Below	122
Figure 4.7	Distribution of Current Work Type at Time of Survey by Gender	123
Figure 4.8	Boxplot of Workers' Time Spent on Interaction Platforms by Percentage of Overall Day (0.0–1.0)	124
Figure 4.9	Various Large Companies with Offices in Singapore and Their Public Policies on the Number of Days of WFH	125
Figure 5.1	Spatial Use Before and During COVID-19	132
Figure 5.2	Examples of Office Configurations Differentiated by the Ability for Workers to Vary Their Seating Locations (Vertical Axis) or Vary Their Working from Office Dates (Horizontal Axis)	135
Figure 5.3	Two Representations of the Same Social Network, Graph (Left) and Adjacency Matrix (Right)	136
Figure 5.4	Key Metrics Used to Evaluate the Performance of a Network	136
Figure 5.5	Indicative Network Configurations	137
Figure 5.6	Hall's Proxemic Distance (Left) and Its Application in a Given Office Configuration (Right)	141

List of Figures   xix

Figure 5.7	Day 2 Snapshot of the Simulation Environment Under Flexible Seating and Schedule with 50 Teams	142
Figure 5.8	Visual Representation of the Independent Model Parameters	143
Figure 5.9	Snapshots of the Spatial Simulation and Resulting Network Model of 5 Teams of Companies in Different Scenarios	144
Figure 5.10	An Example of Individual Social Metrics as Calculated in a Team-Based Network	145
Figure 5.11	Strong Ties Ratio Within Teams (Left) and Among Teams (Right)	147
Figure 5.12	Mean Ties (Frequency) Within Teams (Left) and Among Teams (Right)	148
Figure 5.13	Diversity, Score (Left), and Count (Right)	149
Figure 5.14	Clustering Coefficient	149
Figure 5.15	Mean Distance Between People Within a Team (Left) and With Others (Right)	150
Figure 5.16	Social Network Result at the End of the 4-Week Simulation for a 10-Team Scenario	152
Figure 5.17	Trade-Offs Compared Against Competing Scales of Individuals Flexibility, Intra-Team Interactions and Between-Team Interactions	153
Figire 5.18	Popular Office Configurations Mapped Onto the Trade-Off Diagram	155
Figure 6.1	Data Cleaning Process	169
Figure 6.2	ST–DBSCAN Algorithm to Generate GPS Points Clusters for Each Individual Device	170
Figure 6.3	Land Use Within Centres of Singapore	171
Figure 6.4	Residence Location of Centre's Visitors and Their Mean Centre Weighted by Visiting Frequency	174
Figure 6.5	Daily Average Commuting Number During Weekdays Across Centres From 2019–2022 (Month: April)	175

xx   The City Rebooted: Networks, Connectivity and Place Identities in Singapore

Figure 6.6	Average Trip Count During Weekdays by RTS (MRT+LRT) From April 2019–2022	176
Figure 6.7	Travel Distances Intra- and Inter-towns	177
Figure 6.8	URA Marketing Slogans	180
Figure 7.1	Online Retail Sales Proportion in Singapore From 2019 to 2022	189
Figure 7.2	Online Food and Beverage Sales Proportion in Singapore From 2019 to 2022	190
Figure 7.3	Cloud Kitchen With Seven Brands Occupying a Retail Unit in East Village Shopping Centre	191
Figure 7.4	Licensed Food Establishments in Singapore From 2010 to 2021	204
Figure 8.1	Generation COVID at Our Socially-Distanced University Graduation Ceremony	216
Figure 8.2	An Other-Than-Human's Response to Social Distancing Measures	217
Figure 8.3	Preschools Adjusting for COVID	217
Figure 8.4	One of the Many Unsuccessful Illogical Barricades to Redirect Habitual Foot Traffic	218
Figure 8.5	A COVID Hopscotch? Queueing at Burger King Along Bukit Timah Road	218
Figure 8.6	The 30-Minutes Wait After My First Dose of COVID Vaccination in a Community Centre Turned Into an Emergency Vaccination Hall	219
Figure 8.7	Domestic Travel Experience: Crossing New Border Control at Jurong East Mall	219
Figure 8.8	Record 120 New Coronavirus Cases in Singapore, 2 Foreign Worker Dormitories Gazetted as Isolation Areas	219
Figure 8.9	No More Loud and Convivial Chinese Dinners, Please!	221
Figure 8.10	Ice-Cream Date in a Two-by-Two Box at Salted Caramel Along Lorong Kilat Near Beauty World Metro Station	222
Figure 8.11	All Masked up and Waiting at the Door for Customers to Return During a Peak Dinner Hour in Kovan Neighbourhood	222

List of Figures   xxi

Figure 8.12	The Rise of the Lockdown Circuit Breaker Bento Sets to Minimise Food Sharing in Groups and Make the Lunch Hour While Working From Home Easy	223
Figure 8.13	No Dining in, Takeout Only at the Local Burger King Joint	223
Figure 8.14	Hygiene Dividers Separate Each Seat in a School Canteen From the Front and Sides	224
Figure 8.15	No Group Seating Allowed — Lunching Alone at a Table for Six at Bendemeer Market and Food Centre	225
Figure 8.16	A Taste of Normalcy — Satay at Lau Pa Sat After the Easing of Restrictions	225
Figure 8.17	How Home-Based Learning Shows up Inequality in Singapore — A Look at Three Homes	226
Figure 8.18	An Empty Central Business District During COVID-19	227
Figure 8.19	The Impossible Juggle: Parenting and Working From Home During COVID-19	228
Figure 8.20	Working From Home Right After Maternity Leave Without Being Able to Hire a Helper	229
Figure 8.21	Home Office for a Couple	229
Figure 8.22	Working Hard to Make Iconic Fullerton Bay Singapore Beautiful	230
Figure 8.23	Workers Waiting to be Picked up by the Company Bus After Work in Upper Bukit Timah	230
Figure 8.24	Staying Sane: Neighbourhood Walks and Community Gardening During COVID-19	231
Figure 8.25	Mask-up! Then Play, a Child Catching Frogs at a Farm in Yio Chu Kang	232
Figure 8.26	About a Month Before the Lockdown… Picnicking Outside Somerset Metro Station on a Late Sunday Afternoon	232
Figure 8.27	Solitude in the City at The Guoco Tower in Tanjong Pagar	233

Figure 8.28	Social Distancing Yoga at Capitol Theatre Plaza in Downtown Singapore on a Weekday Night	233
Figure 8.29	A Collage of Safe-Distancing Signs from Singapore Botanic Gardens and Bukit Timah Nature Reserve Created by Bayi Li	234
Figure 8.30	Christmas Wonderland at Gardens by the Bay After the Lifting of Restrictions	235
Figure 8.31	The Flower Dome at Gardens by the Bay During and Post Pandemic	236
Figure 8.32	Silence in the Gallery	237
Figure 8.33	My First Visit to Singapore Started With a 14-Day Quarantine at a Hotel, Where I Could View the Empty Streets	238
Figure 8.34	Great to See the Iconic Symbol Without Tourists in Merlion Park	239
Figure 8.35	A Surreal City of Dreams and Stark Realties Colliding — A View From a Cable Car From Sentosa to Mount Faber	239
Figure 8.36	My Daughter Was Amazed by One of the Exhibitions at Marina Bay Sands	240
Figure 9.1	Traffic Volume Into the City (A.M. Peak) With ALS and ERP Implementation	252
Figure 9.2	Car Ownership Aspirations Among Youths	253
Figure 9.3	EV Purchase Intentions Among Vehicle Owners and Non-Vehicle Owners	253
Figure 9.4	Jurong Innovation District	260
Figure 9.5	Rack Clad High Bay Warehouse Provides Optimal Factory Space Utilisation and Goods Retrieval From Vertical Storage Locations	260
Figure 10.1	Magical Town in Mexico	282
Figure 10.2	Fatahillah Square in Kota Tua, Jakarta	285
Figure 10.3	A Gathering in Kota Tua for a Traditional Music Concert	286
Figure 10.4	Interesting Finds Along Tiong Bahru's Back Alleys	288

Figure 10.5	Tiong Bahru's Low-Rise Flats in Contrast With the Nearby City Centre	289
Figure 10.6	Summary of Case Studies	290
Figure 10.7	Light to Night Festival in Singapore	294

© 2024 World Scientific Publishing Company
https://doi.org/10.1142/9789811287848_fmatter

List of Tables

Table 2.1	Office Transactions in the City Centre from 2019–June 1, 2021	49
Table 2.2	Top 3 Industries for Individual Planning Areas in the City Centre	51
Table 2.3	Inflow and Outflow of Firms to/from the City Centre	52
Table 3.1	Global Ranking of Singapore in e-Trade Indicators	76
Table 3.2	Singapore-Based Unicorn Companies	88
Table 6.1	Visiting Frequency and Clusters (Places) Over Three Years	172
Table 6.2	Descriptive Statistics of Visiting Frequency Change for year 2020 and 2021 Compared to 2019	172
Table 7.1	Summary Table of Typology of Cloud Kitchens in the Singapore Context	192
Table 7.2	Table of the Locations of Key Cloud Kitchens in Singapore	195
Table 7.3	Table of Comparison Between Operating a Cloud Kitchen Operation and a Traditional Kitchen Operation	197
Table 7.4	Summary Table of Comparison of Major Cloud Stores in Singapore	199
Table 7.5	Summary of Key Differences in the Comparison of the Considerations When Setting up Cloud Kitchen and Cloud Stores	203
Table 10.1	Survey on Citizens and the City: Changing Perceptions of Singaporeans (2021)	279
Table 10.2	Demographic Table	300

xxv

Introduction

© 2024 World Scientific Publishing Company
https://doi.org/10.1142/9789811287848_0001

Post Disaster Cities: Reboot, Rethink or Reconfigure?

Chan Heng Chee & Špela Močnik

As the COVID-19 pandemic entered its fourth year, World Health Organization (WHO) Director-General Tedros Adhanom Ghebreyesus said on May 5, "With great hope, I declare COVID-19 over as a global health emergency" (World Health Organization 2023a). According to WHO's Coronavirus Dashboard on the same day, the cumulative cases worldwide stood at 765,222,293, with nearly seven million deaths (World Health Organization 2023b).

At the start of the COVID-19 pandemic in February 2020, there were unknown unknowns. After a year and then two years of the virus, there were known knowns and known unknowns. The COVID-19 virus mutates; vaccinations are essential to protect the community; social-distancing and masks help, but painfully, the physical health recovery and the economic recovery could take a longer time.

The pandemic traumatised cities. The upheaval was sudden and sharp. Lockdowns were imposed to contain the contagion. The streets went dead. The traffic noise ended. There was an unprecedented stillness. Birds came back to the city, and birdsong pierced the air. Initially, there was hyperventilation about the death of the city. Urbanists, urbanologists, architects, realtors, business people, and city leaders have been analysing the trajectory of city recovery and economic recovery; the two are intrinsically related if the return to pre-pandemic activity would be at all possible. The United Kingdom House of Commons' Housing, Communities and Local Government

Committee held a hearing on "Supporting Our High Street after COVID-19" on June 10, 2021 (House of Commons and Levelling Up, Housing and Communities Committee, 2021). It was among the many commissions and committees convened by cities to think through and plan for the post-pandemic phase. The reality is that economic recovery is an existential issue after life/health issues, or in tandem with health issues. The population has been through a great disruption, but it is also a great opportunity for radical rethinking and committed action.

What does the coronavirus pandemic mean for cities? Leading urbanists like Richard Florida argue that great cities will survive the coronavirus; Thomas Campanella postulated that cities through history have endured terrible pandemics, and flourished thereafter, growing larger and more dense. Edward Glaeser is concerned that if the pandemic is the new normal, millions of service jobs in cities will disappear, especially in the retail, leisure, and hospitality sectors, and Bruce Katz optimistically sees new institutions and new government agencies emerge from the crisis (Florida *et al.* 2020). Carlos Moreno, the leading advocate of the "15-minute city" concept, believes "there will never be" a return to city life as it was before the coronavirus (Moreno *et al.* 2021; Yeung 2021).

An avalanche of commentaries, articles and books are being written to imagine the great reset and redesign of cities. Some ideas have already been put in place. How do we jumpstart the economy, reconfigure education, the office, the built environment, redesign health infrastructures, plan travel and recalibrate the work-life dialectic? The strategies and solutions will be different in different cities, regions, and continents. Urbanists and planners already observe the rise of the bicycle and bicycle lanes, the yearning for more green space and parks, people moving to the suburbs, the rise of neighbourhood towns, the preference to work from home, and the ubiquity of food deliveries. These developments have implications on the reshaping of the urban space and could be the new ways people choose to live. The crisis has also rejuvenated long-standing ideas which had been put on the back burner as was the case for the aforementioned 15-minute city with Paris mayor Anne Hidalgo as its strong champion. Moreno believes neighbourhoods can be designed to contain all the amenities we need to live within no more than a 15-minute walk from the person's front door. Besides, this model, it is argued, produces a city built on low-carbon use. Melbourne is interested to design the "20-minute neighbourhood", and in Singapore, the Land Transport Authority's Master Plan for 2040 envision "20-minute towns".

COVID-19 hit Singapore on January 23, 2020 when the first case of a tourist from Wuhan tested positive for the virus. On February 19, 2020, MOH reported cases still at a low — 50 cases in hospital and 34 fully recovered. 2,593 close contacts were placed under quarantine. But by end April 2020, the numbers exploded in the thousands in the foreign workers dormitories, turning Singapore from a gold standard exemplar in its handling of the virus to a cautionary tale. We lived through the Delta variant, and then the Omicron variant. With 80% of the population vaccinated, Singapore prepared in early 2022 to enter the endemic stage of COVID. After nearly two years of lockdowns and circuit breakers, the mood of the city state is to return to normal activity as soon as possible. The rush to return to the office is uneven. Jobs have been lost, businesses face closures. New economic activities have risen, whether of comparable economic value of those lost remains to be seen. But there are lingering concerns for health and safety.

This book proposes to investigate and reimagine the inevitable socio-spatial reconfiguration of the city after the pandemic using the city state of Singapore as a laboratory. Globally, as people struggle to find the new normal in their lives, or living with an endemic challenge, the clear consequence is that whatever the path of the virus, a great reset will take place. Government strategies seek to rebuild the economy, safeguard education space, rework the health infrastructure, and citizens reimagine lifestyle and travel, social gatherings, and review what is important in their lives. It is also an opportunity for planners to tackle some of the larger enduring questions of designing *the* ideal city which will provide a better quality of life for its citizens.

We have an opportunity to redesign our city, not just to introduce new interventions to build our physical environment back better, but also attend to existing ones with a greater sense of urgency. While it was obvious to draw upon studies on urban resilience to provide theoretical grounding for this project, we recognise that in the end, everything can be added to the taxonomy of the resilience framework or considered resilient. The Rockefeller's 100 Resilient Cities launched in 2013 to help cities build resilience to meet the physical, economic, and social challenges of the 21st century produced a framework of drivers with the help of Arup International Development. It focused basically on city risk assessment and dealing with climate adaptation. In 2019, the 100 Resilient Cities programme was ended because of lack of resources and the departure of the champion of the concept. Its lasting legacy was to encourage cities to appoint a City Resilience Officer. The literature on resilience and resilience frameworks highlight ideas and practices that if implemented would make a community, city, or country more resilient — a to-do list, usually highly general in its recommendations, which begs the question of its usefulness. The most important first step is to acknowledge that there are dissimilar and distinct disasters and crises due to scale, complexity, and depth that have overwhelmed cities and countries. In this study, we are not looking at recovery from physical damage to the city from natural disaster or climate change. It is recovery from a collective trauma or mass stress and restarting activity.

The most useful way of adopting the concept of urban resilience when talking about cities in a post pandemic, post-crisis context is offered by Vale and Campanella (2005) in their edited volume *The Resilient City: How Modern Cities Recover from Disaster*. It helps us understand why some cities do better than others and explains the variations in their recovery. After studying a number of cities hit by disasters, from the great fire of Chicago, the earthquake in Tangshan, China to the 9/11 terrorist attacks on the twin towers in New York City, the authors extracted twelve common messages which came out of the stories of urban resilience which could be enormously helpful in any rebuilding or redesign of post-crisis cities.

The axioms resonating with our project are recalled here in the words of the authors (Vale and Campanella 2005):

1. Inventing narratives of resilience are a political necessity. They tend to restore legitimacy to the government presiding over the crisis. And every crisis or disaster must be interpreted as opportunities for progressive reform. Not only should there be physical reconstruction of the built environment, there must be a narrative framework that helps the psychological, emotional, and symbolic recoveries of the people.
2. Urban rebuilding symbolises human resilience. Urban reconstruction is a highly visible enterprise and can be viewed as a heroic sense of renewal and well-being. We rebuild our cities to reassure ourselves about the future.
3. Resilience exploits the power of place. Here, there is every attempt to preserve the old social, religious, and familial networks of the citizens living there before the disaster.
4. Finally, a resilient city is a constructed phenomenon, "not just in the literal sense that cities get reconstructed brick by brick, but in a broader cultural sense."

RECOVERY OF CITIES POST-CRISIS

We begin our investigation into the post-pandemic reconfiguration of Singapore by looking at a few cases in the recent past to understand what might be planned and undertaken. We must assume no two societies, no two cities, will have exactly the same path.

Here, recovery is understood as the measures taken by the government, residents, or anyone who deals with any kind of consequences of a crisis that try to restore, heal, or repair what was destroyed. We will look at different mechanisms that cities employed when dealing with catastrophes of different kinds. We selected cities that were hit by health catastrophes — Singapore, Hong Kong, and Taipei hit by the SARS pandemic in 2003, and cities that suffered terrorism attacks — New York, London, and Paris. Interestingly, despite the different approaches to recovery due to different types, scale, and consequences of each disaster, all the cities studied devised recovery strategies for the tourism sector as a centrepiece for recovery. Tourism is an important economic backbone of many cities and a driving force in urban and economic development.

The tourism industry is all about human movement and activities, be it aviation, shipping, or F&B businesses. When a disaster hits, this industry is among the most affected ones since disasters usually stop human movement. It is also a pillar of many economies and can spur growth in other sectors. Moreover, it can be linked to social capital (McGehee *et al.* 2010). It is an indicator of trust and safety and therefore an expression of social capital. Tourism in post-disaster recovery is important for two reasons. First, its revival is closely linked to boosting the economy and can help recover destinations financially. Second, tourism is about people and trust — once the tourist activities resume, they serve as the key indicator to show that life goes on and that the destination is safe. Post-disaster tourism was shown to serve as a form of resilience for the affected communities (Liu-Lastres *et al.* 2020).

The aim of this section is to understand recovery, to provide a contextual interpretation of the primary mode of recovery for each urban disaster. Each case study contains information about the disaster, its consequences, and the recovery tactics. Six case studies are described in more detail in the next section to shed light for our search for a post COVID-19 recovery.

CASE STUDIES

Severe Acute Respiratory Syndrome 2003

The first reported case of Severe Acute Respiratory Syndrome (SARS) was in the Guangdong Province in China in November 2002 (Chen *et al.* 2009). Soon after, it spread to Hong Kong, Taiwan, and Singapore. Studies have shown that the emergence of SARS had great negative impacts on global tourism and Southeast Asian economies (Chen *et al.* 2009). In Asia, the tourism and aviation industries were hit particularly hard (Barua 2020). There was no precedent on how to react in a pandemic such as SARS. It was scary to say the least, as the fatality rates were high, and many frontline workers and their families were affected.

Singapore: Combatting SARS with intensive public health measures and effective communication

The 2003 SARS outbreak in Singapore began on February 25 and lasted till May 5, 2003, with 238 probable cases and 33 deaths (Ministry of Health, Singapore 2003). The clusters formed mainly in hospitals and 41% of all cases were healthcare workers. When the outbreak began, Singapore did not have any diagnostic tests available, which prompted the city state to set up infrastructure for tests and diagnosis, including the National Centre for Infectious Diseases, which later played a critical role in the COVID-19 pandemic (Amazon Web Services 2020). Despite the initial shock and trauma, SARS was a relatively short (four months) pandemic, after which Singapore economic activity saw a sharp increase (Chan 2021). In 2003, the economy achieved a 1.1% growth despite the pandemic (Monetary Authority of Singapore 2004). This was possible because of the quick reaction of the government, tight prevention measures, an effective communication strategy, and a timely introduction of a relief package of $230 million to assist targeted sectors of the economy, particularly tourism and transport-related industries (Ministry of Finance, Singapore and Ministry of Trade and Industry, Singapore 2003).

The Singapore government responded to SARS with a clear, three-pronged approach to manage the outbreak: 1) prevention and control in hospitals, 2) prevention and control in the community, 3) prevention of trans-border spread (Ministry of Health, Singapore 2003). Having a good communication strategy played a big role in implementing these public health measures. Initially, the government communicated with citizens through press releases and media, and after one month, released a public education campaign to educate the citizens on SARS and the appropriate behaviour to stop the spread (Deurenberg-Yap *et al.* 2005). The introduction of "a very 'wide-net' surveillance, isolation and quarantine policy" proved to be successful in containing the outbreak (Tan 2006). The Ministry of Health adopted a broad definition for suspicious cases which resulted in an early isolation of probable cases, and thus a large number of people being quarantined. It also established a contact tracing centre which helped effectively track potential cases. Furthermore, strict temperature monitoring in schools, airports, and seaports reassured the public that the community was safe (Tan 2006).

During the SARS epidemic, visitor arrivals to Singapore fell by 62% in April and 71% in May 2003 (Deurenberg-Yap *et al.* 2005). To revive the tourism industry, the Singapore Tourism Board (STB) developed two marketing and communication campaigns, *Cool Singapore* and *Step Out Singapore*. The first campaign focused on reassuring residents and visitors that Singapore was a safe destination, while the second campaign introduced special events and offers from retailers and food outlets that regenerated Singapore's vibrant street atmosphere. After the SARS epidemic officially ended in Singapore, the STB and local industry partners launched the *Singapore Roars* campaign, which included "building confidence through testimonial advertisements; media and travel trade familiarisation trips; attractive packages and discounts; and a worldwide advertising blitz in key source markets". These three campaigns helped recover visitors number by 76% in June 2003 and by another 43% in July 2003. Throughout Singapore's SARS crisis, due to their high trust in the government, citizens complied with the health requirements and protocols. Strong political leadership that ensured a coordinated and effective response was crucial in containing the outbreak (Tan 2006).

Reportedly, one of the effects of SARS was to raise hygiene awareness throughout the city state, such as the frequent washing of hands and keeping surfaces clean.

Hong Kong: Launching an international communication campaign for recovery

The 2003 SARS outbreak in Hong Kong lasted from March 11 to June 6. There were 1,750 confirmed cases and 286 deaths (Lee 2003). For Hong Kong, the SARS epidemic was a crisis of exceptional proportion, and the government and health system were not fully prepared to deal with this mysterious illness. The end product of the crisis was to help Hong Kong create a crisis management plan, rehaul its healthcare infrastructure, ensure timely information sharing and build up its communication capabilities (Lai and Wai 2010).

Tourism services and air travel were severely affected during the outbreak. Restaurants and retail sales dropped by 10–50% (Siu and Wong 2004). Chinese restaurants were the most affected and lost as much as 90% of their business during the outbreak (Tse, So, and Sin 2006). In April 2003, the Hong Kong General Chamber of Commerce began lobbying for government relief for SARS-affected businesses. Hong Kong's Chief Executive announced a HK$11.8 billion (S$2 billion) package that included tax rebates, lower rent for shops in public shopping malls and reduced water and sewage charges for restaurants (Tse, So, and Sin 2006). Hong Kong's recovery strategy involved the participation of the business sector, community, and the government, which focused on SARS' impact on the decreased local consumption and lower numbers of foreign travellers (Legislative Council of Hong Kong 2003).

The impact on inbound tourism to Hong Kong was felt almost immediately. Visitor numbers fell by 65% in April, and by 68% in May 2003 (PATA Crisis Resource Center 2020). The Hong Kong Government responded to the crisis in tourism with an economic relief package worth US$1.5 billion and a communication campaign. They dedicated US$130 million to relaunch the economy and tourism industry (Au 2008). The communication campaign consisted of three phases: Response, Reassurance, and Recovery. The goal of the first phase, Response, was to keep locals and foreigners informed about the measures to contain the virus and track the carriers (PATA Crisis Resource Center 2020). The second phase, Reassurance, occurred after the WHO lifted travel advisory to Hong Kong and further reassured key audiences that Hong Kong was free of SARS, which included information about safety, cleanliness standards, and temperature screening. The last phase, Recovery, built a strong image of Hong Kong internationally and promoted it as a desirable destination for both business and leisure (Au 2008).

Taipei: Introducing a standardised epidemic control system

The first SARS case in Taiwan was reported on March 14, 2003 in the Hoping Hospital in Taipei. WHO announced its SARS warning on travel to Taipei from May 8 to June 17, 2003. There were 668 patient cases and 181 deaths (Chen *et al.* 2009). Taipei city's response was directed by the government of Taiwan.

Taiwan's response to SARS was initially chaos and panic (Khaliq 2020). But Taiwan learnt the lessons painfully. A task force was then established with medical experts from the Department of Health and the National Research Institutes to conduct a rapid assessment of every reported case, with isolation, quarantine, contact tracing, and laboratory examinations set up. The government gave twice-daily updates to improve communication as well as briefings to the foreign businesses and embassies.

Taiwan relied heavily on tourism to gain international exposure. A state policy "Challenge 2008: Plan for Multiplying Tourism" was introduced in 2002 to attract five million tourists by 2008 (Chen *et al.* 2009). However, Taiwan's tourism industry was severely affected by the SARS outbreak. The airline and tourism-related sectors suffered the most (Chou, Kuo, and Peng 2004). Arrival numbers fell by around 71% in the second quarter on a year-on-year basis (Mao, Ding, and Lee 2010). The government and private sector jointly created tourism promotion programmes and new tour destinations to attract foreign tourists under the Post-SARS Recovery Plan. As a result, the number of arrivals to Taiwan recovered to 90% of the 2002 level by the end of 2003. To reassure visitors and locals, travel-related procedures, such as screening of travellers for fever and providing tourists with health information, were put in place (Chen *et al.* 2009).

Furthermore, the authorities introduced a NT$300 billion (S$14 billion) budget that expanded public construction and public services over the subsequent three years to buffer the negative SARS impacts. To increase opportunities for businesses, the Ministry of Economic Affairs (MOEA) and the Bureau of Foreign Trade sponsored overseas promotional campaigns for local firms (Waugh 2003). The MOEA also actively promoted video conferencing that was available for free to Taiwan's businesses and their overseas counterparts. In addition to these measures, the government built up an internationally standardised epidemic control system and introduced guidelines to defend Taiwan from SARS (Chou, Kuo, and Peng 2004).

Studying how Hong Kong, Singapore, and Taipei emerged from the SARS crisis, it should be said, the outbreak was, at the start, frightening because the nature and path of SARS as a disease and its spread was baffling. Medical professionals were working in the dark, resulting in many health workers infected and succumbing to the disease. Fortunately, the duration of the epidemic was short, ending abruptly within three months in all three locations. The economic consequences were not as dire as anticipated, although economic assistance packages were swiftly introduced to help business sectors. Interestingly, all three sites bounced back by opening up to tourism again. The major outcome for all the cities was a rehaul of the healthcare system which allowed them to deal better with future health crises. In fact, in early 2020 as COVID-19 emerged, Hong Kong, Singapore, and Taipei were cited as exemplars in managing the health crisis.

New York City: Rebirth after 9/11

On the morning of September 11, 2001, four passenger planes were hijacked by al-Qaeda, and three of them were crashed into buildings. In New York City, two planes crashed into the north and south towers of the World Trade Centre, which killed 2,753 people (CNN 2022). This was a shocking and unprecedented attack that changed the world forever.

Immediately after the attack, 40,000 jobs and 10 million m² of office space were lost (Gotham 2008). In the subsequent months, the economic situation worsened. Around 10% of office space was destroyed, which amounted to US$30 billion in value; in the fourth quarter of 2001, around 100,000 people lost their jobs predominantly in the financial industry, tourism, and air transport; and in the first three months after the attack, the gross city product declined by almost US$12 billion (Eisinger 2007). Furthermore, nearly 18,000 businesses in and around the World Trade Centre complex were dislocated, disrupted, or destroyed, the vast majority of which were small businesses (Makinen 2002). Gross City Product (GCP) was reduced by US$27.3 billion in the subsequent year.

The road to recovery: Investments in high-end commercial real estate

The federal response to the crisis in New York City had two objectives: 1) to reimburse the city for emergency expenditures directly related to the attacks; and 2) to reinvigorate the local economy with economic development incentives. More specifically, by 2002, federal aid was disbursed to serve three different purposes: debris removal and direct aid to individuals and businesses (US$11.2 billion), economic development incentives (US$5 billion), and infrastructure projects (US$5.5 billion) (Makinen 2002). Small businesses were most affected, and therefore a part of the aid was dedicated to them. More than 4,000 loans were made available to firms located in the World Trade Centre complex while the federal government helped small businesses financially in the form of the Community Development Block Grant fund. In the first phase of recovery, US$2.4 billion were made available through the Community Development Block Grant in the form of Business Recovery Grants (BRG) and Residential Recovering Grants (RRG) (Gotham 2008). Almost 40% of the BRG resources were allocated to major corporations and individual financial traders. In the subsequent phase, another US$1.3 billion of funding were used. The Liberty Bond programme of US$8 billion was created, the main beneficiaries of which were developers who would build new towers at the destruction site. In other words, subsidised investment in high-end commercial real estate became the primary mode of recovery to the post 9/11 crisis.

The consequences of the attacks and the subsequent economic recession were strongly felt in the tourism industry. Airlines experienced at least a 30% reduction in demand during the initial shock period (Misrahi 2016). The reduced business-travel budgets severely affected high-spending business travel, especially those relating to conventions and other meetings within the US (Bonham, Edmonds, and Mak 2006). The number of trips abroad by the US residents also diminished, from 60.9 million trips in 2000 to 54.2 million trips in 2003.

The recovery period for the tourist numbers to return to pre-9/11 level was long, around four years. More specifically, it took the hotel industry in New York City 34 months to recover from 9/11 attacks, whereas the wider US hotel market took 45 months (Misrahi 2016). New York City's response to the crisis in tourism comprised an active promotional campaign that promoted visits to New York as a patriotic act as well as deployment of police officers to guard government buildings and landmarks (Fainstein 2002). Other security measures for travellers included the deployment of armed security guards in the city and at the airports, more surveillance cameras, and the establishment of the Office of Homeland Security, among others.

London: Resilience in the face of 7/7 bombings

In the morning of July 7, 2005, less than 24 hours after London was awarded the 2012 Olympic Games, the city of London was subject to four different bombings on underground trains and a double-decker bus. The four terrorist attacks left 52 people dead and more than 700 injured (Holliday 2018). City transportation and road traffic were severely affected, and the mobile phone system broke down.

The 7/7 attacks caused people to perceive the risk of terror to be at major transit hubs (Manelici 2017). There was a 6% fall in house prices near the main rail hubs of London and this decline persisted for one year. Studies have also shown that businesses were negatively impacted as the new firms — especially those relying on foot traffic — were less willing to locate near major public transit stations for up to four years.

There was a short-term negative effect on the tourism industry in the initial month after the attacks, with the tourism falling by 18% compared to the previous year (Savitch 2008). By September 2005, tourism revived, and two records were set that year: foreign visitors made 30 million trips to the United Kingdom (UK), during which they spent a record £14.2 billion (Katz 2006).

The Road to recovery: Rhetoric of resilience forms part of British national identity

London Bombings Relief Charitable Fund (LBRCF) was established within days of the bombings. In one year, it paid almost £12 million to more than 300 people who had been affected by the attack (Harris 2016). Immediately after the attacks, the theme of resilience dominated speeches and responses by political leaders (Bean, Keränen, and Durfy 2011). The theme was used after the attacks to "activate a specific image of British national identity" and as a UK security strategy.

After the terrorist attack, the UK instilled agreed-upon procedures in the case of terrorist attacks, which included establishing crisis management relations among government bodies and the media (APEC Counter-Terrorism Working Group 2017). Numerous counter-terrorism campaigns promoted the idea of a community-in-unity in the face of terrorism.

Culture played an important role in recovery, too. Daniel Craig era Bond movies could be said to "have ultimately rehabilitated post-7/7 London's fallen identity and precarious position on terror alert". These movies recoded the status of London to a *destination*, rather than just a *location* (Holliday 2018). Furthermore, a permanent memorial dedicated to the bombings in London's Hyde Park was unveiled in 2009. The designers worked with the bereaved families to be able to represent their loved ones sensitively and powerfully. Several years after, the London Summer Olympics 2012 brought a further "moment of healing" for the people of London and sent a clear message on embracing multiculturalism (Seidler 2015).

Paris: Getting past horrific terrorist attacks 2015

Paris saw two terrorist attacks in 2015. The attack on the French satirical weekly newspaper Charlie Hebdo took place on January 7, 2015, in Paris, France, by two soldiers of the ISIS/Daesh. In the attacks, 12 people were killed, and many were injured. Only a few months after the attack on Charlie Hebdo, France suffered another terrorist attack. On November 13, 2015, three coordinated attacks happened in Paris. One of the locations was the concert hall Bataclan, where 89 persons were killed; other locations included bars and a soccer stadium.

The tourism industry was hit hard after both attacks in 2015. Tourist numbers from countries like Japan, Russia, and China dropped by over 50%, 35%, and 13% respectively (Chan 2021). However, at the end of 2016, Paris' tourism completely recovered. Paris saw as many visitors at the end of 2016 as it did at the end of 2014, suggesting that the number of tourists returned to pre-attacks figures (Schreuer 2017). This was possible because of the effective response and strategy.

The immediate reaction after the attack on Charlie Hebdo was one of intense solidarity. There were numerous gatherings and marches in *Place de la République*, which became a "living memorial" over the course of 2015 (Titley *et al.* 2017). On the day of the Charlie Hebdo attacks, thousands of people gathered at the *Place de la République*, bringing pens that symbolised freedom of expression and laying candles across the square. Many mourners were carrying placards saying "*Je suis Charlie*". On January 11, 2015, more than one million people of different religions, races and ages joined over 40 presidents and prime ministers on the streets of Paris, which was a strong showcase of solidarity against the threat of Islamic extremism (Alderman and Bilefsky 2015).

The Road to recovery: Effective response and strategy

France undertook serious measures for the tourism industry to recover, which can be summarised in seven steps (World Travel & Tourism Council 2018). First, the French president responded to security concerns fast by deploying more than 10,000 military and police personnel across 830 key locations in the country to assure French citizens and others that France was a safe tourist destination. Second, France created a Made in France campaign worth €2.5 million. The French government, airlines, regional tourist boards, the tourism ministry, and other stakeholders contributed to the development of this campaign. Third, France used social media widely to promote the tourism campaign and counter false news about France and safety. They employed a full-time social media manager and invited over 70 influencers to experience the country and report on it on their social media channels. Fourth, France used a targeted approach for 16 selected markets such as Japan, Russia, and China that supplied the most tourists in the past years. Fifth, France introduced 48-hour visa approvals for countries in Africa, the Middle East, and the Far East. Sixth, France promoted a warm welcome for all tourists, including welcome posters at the airports, information in multiple languages, welcome text messages in visitors' languages, and training for the hospitality sector. Lastly, France used smart technology, e.g., automation for passport control, provision of free Wi-Fi that enabled tourists to share positive messages about France, and the development of apps for tourists.

LESSONS FROM THE SIX CASES

Through the six study cases of two types of urban disasters, we saw that cities and countries employed various measures to recover from them. The way cities reacted depended on the impact of the disaster, culture, national resources, and other factors. The above examples of disasters and recovery responses differed greatly, and it would be difficult to find many commonalities. What, then, can we learn from the experiences of the six case studies?

Despite their varied experiences, we can name at least four generalisable actions that were adopted in all six cities, which could perhaps serve as a sort of a blueprint for future recoveries of disasters. First, all disasters impacted the tourism industry negatively, and therefore all cities and governments prioritised reviving the tourism industry after the event. The tourism industry is "a useful gauge of resilience because of its sensitivity to large-scale, highly publicised violence" (Savitch 2008). Global tourism in the 21st century has been hit by crises such as terrorist attacks and disease outbreaks. However, the impact of these on global tourism was relatively short-term and almost not notable, with the exceptions of SARS (−0.4%) and the global economic crisis (−4.0%) leading to declines in international arrivals (Gössling, Scott, and Hall 2021). Tourism was one of the first sectors to be revived not only because of its importance to the economy, but also because opening up to tourists meant that the destinations were safe again and that trust was strengthened between the government, citizens, and foreigners. Despite tourism as a system being relatively resilient to external shocks, the COVID-19 pandemic might cause an unprecedented impact and delay the recovery period because of the mutation of the virus and the border closures.

Second, to prevent long-term negative economic consequences, authorities reacted quickly in reassuring citizens and visitors that the city or country was safe. Swift action and strong communication campaigns were therefore of utmost importance to achieve this. They also enabled and strengthened trust among people and thus helped build social capital.

Third, funding, loans, tax relief, and other incentives were provided to small businesses. The latter seem to suffer the consequences of disasters the most and efforts were made to alleviate negative impacts. Small businesses are at the heart of every economy, and it is therefore not surprising that they were a huge priority in recovery plans. Fourth, narratives of resilience by political leaders emerged, and they were necessary for the people and place to heal. Often, these narratives would draw on the "power of the place" — resilience of cities is often connected to the attachment that people have to places (Vale and Campanella 2005). This meant that each place capitalised on its own unique resources, image, social, and cultural capital in the recovery phase (e.g., "We are all New Yorkers"; "Made in France" campaign). Social capital in terms of regaining trust, building cohesion, as well as ensuring safety and cooperation played a vital role in all recovery strategies. It is fundamental for community disaster resilience (Partelow 2021).

These generalisable actions might prove useful in recovering from the COVID-19 pandemic, although they will need to be adapted to account for the enormous scale of this urban disaster and the fact that every single country has been affected. Similarly, strategies to sustain and revitalise the economy and the city of Singapore can learn from the traumatic experiences and recovery of other cities while accounting for specific contexts of Singapore and the control of the pandemic. How is the latter different from other urban disasters in the past and what might this mean for the recovery context? We can discuss this through four lenses: symbolism, duration, severity, and spatiality.

Symbolic interpretation of urban disasters changed over time. In the past, being involved in a disaster could result in a feeling of shame and disgrace on the part of those affected. Due to mass media and information technology, urban disasters' symbolic interpretation changed our perception from one of victims to subjects possessing the weight of moral authority (Alexander 2012). Every urban disaster can therefore be interpreted symbolically as "a form of moral outrage" (Alexander 2012). The "story value" (singularity, novelty, human interest, etc.) or the spectacle of a disaster plays an important role in this interpretation. Urban disasters that are novel, shocking, and have an invested human interest in them might leave a city devastated, but at the same time also enable the recovery to start sooner and with greater resources. In the case of COVID-19, the symbolism of suffering and the need to come together as a community might wane with time as the populations everywhere are getting used to the "new normal". The pandemic has ended for most countries, and in early 2023, China was coming out of its zero COVID policy. The momentum of symbolism to enable recovery might need to be substituted. In this new normal, we have to start looking for new solutions to revive city centres, increase opportunities for new businesses and social interactions, and even reinvent the concept of the city as cities in America are discovering.

In terms of *duration*, urban disasters in the above six case studies can be thought of as particular events that ended at some point, including SARS. Their duration varied, some disasters were brief and occurred over a few hours, whereas others lasted several months. In fact, disasters are typically thought of as 'events', i.e., as something that is bounded in time and space (Fuentealba 2021). In the case of the COVID-19 pandemic, the disaster is not so much an event as it is a process, a new way of life. It is therefore difficult to measure the long-term impacts of a pandemic that could have a long tail. Disasters that are short in duration enable us to estimate the immediate impact by comparing the post-disaster economy to its level prior the event (Noy and duPont IV 2018). Scholarship pays less attention to long-term impacts as they are more difficult to measure. For long-term disasters, assessing long-term impacts might be even more challenging.

The *severity* of an urban disaster can be measured in terms of casualties, shock, destroyed infrastructure, and economic consequences, among others. We can distinguish direct damages and indirect losses of a disaster (Noy and duPont IV 2018). Direct damages are an immediate consequence of the disaster and may include damages to infrastructure or capital as well as mortality. They are relatively easy to estimate and address. Indirect losses, on the other hand, include diminished economic activities that occurred because of a disaster. They are more difficult to measure, especially if a disaster lasts for a longer period, and may include emergency costs, business interruptions, falls in demand, negative economic growth, negative health consequences, social and community network disruptions, poverty, and impacts on security and stability. However, disasters might also cause some unexpected indirect benefits, e.g., growth in construction industries as a result of a higher demand for construction services after natural disasters. There are sectors that are booming because of the COVID-19 pandemic, some that successfully adapted, and others that emerged because of it.

The COVID pandemic economic recovery has been exacerbated by two factors. Firstly, the enforced lockdowns posed significant challenges for supply chains globally. Manufacturing was disrupted with the stoppage of flows of raw materials and finished goods. Adapting to a more resilient and sustainable supply chain has been the focus of most discussions and actions. The economic situation has been made more difficult because the Russian invasion of Ukraine sparked off a round of comprehensive economic and financial sanctions which has dragged out recovery due to further supply chain disruptions, reconfiguring economic activities or cutting off activities and causing inflation.

The *spatiality* of a disaster matters as it is linked to scale. There can be a single focal point (e.g., Charlie Hebdo attack), it can affect one or more countries (e.g., SARS), or it can be global (e.g., COVID-19). Urban disasters that are global in nature are rare, but there are cases where several countries are affected by the same disaster (e.g., tropical cyclones or tsunamis in the Asia-Pacific region). Furthermore, modern-day national or regional disasters can become global phenomena because of the instant international communications and cross-border threats such as climate change (ESCAP 2015). In the case of the COVID-19 pandemic, it was global (albeit it became so progressively), but unfortunately the international cooperation came late with developed countries turning inward initially before they offered help to other afflicted countries. Regional collaboration was more effective in Asia. One clear unique spatial element of the COVID-19 pandemic was the lost/diminished interconnectedness between nations, cities, businesses, and people, but immediately new ways were found for connecting or reconnecting — virtually, physically, and above all, safely. Whereas the catastrophic events discussed here forced the cities to adapt rather than totally transform themselves, COVID-19 required a different socio-spatial reconfiguration, which is grappling with increased digitalisation and a hybrid form of interactions.

The preceding section briefly presented the essence of how cities recovered from traumatic crises and the economic consequences of urban disasters with some attention on the tourism industry. This is not to say there were no other consequences of a psychological, social, and political nature. But it is a good place to start when thinking about the socio-spatial reconfiguration of Singapore after the pandemic.

Singapore, like other global cities, will focus on reviving travel and enabling free flows of people safely across borders, but most importantly assist the business sector, especially the SMEs, to achieve a steady and strong recovery. In fact, Singapore responded fast by being one of the earlier Asian countries to open up and managed its workforce relatively well, having not laid off workers completely. Most countries underestimated the pent-up travel demands or 'revenge travel' that would take place, and airports were scenes of confusion and chaos. In reality, the supply and demand pressures were mismatched. Airports could not get workers fully back to work, which posed major issues.

In Singapore, besides urban planners, residents and users of the city have clear ideas how they would like to reimagine the city. Exiting a wrenching experience helps to clarify priorities and rethink how one wants to live. Thirty-eight C-Suite inhabitants of the city centre in an illuminating interview with *The Business Times* provided articulate and innovative ideas on how to repurpose the Central Business District (CBD) (The Business Times 2021). Some questioned if it was necessary in these contemporary times to have a CBD at all. Professor Lawrence Loh of the National University of Singapore (NUS) saw the CBD challenged by Work from Home (WFH). The CBD, he argues, will in the future be a Coordinating Business Duplex, 1) "providing a core but minimalist nerve centre for co-ordinating planning activities" and 2) "fostering work processes across multiple decentralised localities". Many users of the city highlighted it should be repurposing of the city post-COVID rather than redevelopment, emphasised the need for mixed development, multifunctional and multi-generational spaces, and above all a city centre that allows for affordable housing, a place for people to live, work, and play (The Business Times 2021).

But as we come out of the pandemic, the experience of the isolation, the lockdowns, the work-from-home regime, forced online education for school children and the institutes of higher learning, one consequence of the entire experience demands our attention. In the workplace, remote collaboration results in a loss of creativity, innovation, and the organisational culture. The ability to mentor and coach employees to work in a team compared to the pre-pandemic level is far lower. Indeed, the question has been raised as to what the consequences would be of long-term remote work (Kane *et al.* 2021). We are now learning anecdotally that senior executives and CEOs are saying the work-from-home regime does not produce the same level of productivity of the pre-pandemic office, but they recognise it would be difficult to return to the full work-from-office regime. It is instructive though that many US companies such as Meta and Google are trying to rebalance the remote work policy with in-person work. Wall

Street banks such as JP Morgan have emphasised a back-to-the-office strategy after allowing for remote work wholeheartedly. Remote work is allowed but the emphasis is on the office as the primary workplace.

The value of weak ties as Granovetter so brilliantly highlighted in his now classic study of networks is a useful reminder of opportunity cost (Granovetter 1973; Pentland 2015). It is the loss of community and social interaction, leading to a *social deficit* we will incur in our work and lives if we choose not to meet and work together in a same space. This must lead to the weakening of identity and diminishing of the social *capital* of a community, city, and country (Putnam 2000; Jacobs 2016). The consequence is great as this means loss of trust (Fukuyama 1996): the social glue that binds society and organisations together and makes the achievement of results smoother and more efficient. One can almost predict the fraying of democracy in the US today in Putnam's conclusions foretold.

ORGANISATION OF THE BOOK

Our study, *The City Rebooted*, is meant to explore the possibilities of reimagining and rethinking the city space. We are approaching our task through an interdisciplinary perspective of architects, geographers, urban planners, sociologists, political scientists, and data scientists collaborating together. We have gathered data, big data and small data, through surveys and field observations and insight from articles and books relevant to our topic. We ask long-standing questions about urban development and change, but importantly, these are questions which have taken on greater (or in some cases, different) significance for cities like Singapore, which have begun to take tentative steps out of the crisis.

Following this introductory chapter, the first of four thematic sections, The New Economic Trends of Singapore City, will revisit a long-standing question many cities across the world have been asking for decades of their city centres as well as how the digital economy reshape the form and function of Singapore. For the former, Sara Ann Nicholas and Winston Yap took the pandemic, arguably the biggest crisis city centres have faced, as a springboard to determine if indeed the city centre in Singapore has been hollowing out (in the economic sense). Core to their argument is that if the city centre stands strong in the aftermath of such a blow, it is unlikely that the city centre will hollow out in the near future. Their chapter marshals a variety of urban data that points to the continued resilience, relevance, and repurposing of the city centre. Amongst the many key takeaways from the pandemic is the importance of digitisation as well as the free flow of global talent for cities. In their chapter, Dinithi Jayasekara and Fredrik Hansson examine the nature and implications of a digital economy, drawing on the experiences of Singapore, Sweden, and Estonia. In turning their attention to the future of Singapore's digitisation process, the authors suggest post-pandemic Singapore need not diverge from its key digitisation strategies, but in fact more aggressively work on them.

The second section looks at the future of the office from two analytical lenses, Sam Conrad Joyce's chapter takes one through the developmental history of the concept of office, in both spatial and social terms, and affirms the relevance of the office despite post-pandemic calls to "cancel office". He sees the pandemic as being the latest in a long list of shifts in socio-economic and planning norms that compel the office to morph once more. The chapter following his takes this morphing to be a hybrid office work arrangement. Sam Conrad Joyce and Nazim Ibrahim then ask the question many have asked: "What kinds of hybrid work arrangement for what kinds of industries?"

The third section, The Future of Polycentres, looks at two topics which have been "boosted" by the pandemic experience. In laying out the developmental trajectory of Singapore's long-standing interest in polycentricity (in the form of regional centres), Harvey Neo and Bayi Li argue that the pandemic offers pathways to rejuvenate and accelerate the "regionalism" planning concept which, amongst other things, place critical importance to place identity and community buy-ins. Following their chapter, Samuel Chng deep dives into the rapid rise of cloud kitchens and cloud stores (a development which was just nascent pre-pandemic but has since witnessed tremendous growth). Chng provides an overview of the current status of this urban-economic phenomenon and highlights the neglected social externalities that may result from cloud kitchens and stores should they become mainstream.

The affirmation of the continued relevance of the city centre in several of the earlier chapters sidestep core questions which the final thematic section will address. First, that city centres continue to stake its *economic* relevance begs the question of what the allure and attraction of the city centre is. Authors Chan Heng Chee, Winston Yap and Sara Ann Nicholas posit that the city, along with its relevance (or irrelevance), cannot be understood in purely economic and functional terms and develop an intricate argument of the magic of the city as intimately tied to the notion of modernity, using Singapore as an example. In the chapter that follows, Rafael Martinez, Sara Ann Nicholas and Špela Močnik ask if indeed there is "magic" in the city, how then can it be cultivated? The two chapters in this section are preceded by a collection of photo-essays which we hope will help readers see the city in a different, more visceral light, enabling them to discover the magic and mystery of the city in their own terms.

In our concluding chapter, we recall the conceptual motifs that have strung the chapters in this collection. We reiterate the importance of place identity, social capital, and human centricity in making better cities.

REFERENCES

Alderman, Liz, and Dan Bilefsky. 2015. "Huge Show of Solidarity in Paris Against Terrorism." The New York Times. January 11, 2015. https://www.nytimes.com/2015/01/12/world/europe/paris-march-against-terror-charlie-hebdo.html.

Alexander, David. 2012. "Models of Social Vulnerability to Disasters." *RCCS Annual Review* 4 (October). https://doi.org/10.4000/rccsar.412.

Amazon Web Services. 2020. "A Peek into the Frontlines of Healthtech." GovInsider. September 8, 2020. https://govinsider.asia/intl-en/article/aws-amazon-web-services-cloud-a-peek-into-the-frontlines-of-healthtech.

APEC Counter-Terrorism Working Group. 2017. "Strengthening Tourism Business Resilience against the Impact of Terrorist Attack." Report on the APEC Counter-Terrorism Working Group's Workshop on 9–10 May 2017, Bali, Indonesia. https://www.apec.org/docs/default-source/

Publications/2017/9/Strengthening-Tourism-Business-Resilience-against-the-Impact-of-Terrorist-Attack/217_CTWG_Draft-APEC-Final-Report.pdf.

Au, King-chi. 2008. "Collaboration Key to Tourism Recovery." November 16, 2008. https://www.news.gov.hk/isd/ebulletin/en/category/ontherecord/081117/html/081117en11001.htm.

Barua, Akrur. 2020. "Economic Impact of Epidemics and Pandemics in Asia." Deloitte Insights. May 20, 2020. https://www2.deloitte.com/us/en/insights/economy/asia-pacific/economic-impact-of-epidemics-and-pandemics.html.

Bean, Hamilton, Lisa Keränen, and Margaret Durfy. 2011. "'This is London': Cosmopolitan Nationalism and the Discourse of Resilience in the Case of the 7/7 Terrorist Attacks." *Rhetoric & Public Affairs* 14 (3): 427–464. https://doi.org/10.1353/rap.2011.0018.

Bonham, Carl, Christopher Edmonds, and James Mak. 2006. "The Impact of 9/11 and Other Terrible Global Events on Tourism in the United States and Hawaii." *Journal of Travel Research* 45 (1): 99–110. https://doi.org/10.1177/0047287506288812.

Chan, Heng Chee. 2021. *World in Transition: Singapore's Future*. World Scientific Publishing.

Chen, Chun-Da, Chin-Chun Chen, Wan-Wei Tang, and Bor-Yi Huang. 2009. "The Positive and Negative Impacts of the SARS Outbreak: A Case of the Taiwan Industries." *The Journal of Developing Areas* 43 (1): 281–293.

Chou, Ji, Nai-Fong Kuo, and Su-Ling Peng. 2004. "Potential Impacts of the SARS Outbreak on Taiwan's Economy." *Asian Economic Papers* 3 (1): 84–99. https://doi.org/10.1162/1535351041747969.

CNN. 2022. "September 11 Terror Attacks Fast Facts." CNN. August 25, 2022. https://edition.cnn.com/2013/07/27/us/september-11-anniversary-fast-facts/index.html.

Deurenberg-Yap, M., L. L. Foo, Y. Y. Low, S. P. Chan, K. Vijaya, and M. Lee. 2005. "The Singaporean Response to the SARS Outbreak: Knowledge Sufficiency versus Public Trust." *Health Promotion International* 20 (4): 320–326. https://doi.org/10.1093/heapro/dai010.

Eisinger, Peter. 2007. "Business as Usual: New York City after 9/11: Review Essay." *International Journal of Urban and Regional Research* 31 (4): 875–879. https://doi.org/10.1111/j.1468-2427.2007.00762.x.

ESCAP. 2015. "Disasters Without Borders: Regional Resilience for Sustainable Development." Asia-Pacific Disaster Report 2015. ESCAP. file:///Users/coolkid/Downloads/ESCAP-2016-FS-Disasters-without-borders.pdf. https://www.unescap.org/sites/default/files/Full%20Report%20%20%5BLow-Res%5D.pdf?

Fainstein, Susan S. 2002. "One Year on. Reflections on September 11th and the 'War On Terrorism': Regulating New York City's Visitors in the Aftermath of September 11th." *International Journal of Urban and Regional Research* 26 (3): 591–595. https://doi.org/10.1111/1468-2427.00401.

Florida, Richard, Edward Glaeser, Maimunah Mohd Sharif, Thomas J. Campanella, Heng Chee Chan, Dan Doctoroff, *et al.* 2020. "How Life in Cities Will Change Due to the Coronavirus Pandemic." Foreign Policy. January 5, 2020. https://foreignpolicy.com/2020/05/01/future-of-cities-urban-life-after-coronavirus-pandemic/.

Fuentealba, Ricardo. 2021. "Divergent Disaster Events? The Politics of Post-Disaster Memory on the Urban Margin." *International Journal of Disaster Risk Reduction* 62 (August): 102389. https://doi.org/10.1016/j.ijdrr.2021.102389.

Fukuyama, Francis. 1996. *Trust: The Social Virtues and the Creation of Prosperity*. Simon and Schuster.

Gössling, Stefan, Daniel Scott, and C. Michael Hall. 2021. "Pandemics, Tourism and Global Change: A Rapid Assessment of COVID-19." *Journal of Sustainable Tourism* 29 (1): 1–20. https://doi.org/10.1080/09669582.2020.1758708.

Gotham, K. F. 2008. "From 9/11 to 8/29: Post-Disaster Recovery and Rebuilding in New York and New Orleans." *Social Forces* 87 (2): 1039–1062. https://doi.org/10.1353/sof.0.0131.

Granovetter, Mark S. 1973. "The Strength of Weak Ties." *American Journal of Sociology* 78 (6): 1360–1380.

Harris, Toby. 2016. "London's Preparedness to Respond to a Major Terrorist Incident." Independent Review for the Mayor of London. Greater London Authority. https://www.london.gov.uk/sites/default/files/londons_preparedness_to_respond_to_a_major_terrorist_incident_-_independent_review_oct_2016.pdf.

Holliday, Christopher. 2018. "London, the Post-7/7 Bond Films, and Mourning Work." *Journal of Popular Film and Television* 46 (1): 56–63. https://doi.org/10.1080/01956051.2018.1423210.

House of Commons and Levelling Up, Housing and Communities Committee. 2021. "Supporing Our High Street after COVID-19." Sixth Report

of Session 2021–2022, House of Commons. https://committees.parliament.uk/publications/8172/documents/83568/default/.
Hung, Lee Shiu. 2003. "The SARS Epidemic in Hong Kong: What Lessons Have We Learned?" *Journal of the Royal Society of Medicine* 96 (8): 374–78. https://doi.org/10.1177/014107680309600803.
Jacobs, Jane. 2016. *The Death and Life of Great American Cities.* Vintage.
Kane, Gerald C., Rich Nanda, Anh Phillips, and Jonathan Copulsky. 2021. "Redesigning the Post-Pandemic Workplace." *MIT Sloan Management Review* 62 (3): 12–14.
Katz, Liane. 2006. "UK Tourism Has Record Year despite London Bombs." *The Guardian*, November 8, 2006. https://www.theguardian.com/travel/2006/nov/08/travelnews.uknews.
Khaliq, Riyaz ul. 2020. "'Taiwan's SARS Experience Helped It Beat COVID-19.'" AA. May 6, 2020. https://www.aa.com.tr/en/asia-pacific/-taiwan-s-sars-experience-helped-it-beat-covid-19-/1830547.
Legislative Council of Hong Kong. 2003. "Communicating Hong Kong's Recovery." https://www.legco.gov.hk/yr02-03/english/panels/fa/papers/fa0512cb1-1658-e.pdf.
Liu-Lastres, Bingjie, Dini Mariska, Xiaoyuan Tan, and Tianyu Ying. 2020. "Can Post-Disaster Tourism Development Improve Destination Livelihoods? A Case Study of Aceh, Indonesia." *Journal of Destination Marketing & Management* 18: 100510.
Makinen, Gail. 2002. "The Economic Effects of 9/11: A Retrospective Assessment." Report for Congress. Congressional Research Service, Library of Congress. https://apps.dtic.mil/dtic/tr/fulltext/u2/a469198.pdf.
Manelici, Isabela. 2017. "Terrorism and the Value of Proximity to Public Transportation: Evidence from the 2005 London Bombings." *Journal of Urban Economics* 102 (November): 52–75. https://doi.org/10.1016/j.jue.2017.09.001.
Mao, Chi-Kuo, Cherng G. Ding, and Hsiu-Yu Lee. 2010. "Post-SARS Tourist Arrival Recovery Patterns: An Analysis Based on a Catastrophe Theory." *Tourism Management* 31 (6): 855–861. https://doi.org/10.1016/j.tourman.2009.09.003.
McGehee, Nancy Gard, Seungwoo Lee, Teresa L. O'Bannon, and Richard R. Perdue. 2010. "Tourism-Related Social Capital and Its Relationship with Other Forms of Capital: An Exploratory Study." *Journal of Travel Research* 49 (4): 486–500.
Ministry of Finance, Singapore and Ministry of Trade and Industry, Singapore. 2003. "Government Unveils $230 Million SARS Relief

Package." Ministry of Finance. April 17, 2003. https://www.mof.gov.sg/news-publications/press-releases.

Ministry of Health, Singapore. 2003. "Special Feature: Severe Acute Respiratory Syndrome (SARS)." Communicable Diseases Surveillance in Singapore 2003. Ministry of Health, Singapore. https://www.moh.gov.sg/docs/librariesprovider5/resources-statistics/reports/special_feature_sars.pdf.

Misrahi, Tiffany. 2016. "How Destinations Can Bounce Back after Terrorist Attacks." World Economic Forum. March 23, 2016. https://www.weforum.org/agenda/2016/03/how-destinations-can-bounce-back-after-terrorist-attacks/.

Monetary Authority of Singapore. 2004. "Monetary Authority of Singapore Annual Report 2003/2004." Monetary Authority of Singapore. https://www.mas.gov.sg/-/media/mas/about-mas/reporting/annual-reports/past-ar-pdf/20032004.pdf.

Moreno, Carlos, Zaheer Allam, Didier Chabaud, Catherine Gall, and Florent Pratlong. 2021. "Introducing the '15-Minute City': Sustainability, Resilience and Place Identity in Future Post-Pandemic Cities." *Smart Cities* 4 (1): 93–111. https://doi.org/10.3390/smartcities4010006.

Noy, Ilan, and William duPont IV. 2018. "The Long-Term Consequences of Disasters: What Do We Know, and What We Still Don't." *International Review of Environmental and Resource Economics* 12 (4): 325–354. https://doi.org/10.1561/101.00000104.

Partelow, Stefan. 2021. "Social Capital and Community Disaster Resilience: Post-Earthquake Tourism Recovery on Gili Trawangan, Indonesia." *Sustainability Science* 16 (1): 203–220.

PATA Crisis Resource Center. 2020. "Case Study Hong Kong's Recovery from SARS." PATA Crisis Resource Center. https://src.pata.org/wp-content/uploads/Case-Study-Hong-Kongs-Recovery-from-SARS.pdf.

Pentland, Alex. 2015. *Social Physics: How Social Networks Can Make Us Smarter*. Penguin.

Putnam, Robert D. 2000. *Bowling Alone: The Collapse and Revival of American Community*. Simon and Schuster.

Savitch, Hank V. 2008. "Cities in a Time of Terror: Space, Territory, and Local Resilience". ME Sharpe, Inc., 135–138.

Schreuer, Milan. 2017. "Paris Tourism Has Recovered From 2015 Attacks, Officials Say." The New York Times. April 14, 2017. https://www.nytimes.com/2017/04/14/world/europe/paris-tourism.html.

Seidler, Victor. 2015. "Why Don't Londoners Remember 7/7 like New York Remembers 9/11?" The Conversation. July 6, 2015. http://theconversation.com/why-dont-londoners-remember-7-7-like-new-york-remembers-9-11-44214.
Siu, Alan, and YC Richard Wong. 2004. "Economic Impact of SARS: The Case of Hong Kong." *Asian Economic Papers* 3 (1): 62–83.
Tan, Chorh-Chuan. 2006. "SARS in Singapore — Key Lessons from an Epidemic." *Annals of the Academy of Medicine Singapore* 35 (5): 345.
The Business Times. 2021. "CBD Reimagined and Repurposed." *The Business Times.* July 26, 2021. https://www.businesstimes.com.sg/cbd-reimagined-and-repurposed.
Thomas, Sik To Lai, and Cho Yu Wai. 2010. "The Lessons of SARS in Hong Kong." *Clinical Medicine* 10 (1): 50.
Titley, Gavan, Des Freedman, Gholam Khiabany, and Aurélien Mondon. 2017. *After Charlie Hebdo: Terror, Racism and Free Speech.* Bloomsbury Publishing.
Tse, Alan C.B., Stella So, and Leo Sin. 2006. "Crisis Management and Recovery: How Restaurants in Hong Kong Responded to SARS." *International Journal of Hospitality Management* 25 (1): 3–11. https://doi.org/10.1016/j.ijhm.2004.12.001.
Vale, Lawrence J., and Thomas J. Campanella, eds. 2005. *The Resilient City: How Modern Cities Recover from Disaster.* Oxford University Press.
Waugh, Butler. 2003. "Economic Recovery in the Wake of SARS." Taiwan Today. Ministry of Foreign Affairs, Republic of China (Taiwan). October 1, 2003. https://taiwantoday.tw/news.php?unit=8&post=12681.
World Health Organization. 2023a. "WHO Chief Declares End to COVID-19 as a Global Health Emergency." UN News. May 5, 2023. https://news.un.org/en/story/2023/05/1136367.
World Health Organization. 2023b. "WHO Coronavirus (COVID-19) Dashboard." May 5, 2023. https://covid19.who.int.
World Travel & Tourism Council. 2018. "Tourism Recovery after Terrorism: How France Bounced Back." *Medium* (blog). July 5, 2018. https://worldtraveltourismcouncil.medium.com/tourism-recovery-after-terrorism-how-france-bounced-back-ff2d25c2834a.
Yeung, Peter. 2021. "How '15-Minute Cities' Will Change the Way We Socialise." BBC. April 1, 2021. https://www.bbc.com/worklife/article/20201214-how-15-minute-cities-will-change-the-way-we-socialise.

The New Economic Trends of
Singapore City

© 2024 World Scientific Publishing Company
https://doi.org/10.1142/9789811287848_0002

Is the City Centre Hollowing Out?

Sara Ann Nicholas & Winston Yap

In the feverish early days of the pandemic, when people scrambled to stay indoors, and work-from-home became the norm, many believed that city centres globally would face a "donut effect" wherein activities would shift out of the city centre and into surrounding areas (Ramani and Bloom 2021). This prompted important questions about the fate of the city centre, a space which has long held a sacrosanct position for the cardinal functions it performs. Who is using the city centre now, and which players have left? Where are social and economic activities taking place at present? Will the city centre remain relevant post-COVID-19?

It is our objective to provide the answers to these questions and more, in the context of Singapore. While we acknowledge that the pandemic and its multifarious consequences are and have been hallmarked by unpredictability, we hope that this chapter will provide a coherent entry-point into understanding the effects of COVID-19 on Singapore's city centre — past, present, and prospective. Through our analysis of various components of the city centre, we argue that it is not all doom and gloom for Singapore — her city centre will continue to remain relevant post-pandemic, albeit with a changing identity.

We begin by explicating the salience of Singapore's city centre as a national and global icon. Thereafter, we adopt an urban economics lens to understand the spatial structure of the city centre at large, and later scrutinise the changing landscape of individual planning areas in the city centre. Finally, we conclude with trends that have emerged in the city centre as a result of the pandemic.

THE CITY CENTRE

Over five decades of nation-building has transformed Singapore from a backward British colony into a modern and leading global business hub. The Forbes 2017 Global 2000, which lists the world's largest public companies according to economic worth, ranks Singapore as the top regional headquarters among technology multinational corporations (MNCs) in Asia (KPMG 2017). On innovation, Singapore is consistently ranked as one of the most innovative cities in the world (Dutta *et al.* 2019). Much of Singapore's current distinction as a world-class city is epitomised by its contemporary cityscape of which the city centre forms the heart. During the pandemic, Singapore further enhanced its status as a safe haven for wealthy families who wished to invest and live in security and peace.

Singapore's city centre consists of two key districts — the Central Business District (CBD) and Civic District. Since independence, the area has played a significant role in Singapore's transformation into a first world city. As a global business platform, the CBD remains the foremost gateway connecting Singapore to the international economy. It stands out as the meridian location of choice for businesses and serves to anchor numerous transnational corporation headquarters within the region. Juxtaposing the CBD is the Civic District which beholds corporeal evidence of Singapore's historic and cultural roots. As aptly mentioned by Goh and Heng (2016, 212–213): "Here, the beginnings of Singapore's urban planning and administrative foundations can be traced, (…), the Civic District is arguably the soul of Singapore's city centre as it is communicative of our nation's past and future in both colonial and modern terms." Holistically, the CBD and Civic District jointly bear testament to some of the most monolithic and complex civil engineering tasks undertaken in Singapore's national history. In this sense, the city centre symbolises the aspirations and sentiments of a young nation state. The present state of development is a corollary of sustained, strong political

Is the City Centre Hollowing Out? 37

will, driven by an insatiable socio-political climate for renewal and improvement.

The remainder of this section will introduce the city centre in greater geospatial granularity and elaborate on its significance as a special space for Singapore and Singaporeans.

PRIME LOCATION

Singapore's city centre is in the central region of Singapore and falls within the larger Central Area, consisting of 11 adjoining planning areas (Figure 2.1). While there are no clear-cut boundaries, the Downtown Core, Outram, and Singapore River planning areas are generally recognised as the Central Business District while most of the Civic District occupies the Museum planning area. At the northern tip lies the Orchard planning area which serves as the premier retail

Figure 2.1: Singapore's city centre (*Source*: Urban Redevelopment Authority 2019)

precinct in Singapore. Since the mid-1960s, subsequent land reclamation efforts helped to extend the southern foreshore, contributing to a 139 km^2 increase in land mass. Today, the extended Marina Bay waterfront area harbours the iconic Gardens by the Bay and the Marina Bay Sands Integrated Resort. Decades of careful urban intervention guided by a well-thought through strategic urban design vision has helped transform the city centre into a liveable, vibrant, and attractive cityscape.

GATEWAY TO THE GLOBAL KNOWLEDGE ECONOMY

The CBD serves as Singapore's predominant connection to the global economy. As of end-2020, Singapore's financial district is reported to host $4.7 trillion SGD of financial assets (Monetary Authority of Singapore 2021). In addition, 46% of regional headquarters in Asia are estimated to be based in Singapore, and this number climbs to 59% for technology MNCs headquarters (Singapore Economic Development Board 2021). It is estimated that a large majority of these headquarters are located within the Central Business District.

The economic importance of the CBD was recognised by policymakers from as early as the 2000s. While decentralisation was a key strategy in the 1991 concept plan, the subsequent 2001 concept plan stressed the importance of keeping the majority of office spaces within the city area. Towards this objective, land-use zoning was one of the main tools employed to keep core business and financial activities in the city centre. Subsequent planning efforts focused on addressing global socio-economic transitions, such as the changing nature of the way people work and play. Over the years, the city centre has continuously strived to remain competitive and appeal to the creative class. During a 2005 parliamentary session, Singapore's founding Prime Minister, Mr. Lee Kuan Yew, mentioned the importance of staying globally competitive: "The old model on which I worked was to create a first world city in a third world region, (…), these virtues are valuable but no longer sufficient. Now, we also have to be not just economically vibrant, but also an exciting, fascinating city to visit, with top-class symphony orchestras, concerts, dramas, plays, artists, singers, and popular entertainment" (Lee 2005 in The Straits Times 2015). The zoning strategy shifted to include more "white-site" land parcels, helping to promote greater development flexibility and diversity in land use. New extensions to the urban skyline also helped to expand the city centre's role in arts and culture with the addition of monumental structures such as the Esplanade and Art Science Museum. Today, modern Singaporeans generally recognise the city centre as a precinct with excellent accessibility to amenities and an ample selection of business and recreational opportunities.

ECONOMIC STRUCTURE OF THE CITY CENTRE

In this section, we adopt an urban economics lens to analyse and understand the spatial structure underlying Singapore's city centre. Our analysis draws on office and retail transactions data obtained from the Real Estate Information System (REALIS) database provided by the Urban Redevelopment Authority (URA). The REALIS database records up-to-date and comprehensive statistics of property transactions and rental rates for various planning areas in Singapore. More details on data pre-processing and transformation will accompany in the following sub-sections.

URBAN AGGLOMERATION ECONOMIES AND CLUSTERS

Early discourse on city cores engaged with the urban spatial structure of cities. Urban spatial structure was understood to have a strong influence on people's daily lives, having underpinnings for economic growth, social equity, and the sustainable development of cities. Within the urban structure of cities, the city core was understood as a place of strategic functional importance and one with size and geographic extent delimited by the laws of urban economics. The density and diversity of economic activities in the city centre allowed it to develop specialisation and economies of scale for production and delivery of services. This phenomenon is termed in urban economics parlance as agglomeration economies. In her renowned book on the global city, Saskia Sassen describes the presence of urban agglomeration economies as a necessary prerequisite for the transformation of economies towards the production of global, high-value goods and services (Sassen 2001).

While planning boundaries go some way to aid our understanding of what constitutes the urban core, it is not an infallible concept. As a form of social artifact, planning boundaries are inherently subjective constructs which lend themselves to easy manipulation. This issue of how different planning zonings can result in spurious correlations is well documented in the field of Geographic Information Sciences (GIS) and is generally termed the modifiable areal unit problem. Subsequently, this raises the critical question of how one can objectively hope to measure the spatial extent, or hope to detect the presence of urban agglomeration clusters in the city centre. Towards this issue, we refer to the literature on urban economics and urban spatial analysis, and adopt a similar approach to studies published in the literature. Broadly speaking, methods for delineating the city core can be segregated into objective and subjective methods. Objective methods consider the physical or measurable aspects of the built environment and its functions. These methods generally strive to identify the city core through density and proximity of urban activities. Studies include examples that look at built density thresholds, travel survey data flows, and marked point pattern analysis of activity locations. On the other hand, subjective methods aim to understand urban symbology through the perceptions of urban residents and how they map the city mentally (Lynch 1960).

In this study, we focus on objective methods of defining the city core and employ real estate commercial transaction data as a proxy for human activity. This is a reasonable assumption given that areas where a large number of transactions occur can be viewed as competitive business sites with high commercial potential. This understanding is consistent with the understanding of bid rent in urban economics theory where central sites tend to command the highest rents.

URBAN SPATIAL STRUCTURE

For our analysis, we examined REALIS commercial transaction data drawn from the period spanning January 2017 to June 2021. Transaction data was geocoded to obtain longitude and latitude coordinates via open source MapBox application programming interface (API) and processed in RStudio. The point pattern distribution for office transactions show clear sub-clusters located at the Outram/Downtown Core and Rochor areas (Figure 2.2). The Outram/Downtown Core sub-cluster displays the highest density of transactions and is likely the main cluster of office activity in the city centre. This finding makes intuitive sense as the Outram/Downtown Core area is the primary location where majority of Grade A office buildings are located. On the other hand, retail transactions seem more spread out throughout the CBD. Three areas report active retail activity: Orchard, Rochor, and Outram/Downtown Core. The co-occurrence of retail and office activity is hardly surprising as office crowds remain the main sources of demand for services in the city centre.

While point pattern visualisations are effective to show spatial distribution, they lose their effectiveness at higher spatial resolutions. For example, if there are a large number of overlapping points at the same location, points might overshadow one another and create a false impression of few points in the area. To improve our

Figure 2.2: Point pattern distribution of office, retail, and shop house transactions (*Source*: REALIS 2021)

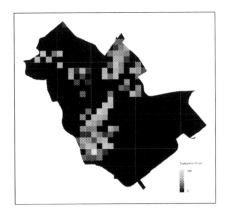 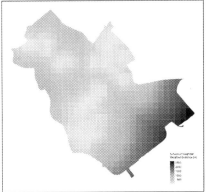

Figure 2.3.1: Transaction count aggregation

Figure 2.3.2: K-nearest neighbour (KNN-30) weighted distance to nearest transaction

Figures 2.3: Density and proximity of transactions (200m raster grid) (*Source*: REALIS 2021)

analysis, we created a mesh grid of 200 by 200 metre raster cells, and plotted the aggregated number of transactions within each grid (Figure 2.3.1). Two interesting observations can be obtained from the plot: 1) within the Downtown Core, Tanjong Pagar sub-zone has the highest level of economic activity, and 2) aside from Tanjong Pagar, commercial activity throughout the city centre seems to be well spread out, indicating the presence of multiple clusters of economic activity.

Another measure of economic agglomeration is node proximity. This measure assumes that points are located closer to one another (distance-wise) within a cluster as compared to when they are not part of a cluster. To compute this measure, we implemented a K-Nearest-Neighbour-30 (KNN-30) algorithm that measures the average Euclidean distance (crow's flight) between each grid centroid to thirty nearest transactions. Overall, the results (Figure 2.3.2) display similarity with the patterns observed in the aggregated count plot. Aside from helping to validate our previous observations, the proximity gradient plot allows us a finer-grained understanding of how proximity to economic activity changes throughout the city centre.

URBAN LAND MARKETS

A bid-rent model is often employed to understand spatial patterns of built density and land price of urban markets. Building density and rental rates are often highest at the urban core, as reflective of locational demand. The model shown in Figure 2.4 suggests a typical monocentric model where rental rates decrease with increasing distance from the urban core. In commercial terms, larger distance from the city core is associated with reduced accessibility to complementary services, core markets, critical masses of employment, and locational prestige, all of which justify lower rents.

In comparison, the bid-rent model for Singapore is starkly different, and aligns with the findings from previous sections. Notably, Figure 2.5 shows two peaks with the first peak at Downtown Core, and another peak close to 2,800 metres from the urban core. This observation validates our findings of a polycentric urban market

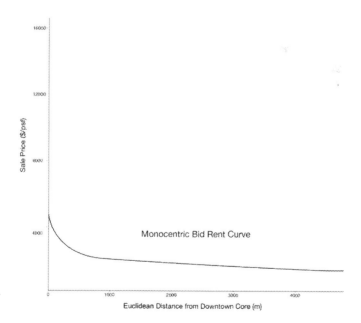

Figure 2.4: A theoretical monocentric bid-rent curve as specified by von Thünen (1826/1966). The graph displays a gradual and smooth decline in price with increasing distance from the central core.

in the city centre. In other words, while there is critical density at Downtown Core, there is no clear market leader in commercial land value throughout the city centre. A possible explanation might be that given the small size of the city centre, firms are able to enjoy relatively good access to supporting services, proximity to ancillary businesses, and excellent transportation and utilities infrastructure, regardless of their location in the city centre.

To examine the ramifications of COVID-19, the data was further split into two time bands: 1) transactions before January 23, 2020 (first COVID-19 case reported in Singapore); 2) transactions extending from January 23, 2020 till March 1, 2021 (latest record available at time of study). As shown in Figure 2.5, the upper dashed line

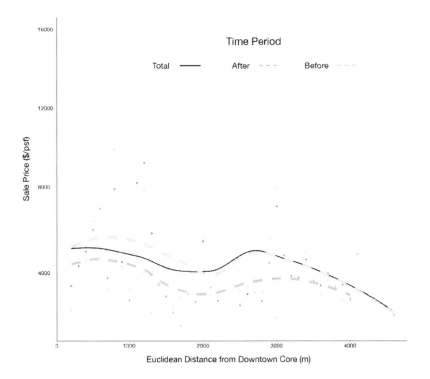

Figure 2.5: Singapore's city centre's bid-rent curve. Mean sale price per square feet aggregated by 100m distance band from downtown core. Transactions are further split into before and after January 23, 2020 — first COVID-19 case reported in Singapore. (*Source*: REALIS 2020)

shows the price before the pandemic hit Singapore, and the lower dashed line indicates rents recorded during COVID-19. Notably, while the trends display similar fluctuations according to distance from the city core, transactions recorded during COVID-19 are on average significantly lower than those recorded pre-COVID-19. This is strong evidence of the economic ramifications of COVID-19 on commercial land value in the city centre. Another point worth mentioning is that the land rent differential is constant throughout the city centre and appears to taper off at large distances from the city centre — potentially suggesting that commercial rents outside the city centre are less affected by the COVID-19 pandemic. This provides support for the premise that regional/heartland commerce largely cater to local markets with less global exposure. As of May 10, 2023, the city core commercial rental market displays signs of stable economic recovery, mainly fuelled by a robust office sector that has exceeded pre-COVID-19 levels.

CHANGES TO INDIVIDUAL PLANNING AREAS

In the preceding section, we examined the economic structure of the city centre at large. Here, we home in on the individual planning areas (Figure 2.1) of the city centre. We provide an account of key indicators such as vacancy and rental trends, office transactions, industry compositions, as well as movements of firms to an overview of changes that have been taking place from pre-pandemic times to the present.

VACANCY RATES

Figure 2.6 shows the vacancy rates for commercial land across nine planning areas in the city centre from Q1 2019 to Q1 2021. During this period, vacancy rates decreased for most areas with the exception of Orchard, Outram, Rochor, and Singapore River. This is despite a general increase in vacancy rates from Q1 2020 to Q2 2020, when Circuit Breaker measures were implemented. The increase in vacancy rates for some of the abovementioned areas could be attributed to the fact that they predominantly serve retail functions (Figure 2.2), which

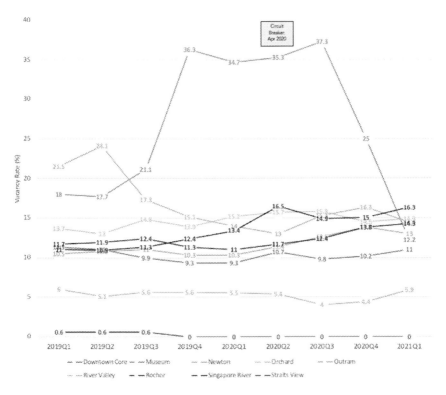

Figure 2.6: Vacancy rates in the city centre from 2019 to Q1 2021 (*Source:* REALIS 2021)

were heavily impacted by the pandemic. Vacancy rates display similar trends across all areas except for Museum and Straits View, which recorded the highest and lowest vacancy rates respectively.

RENTALS

Figure 2.7 depicts the median rental for commercial land across eight areas in the city centre from January 2019 to April 2021. During this period, median rental decreased for all areas apart from Orchard, River Valley, and Rochor. Akin to the vacancy graph, similar rental trends can be observed across all areas save for Museum, which is the most volatile in terms of rental price fluctuations from 2019–2021.

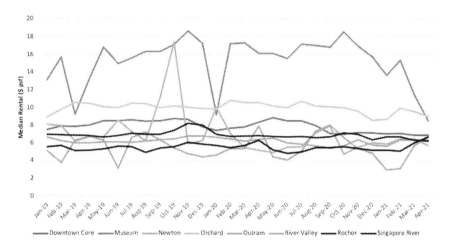

Figure 2.7: Median rental in the city centre from 2019 to April 2021 (*Source*: REALIS 2021)

OFFICE RENTALS

While we have hitherto explored commercial rental trends, this section spotlights office rental data from January 2018 to August 2021. Missing values were accounted for through a forward-fill imputation method which takes the values from the previous month as replacement. Finally, a five-month moving average window was employed to smooth out volatility and identify broader rental movement trends.

As shown in Figure 2.8, office rental rates have generally been on a steady increase for the entire duration of 2018 to 2019. However, this trend which peaked in December 2019 started to pivot and rapidly decline since the beginning of 2020. This fall in office rental rates coincides with the rise in COVID-19 cases in Singapore, and likely reflects the ramifications of the global pandemic on businesses. Unsurprisingly, the Downtown Core area (blue solid line) has the highest office rental rates, while the Rochor area has the lowest office rentals. Most of the offices in Downtown Core comprise of high density, modern, Grade A office blocks including Asia Square Tower and CapitaGreen, while the offices in Rochor comprise relatively smaller, low-rise, and older office blocks, such as those located along Prinsep Street. The rent divergence between Downtown Core and Rochor

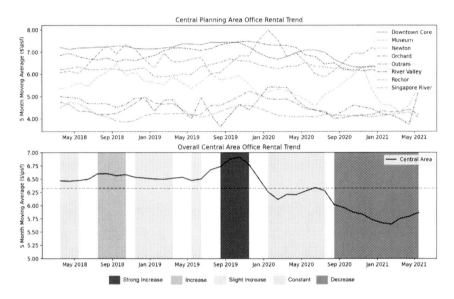

Figure 2.8: Office rental rate across different planning areas (upper plot) and overall central area office rental rate (lower plot) (*Source*: REALIS 2021)

offices approximates to an average of four-dollar differential per square foot. The large difference validates the presence of multiple clusters and sub-markets within the city centre.

OFFICE TRANSACTIONS

Number of transactions

Table 2.1 illustrates the number of office transactions across six planning areas from 2019 to June 1, 2021. Office transactions include new sales, sub-sales, and resale instances. The number of transactions generally decreased across all areas from 2019 to 2020. However, there is evidence of strong growth from 2020 to 2021, with the number of transactions in some areas like Orchard and Outram almost matching or exceeding pre-COVID-19 (i.e., 2019) levels.

Notably, from April to May 2019, the total number of office transactions recorded across all areas was 56. For the same period in 2020, during which Singapore implemented its Circuit Breaker, there were only 8 transactions. However, from April to May 2021, 31

Table 2.1: Office transactions in the city centre from 2019–June 1, 2021

Planning Area	2019	2020	2021 (up till 1st June)
Downtown Core	109	70	45
Museum	—	1	—
Orchard	22	7	10
Outram	14	11	8
Rochor	26	17	8
Singapore River	49	15	15
TOTAL	220	121	86

Source: REALIS 2021

transactions were recorded. Hence, while the pandemic caused a decrease in the number of office transactions, recent figures indicate signs of an upswing.

Additionally, Downtown Core accounted for the majority of office transactions across all three years.

Area transacted

Figure 2.9 shows the total office space transacted across six planning areas from 2019 to June 1, 2021. The total transacted area of office space generally decreased across all areas from 2019 to 2020. Downtown Core similarly accounted for the majority of office space transacted across all three years.

A noteworthy anomaly is Outram, which in 2021 saw a 1193% increase in office area transacted compared to 2019. This was attributed to the en bloc sale of Maxwell House, a 13-storey commercial development comprising 145 strata units (Leong 2021). The project alone accounted for 98% of the total transacted area in Outram, and 44% of the total transacted area across all areas. Therefore, prudence must be exercised when gauging future trends as such projects are the exception rather than the rule. Hence, while figures for 2020 to June 1, 2021 show signs of growth, it seems unlikely that total office space transacted will match pre-pandemic levels, although the

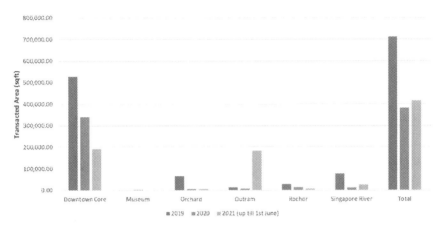

Figure 2.9: Transacted office space in the city centre from 2019–June 1, 2021 (*Source*: REALIS 2021)

number of office transactions in the city centre seems to be growing. This could be explained by companies: 1) downsizing their offices due to the increase in remote working, 2) cutting costs in an uncertain economic climate, and 3) adopting hub-and-spoke models to spread out the workforce beyond the CBD.

INDUSTRY COMPOSITION

In this section, we examine the industry composition of the city centre. The data, which comprises the number of employed residents aged 15 years and over by industry based on Census data for 2020, was gleaned from SingStat, the database of the Singapore Department of Statistics (DOS). The highest concentration of workers in the city centre came from the Financial & Insurance Services industry (26.5%) (Figure 2.10). This was followed by the following industries: Professional Services (16.0%), Wholesale & Retail Trade (13.4%), Accommodation & Food Services (8%), and Information & Communications (8%). Thus, the industrial composition of Singapore's city centre indeed reflects its role as the Central Business District.

Table 2.2 shows the top three industries for individual planning areas in the city centre. The data chimes with previous findings.

Is the City Centre Hollowing Out? 51

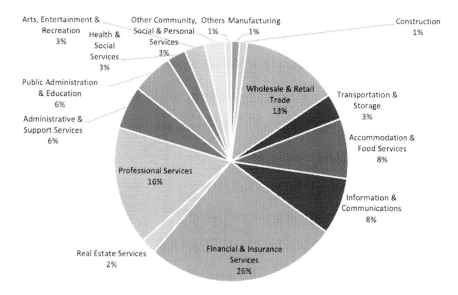

Figure 2.10: Concentration of employed residents aged 15 years and over in different industries in the city centre in 2020 (*Source*: DOS 2020)

Table 2.2: Top 3 industries for individual planning areas in the city centre

Planning area	Top 3 industries (in descending order from left to right)		
Downtown Core	Financial & Insurance Services	Professional Services	Wholesale & Retail Trade
Museum	Public Administration & Education	Financial & Insurance Services	Professional Services
Newton	Financial & Insurance Services	Others	Health & Social Services
Orchard	Wholesale & Retail Trade	Accommodation & Food Services	Information & Communications
Outram	Professional Services	Financial & Insurance Services	Wholesale & Retail Trade
Rochor	Wholesale & Retail Trade	Accommodation & Food Services	Professional Services
Singapore River	Accommodation & Food Services	Professional Services	Wholesale & Retail Trade

Source: DOS 2023

For instance, Downtown Core and Outram remain critical locations for office activity, while Orchard remains the premier retail precinct, followed closely by Rochor. Interestingly, Public Administration and Education is the top industry for the Museum planning area — possibly, Museum acts as a sub-market in the city centre, which explains why its commercial vacancy and rental trends (Tables 2.2 and 2.3) seem to digress from the other areas.

Table 2.3: Inflow and outflow of firms to/from the city centre

Inflow of Firms into Central Business District

Sector	Company	Period	Floorspace (sqft)	Address
Tech & ICT				
	IRESS Market Tech	Q2 2020	4,680	18 Robinson
	Shutterstock	Q2 2020	8,850	18 Robinson
	Delivery Hero	Q3 2020	50,000	Afro-Asia i-Mark
	Rackspace Technology	Q4 2020	4,876	One Raffles Place
	ByteDance (TikTok)	Q4 2020	60,000	One Raffles Quay
	Alibaba & Lazada	Q4 2020	140,000	5One Central
	Tencent (WeChat)	Q4 2020	10,000	OCBC Centre East
	Spotify	Q4 2020	37,000	5One Central
	Amazon	Q4 2020	90,000	Asia Square Tower 1
	Equinix	Q1 2021	80,000	79 Robinson Road
	Twitter	Q2 2021	22,000	Capitagreen
	LinkedIn	Q3 2021	22,000	Marina Bay Financial Tower 2
Flexi-work				
	Arcc Spaces	Q2 2020	19,000	One Marina Boulevard
	The Great Room	Q2 2020	37,000	Afro-Asia i-Mark
	JustCo	Q2 2020	45,000	OCBC Centre East

Table 2.3: (*Continued*)

		Inflow		
Sector	Company	Period	Floorspace (sqft)	Address
	Work Project	Q3 2020	21,500	Capitagreen
	JustCo	Q4 2020	60,000	Centrepoint
	WeWork	Q4 2020	82,000	30 Raffles Place
	IWG Regus	Q2 2021	22,000	PLUS building
	The Executive Centre	Q3 2021	38,736	One Raffles Quay North Tower
Finance				
	Citadel Enterprise	Q1 2021	30,000	Asia Square Tower 2
	QBE Insurance	Q4 2020	31,000	Guoco Tower

		Outflow	
Sector	Company	Floorspace surrendered (sqft)	Remarks
Finance			
	Citigroup	90,000 (by Amazon)	Some functions to be relocated to Changi Business Park.
	DBS Bank	75,000	Existing office space in Changi Business Park.
	Mizuho Bank	16,800	Has back-up office at Changi Business Park.
	Sumitomo Mitsubishi Banking Corporation	70,000	Remainder of back-office functions will move to Changi Business Park.
	Australia and New Zealand Banking Group	20,000	N.A.
	Standard Chartered	80,000 or more[†]	Upgrading facility at Changi. Business Park.

(*Continued*)

Table 2.3: (*Continued*)

Sector	Company	Period	Floorspace (sqft)	Address
	Sompo Insurance		10,400	N.A.
Tech & ICT				
	Grab		54,000	Moving to One-North H.Q.

†Exact floorspace to be confirmed.
Compiled from various sources: *The Business Times* 2020a, 2020b, 2021; *The Straits Times* 2020a, 2020b, 2020c, 2021; Chin 2021; Chow 2019; Commercial Guru 2020; Corporate Locations 2020a, 2020b, 2020c, 2021a, 2021b; Knowles 2020; Office Finder 2021; Rashiwala and Lee, 2016; Rashiwala 2020; Siow 2020

INFLOW AND OUTFLOW OF FIRMS

In this final section, we turn our attention to current and future commercial trends concerning Singapore's city centre. As outlined in the beginning of our chapter, the city centre plays a critical role in Singapore's success as a global hub for talent and business. Yet, the ongoing socio-spatial reconfiguration of work has changed the way offices are meant to function. Trends such as work-from-home and remote work are gaining regularity in the new state of work, and companies are readjusting their positions towards commercial space.

A fundamental question is whether the CBD will lose its competitive edge, or the basis of its existence as a cluster of economic activity. Our sampling of recent transaction data suggests otherwise (Table 2.3). Instead, commercial uptake of office space seems to be picking up speed. At the outset of COVID-19 (Q2 2020), we see strong initial demand from the flexi-work sector, perhaps driven by companies slashing office space or diversifying their workforce across various locations. Unsurprisingly, the greatest uptake of office space occurred in the fourth quarter of 2020 — when Singapore implemented Phase 3 of its Circuit Breaker, and there was further resumption of activities. Demand was led by global technology companies, possibly because such firms were 1) capitalising on decreasing office rentals, and 2) undertaking their own global risk diversification strategies, where Singapore was perceived as a safe location relative to the global situation. Uptake of office space in 2021 has similarly been dominated by technology firms.

In terms of outflow, many companies in the finance industry (mostly banks) have surrendered or are planning to give up prime office space in the CBD for peripheral areas such as Changi. However, these CBD office spaces are readily snapped up by technology firms. On the whole, these changes signify both the increasing affluence and supremacy of the technology sector and the continued international confidence in Singapore's CBD commercial space.

IMPLICATIONS OF COVID-19 ON THE CITY CENTRE

This chapter has heretofore discussed various components of the city centre and tracked their changes from pre-COVID-19 to the present. Contrary to popular belief that city centres will hollow out, our analysis gestures towards a more sanguine outcome for Singapore's city centre, which we encapsulate in three broad trends: 1) the continued relevance of the physical office, 2) the changing industrial composition of the city centre, and 3) the transformation of the city centre into a mixed-use precinct.

CONTINUED RELEVANCE OF THE PHYSICAL OFFICE

Our analysis has demonstrated that vacancy rates in Singapore's central area have generally decreased from 2019 to 2021, and office transactions show strong signs of growth post-pandemic. These indicate that the city centre, as well as physical offices, remain requisite despite the rise in remote and hybrid forms of work in recent times.

The pandemic has not dampened the traditional appeal of the city centre. For instance, city centres continue to epitomise modernity and prestige, which remain significant pull factors for companies and workers (Clark 2020). Furthermore, agglomeration economies afforded by city centres are growing in importance: According to a study by Ernst & Young, companies are increasingly stressing the importance of being close to clients and businesses (57% in 2020 compared to 46% in 2017) (Lhermitte 2020). In Singapore, Downtown Core remains the prime central area, with its critical density of office transactions and large office spaces transacted.

Physical offices have also remained vital, largely attributed to the social environments they offer. According to a survey[1] conducted by the Lee Kuan Yew Centre for Innovative Cities (LKYCIC) titled "Survey on Citizens and the City: Changing Perceptions by Singaporeans" in February 2021, the top three reasons why people prefer working from the office are access to resources, collaboration, and increased productivity (see Chapter 10's Annex). Similarly, the top three reasons why people feel less productive working from home are more distractions, difficulty interacting/communicating with colleagues, and poorer access to resources and business partners/services. Evidently, the social functions afforded by the office are indispensable. Moreover, Jones Lang LaSalle (JLL) reported that workers in Singapore are growing tired of working from home, and desire returning to the office as they crave face-to-face interactions with their colleagues (Tay 2021). In the study by JLL, it was found that the ideal number of days employees want to work from the office has risen from 1.7 days in October 2020, to 2.3 days in March 2021 (Tay 2021). Therefore, the physical office will continue to be relevant in the future as the fundamental social functions it has traditionally served — such as enabling collaboration and fostering camaraderie — remain abiding.

CHANGING INDUSTRIAL COMPOSITION OF THE CITY CENTRE

The finance sector has been at the helm of Singapore's city centre for decades, with major banks serving as anchor tenants for many of its skyscrapers. Today, as a result of the pandemic, Singapore is witnessing an emigration of banks from its city centre. Yet, this phenomenon is not nascent: banks have been restructuring and downsizing prime office space since the Global Financial Crisis in 2009 (Shiao 2021). Over the past decade, many banks have relocated back- and middle-office operations to cheaper areas such as Changi Business Park and Mapletree Business City (Shiao 2021). While the pandemic has accelerated this trend as banks learn they can operate effectively without most employees working from a physical office, it is worth noting that banks still typically choose to locate their headquarters in the city centre given the prestige of a CBD address (Ong 2019).

Moreover, the departure of banks from Singapore's city centre will not spell long-term trouble for its office market. This is attributed to strong demand from technology firms which are drawn to Singapore for her close proximity to Southeast Asia, business-friendly regulations, robust political environment, sophisticated infrastructures, and talented pool of labour (Tay, Goh, and Tee 2020). Moreover, the city centre is a popular location for these companies due to its accessibility and connectivity, amenities and offices, and ease of attracting talent (Tay, Goh, and Tee 2020). Notably, strong demand drivers include US and Chinese technology behemoths such as Amazon, Twitter, ByteDance, and Tencent, who are capitalising on Singapore's geopolitical neutrality amidst growing tensions between the United States and China (Ng 2021). Hence, as technology firms increasingly prevail over the finance sector, we are witnessing a transformation in the industrial composition of Singapore's city centre.

A CITY CENTRE FOR WORKING, LIVING AND PLAYING

One thing the pandemic has crystallised for occupiers is the importance of flexibility. In terms of lease flexibility, firms are increasingly seeking shorter-term commitments in light of the volatilities and uncertainties of the pandemic (Wright and Kunhiraman 2020). In terms of space flexibility, the ability to expand or shrink footprints at short notice has become a fundamental consideration for companies (Wright and Kunhiraman 2020). Indeed, demand for flexible working spaces has grown since the onset of the pandemic.

Prime office buildings with technology-centric specifications offer the agility that firms now desire, putting ageing office stock at risk of increasing vacancy rates (CBRE Research 2021). This places pressure on landlords of old buildings to redevelop to stay fashionable and competitive. Thus, many might leverage the URA's Central Business District Incentive Scheme and Strategic Development Incentive (SDI) (both implemented in 2019), which encourage the conversion of older buildings into mixed-use developments offering live, work, and play options (Wong 2019). One example of a building which has adopted the CBD Incentive Scheme is the Fuji Xerox Tower. Slated for redevelopment in 2020 owing to profit losses engendered by the pandemic, the new building will serve office, retail, and residential functions (Burgos 2020). Complementing these schemes are the government's plans to rejuvenate Orchard Road to bolster its position as a vibrant lifestyle destination, as well as plans to transform the Greater Southern Waterfront into an urban living space (Song and Wong 2021). In all, these initiatives will help reverse the increase in vacancy rates for areas such as Orchard, Outram, Rochor, and Singapore River.

Furthermore, the rise in the number of homes built in the city centre speaks to its shift from a mono-use to mixed-use space. Notable examples are luxury condominiums Midtown Modern and Midtown Bay near Bugis, and One Bernam near Tanjong Pagar, launched in 2021 (Yee 2021). Plans were also announced for the redevelopment of a white site in Marina View: most of the site will be dedicated for residential use (min. 51,000 m^2) and hotel use (min. 26,000 m^2), while a maximum of 2,000 m^2 each will be dedicated for office use and commercial use (including retail and F&B) respectively (Yee 2021). Most recently, the Housing and Development Board (HDB) announced the new Prime Location Public Housing (PLH) scheme, which will see the construction of more public housing projects in the city centre (Lim 2021). The first project under the new scheme will be built in Rochor, and was launched at the recent Build-to-Order (BTO) exercise (Ng 2021). With the influx of homes in the city centre, a very possible corollary would be a rise in lifestyle and recreational amenities to cater to residents, including grocery stores, schools, parks, and gyms. Indeed, the pandemic has reinforced desires for a lively, mixed-use city centre: According to Singapore's C-Suite executives, planners must create exciting and versatile spaces in the CBD in order to safeguard its vibrancy post-pandemic (Wong 2021).

CONCLUSION

By way of summary, this chapter has demonstrated the value of Singapore's city centre, delved into its spatial structure, investigated its individual planning areas, and presented trends that have emerged from the pandemic. While being careful not to undermine the devastations that COVID-19 has brought in its wake, we posit that the pandemic has offered Singapore salutary lessons: that physical offices remain integral assets, the traditional dominance of banks is eroding while technology firms are growing in prominence, and the city centre is increasingly being transformed into a mixed-use precinct. Now, three years into the pandemic, Singapore's city centre appears resilient, displaying a strong economic outlook with office rental rates surpassing pre-COVID-19 levels. Contrary to expectations, the emergence of home offices and third spaces in regional areas has not diminished the significance of the city centre. Therefore, it is our belief that the pandemic has not led and will not lead to the demise of Singapore's city centre, which will continue to remain relevant, albeit with a changing identity. As the pandemic evolves, let us not underestimate the robustness of Singapore's city centre — it has stood the test of time, and will continue to do so.

ENDNOTE

A total of 2,000 respondents were surveyed, comprised primarily of Singapore Citizens/Permanent Residents working in various industries.

REFERENCES

Burgos, Jonathan. 2020. "CDL to Redevelop Fuji Xerox Towers, Central Mall." Mingtiandi. August 13, 2020. https://www.mingtiandi.com/real-estate/projects/cdl-to-redevelop-fuji-xerox-towers-central-mall/.

CBRE Research. 2021. "Capitalising on Bifurcated Real Estate." CBRE. https://www.cbre.com/-/media/project/cbre/shared-site/insights/books/singapore-real-estate-market-outlook-2021/singapore-market-outlook-2021.pdf.

Chin, Charlene. 2021. "Committed office leases helped mitigate occupancy declines last year: Knight Frank." January 20, 2021. https://www.edgeprop.sg/property-news/committed-office-leases-helped-mitigate-occupancy-declines-last-year-knight-frank.

Chow, Cecilia. 2019. "The Great Room and owners of Afro-Asia i-Mark adopt revenue-sharing model." October 11, 2019. https://sg.news.yahoo.com/great-room-owners-afro-asia-021259718.html.

Clark, Greg. 2020. "The Planet of Cities: Business Districts as Usual?" RICS. October 16, 2020. https://www.rics.org/news-insights/wbef/the-planet-of-cities-business-districts-as-usual.

CommercialGuru. 2020. "AXA to exit AXA Tower amid redevelopment plans for the iconic building." December 8, 2020. https://www.commercialguru.com.sg/property-management-news/2020/12/195115/axa-to-exit-axa-tower-amid-redevelopment-plans-for-the-iconic-building.

Corporate Locations. 2020. "Office Market Update." https://www.corporatelocations.com.sg/pdf_2020/SG_Market_Update_JAN20.pdf.

Corporate Locations. 2020. "Singapore Office Leasing Update: Recent Relocations." https://www.corporatelocations.com.sg/updates/singapore-office-leasing-update-nov20.php.

Corporate Locations. 2020. "Singapore Office Market Review Q3/Q4 2020." https://www.corporatelocations.com.sg/pdf_2020/CL-Market-Review-OCT20.pdf.

Corporate Locations. 2021. "DBS Group Holdings trimming their office space footprint in the CBD." https://www.corporatelocations.com.sg/updates/dbs-office-space-footprint-cbd.php.

Corporate Locations. 2021. "Office Market Review Q2 2021." https://www.corporatelocations.com.sg/market-research/Q3-2021/forecast.php.

Dutta, Soumitra, Rafael Escalona Reynoso, Sacha Wunsch-Vincent, Lorena Rivera León, and Cashelle Hardman. 2019. "The Global Innovation Index 2019: Creating Healthy Lives — The Future of Medical Innovation." Cornell University, INSEAD, and the World Intellectual Property Organization. https://www.wipo.int/edocs/pubdocs/en/wipo_pub_gii_2019-chapter1b.pdf.

Goh, Hup Chor, and Chye Kiang Heng. 2016. "Shaping Singapore's Cityscape through Urban Design." In Heng, Chye Kiang (ed.) *50 Years of Urban Planning in Singapore*, 211–234. World Scientific Publishing. https://doi.org/10.1142/9789814656474_0012.

Knowles, Catherine. 2020. "Rackspace Technology Opens New Singapore Office." DataCenterNews Asia Pacific. October 28, 2020. https://datacenternews.asia/story/rackspace-technology-opens-new-singapore-office.

KPMG. 2017. "The Case for a Hong Kong RHQ Tax Incentive." KPMG. https://assets.kpmg.com/content/dam/kpmg/cn/pdf/en/2017/10/the-case-for-a-hk-rhq-tax-incentive-report.pdf.

Leong, Grace. 2021. "Maxwell House Sold En Bloc to Chip Eng Seng, SingHaiyi for $276.8m, above Asking Price." *The Straits Times*. May 7, 2021. https://www.straitstimes.com/business/property/maxwell-house-sold-en-bloc-to-chip-eng-seng-singhaiyi-for-2768-million-above.

Lhermitte, Marc. 2020. "Is This the End of the Central Business District?" EY Consulting. May 19, 2020. https://www.ey.com/en_sg/real-estate-hospitality-construction/is-this-the-end-of-the-central-business-district.

Lim, Janice. 2021. "MND Announces Stricter Ownership Criteria for HDB Flats in Prime Locations, Including 10-Year Minimum Occupancy Period." *TODAY*. October 27, 2021. https://www.todayonline.com/singapore/least-10-year-occupancy-new-hdb-flats-prime-areas-prevent-build-wealthy-enclaves.

Lynch, Kevin. 1960. *The Image of the City*. Publication of the Joint Center for Urban Studies. M.I.T. Press.

Monetary Authority of Singapore. 2021. "Remarks by Mr Ravi Menon, Managing Director, MAS at the MAS Annual Report 2020/2021 Virtual Media Conference on 30 June 2021." June 30, 2021. https://www.mas.gov.sg/news/speeches/2021/remarks-by-mr-ravi-menon-managing-director-mas-at-the-mas-annual-report-2020-2021-virtual-media-conference-on-30-june-2021.

Ng, Jun Sen. 2021. "The Big Read: As Tech Titans Converge in Singapore, Can It Truly Become Asia's Silicon Valley?" *can*. February 8, 2021. https://www.channelnewsasia.c25ingaporeore/big-read-tech-titans-converge-singapore-asia-silicon-valley-324046.

Office Finder. 2021. "Office Space Downsizing By Banks Started Over 10 Years Ago." 12 April, 2021. https://officefinder.com.sg/office-space-downsizing-by-banks-started-over-10-years-ago/.

Ong, Yunita. 2019. "Beyond the Core: Singapore's Office Decentralisation." *Business Times*. March 30, 2019. https://www.businesstimes.com.sg/opinion-features/features/beyond-core-singapores-office-decentralisation.

Ramani, Arjun, and Nicholas Bloom. 2021. "The Donut Effect of Covid-19 on Cities." Working Paper. Working Paper Series, National Bureau of Economic Research. https://doi.org/10.3386/w28876.

Rashiwala, Kalpana, and Jamie Lee. 2016. "More Banks May Cut Back on Office Space amid Weakening Outlook." March 22, 2016. https://www.businesstimes.com.sg/companies-markets/banking-finance/more-banks-may-cut-back-office-space-amid-weakening-outlook.

Rashiwala, Kalpana. 2020. "A Stream of Office Space Leasing Deals in Pipeline despite Uncertain Business Climate." The Business Times. July 17, 2020. https://www.businesstimes.com.sg/real-estate/a-stream-of-office-space-leasing-deals-in-pipeline-despite-uncertain-business-climate.

REALIS (various years) https://www.ura.gov.sg/reis/index.

Sassen, Saskia. 2001. *The Global City: New York, London, Tokyo*. 2nd ed. Princeton University Press.

Shiao, Vivien. 2021. "Banks to Speed up Shrinking and Shifting of CBD Space amid Hybrid Work." *Business Times*. April 12, 2021. https://www.businesstimes.com.sg/banking-finance/banks-to-speed-up-shrinking-and-shifting-of-cbd-space-amid-hybrid-work.

Singapore Economic Development Board. 2021. "Headquarters." 2021. https://www.edb.gov.sg/en/our-industries/headquarters.html.

Siow, Li Sen. 2020. "Original Ideas for Guoco Midtown Still Relevant Even in the New Normal, Says Group MD." The Business Times. August 20, 2020. https://www.businesstimes.com.sg/property/original-ideas-guoco-midtown-still-relevant-even-new-normal-says-group-md.

Song, Tricia, and Shirley Wong. 2021. "Singapore Market Outlook 2021." Colliers International. https://www.colliers.com/download-article?itemId=018f9556-b21e-4efe-b1e9-f1cfe5f07a75

Tay, Huey Ying, Doreen Goh, and Michelle Tee. 2020. "Lure of Singapore for Tech Firms." Jones Lang LaSalle. April 21, 2020. https://www.jll.com.sg/en/trends-and-insights/resear25ingaporeore-a-lure-for-tech.

Tay, Huey Ying. 2021. "Singapore's Future of Work Is Shaping up." July 27, 2021. https://www.joneslanglasalle.cn/en/trends-and-insights/research/singapores-future-of-work-shaping-up.

Tay, Timothy. 2021. "The Executive Centre Opens New Extension at One Raffles Quay." Yahoo News. June 17, 2021. https://sg.news.yahoo.com/executive-centre-opens-extension-one-213000152.html.

The Business Times. 2020a. "TikTok Owner Bytedance Moving to Bigger Singapore Office at One Raffles Quay." October 15, 2020. https://www.businesstimes.com.sg/startups-tech/startups/tiktok-owner-bytedance-moving-bigger-singapore-office-one-raffles-quay.

The Business Times. 2020b. "Tencent chooses co-working space for first Singapore office." October 16, 2020. https://www.businesstimes.com.sg/garage/news/tencent-chooses-co-working-space-for-first-singapore-office.

The Business Times. 2021. "DBS to cut Singapore office space: sources." April 9, 2021. https://www.businesstimes.com.sg/companies-markets/dbs-to-cut-singapore-office-space-sources.

The Straits Times. 2015. "In His Own Words: IRs Needed for S'pore to Keep Abreast of the Top Cities," March 27, 2015. https://www.straitstimes.c25ingaporeore/in-his-own-words-irs-needed-for-spore-to-keep-abreast-of-the-top-cities.

The Straits Times. 2020a. "Amazon to Take Three Floors of Citigroup Office Space in Singapore's Asia Square Tower 1, Say Sources," September 30, 2020. https://www.straitstimes.com/business/property/amazon-to-take-three-floors-of-citigroup-office-space-in-singapores-asia-square.

The Straits Times. 2020b. "Singapore office rents drop further in Q3, tenants asking for short-term renewals: Report." October 6, 2020. https://www.straitstimes.com/business/property/singapore-office-rents-drop-further-in-q3-tenants-ask-for-short-term-renewals.

The Straits Times. 2020c. "Mizuho to cut Singapore office space in workplace revamp: Sources." November 20, 2020. https://www.straitstimes.com/business/banking/mizuho-to-cut-singapore-office-space-in-workplace-revamp-sources.

The Straits Times. 2021. "Standard Chartered bank considers slashing Singapore office space: Sources." April 28, 2021. https://www.straitstimes.com/business/banking/standard-chartered-bank-considers-slashing-singapore-office-space.

Urban Redevelopment Authority. 2019. "The Planning Act Master Plan Written Statement 2019." Urban Redevelopment Authority. https://www.ura.gov.sg/-/media/Corporate/Planning/Master-Plan/MP19writtenstatement.pdf?la=en.

Von Thünen, Johann Heinrich. 1966. *Isolated State* (Carla M. Wartenberg, Trans.). Pergamon Press (Original work published 1826).

Wong, Derek. 2019. "URA Unveils Plan to Revitalise Orchard Road, CBD." *The Straits Times*. March 27, 2019. https://www.straitstimes. c26ingaporeore/orchard-road-cbd-to-be-boosted-with-greater-connectivity-and-ura-schemes-encouraging.

Wong, Shirley. 2021. "*Expect a turnaround in H2 2021* (Q2 2021)." Colliers International.

Wong, Shirley. 2021. "*Office Q3 2021: Rents see an upturn* (Q3 2021)." Colliers International.

Wong, Valerie. 2021. "CBD Reimagined and Repurposed." *Business Times*. July 26, 2021. https://www.businesstimes.com.sg/cbd-reimagined-and-repurposed.

Wright, Jonathan, and Rakesh Kunhiraman. 2020. "Flexible Workspace Outlook Report 2020." Colliers International. https://www.colliers.com/download-article?itemId=76e934c0-2461-4dba-a7bc-5a4692366e00.

Yee, Leslie. 2021. "Marina View: Testing the 'Work, Live, Play' Concept within CBD." *Business Times*. September 7, 2021. https://www.businesstimes.com.sg/property/marina-view-testing-work-live-play-concept-within-cbd.

© 2024 World Scientific Publishing Company
https://doi.org/10.1142/9789811287848_0003

The Digital Economy Takes Over

Dinithi Jayasekara & Fredrik Hansson

The COVID-19 pandemic was a catalyst that moved work, commerce, and social relations into the digital space. In the wake of the pandemic, Singaporeans were advised to work from home and limit social interactions. This caused internet traffic to increase by as much as 60% (Wong 2020), while the number of contactless payments through payment services such as PayNow doubled (Yong 2021). As people struggled to avoid physical contact, digital innovation in the private sector accelerated to meet the growing demand for contactless communication and transactions. Traditional bricks-and-mortar businesses supplemented their storefront locations with online services through digital platforms; general practitioners (GPs) offered telemedicine for patients in home recovery, and employers adopted new routines and means of communication to facilitate remote work. By some estimates, the value of the consumer and business adoptions of digital solutions in the first month of the pandemic was equal to the adoption usually seen over a five-year period (Baig *et al.* 2020). Although safe-distancing restrictions were gradually lifted, and life slowly returned to normal, new digital technology and online habits permanently changed the digital economy in which we work and do commerce.

However, for Singapore, accelerating digital technology adoption during the pandemic was not drastic as it was for many other countries. Singapore was one of the first nations to recognise the digital economy's potential for job creation. In 2014, the Singapore government created the Smart Nation initiative to promote infocomm technologies, and in 2018, the Infocomm Media Development Authority (IMDA) launched the Digital Economy Framework for Action to increase the competitiveness of firms and support the growth of the digital economy. Despite Singapore's previous initiatives, the speed of technological innovation has exceeded all expectations during the COVID-19 pandemic, and regulations have created bottlenecks that slowed down the deployment of new digital solutions. The Singapore government has responded by stepping up its efforts in lifting red tape to facilitate new means of interaction between business, consumers, as well as government agencies. For example, 99% of all government transactions with citizens can now be done digitally, years ahead of schedule (Chia 2022). Due to its early recognition of the importance of the digital economy, Singapore was better positioned to transition to a digital economy in the beginning of the COVID-19 pandemic. However, future macroeconomic uncertainties pose new challenges. Globally, as well as for Singapore, rising energy prices following the Russian invasion of Ukraine has increased operational costs of large energy-hungry data centres; the China–United States trade war has deepened the global shortage of semiconductors, and rising inflation and interest rates have reduced the appetite for investments in risky growth industries. The rapid changes brought by the expansion of digital economy has motivated us to dive deep to understand what is truly entailed in a digital economy, the opportunities and challenges faced by Singapore and other leaders of the digital economy, and what needs to be done to ensure a thriving digital economy post COVID-19.

WHAT IS A DIGITAL ECONOMY?

The Smart Nation Singapore defines the digital economy as the adoption of the latest technology to digitalise processes and drive business growth. However, there is no agreed upon definition of what makes up a digital economy. One report by the International Monetary Fund (IMF) notes that the digital economy "is sometimes defined narrowly as online platforms, and activities that owe their existence to such platforms, yet, in a broad sense, all activities that use digitised

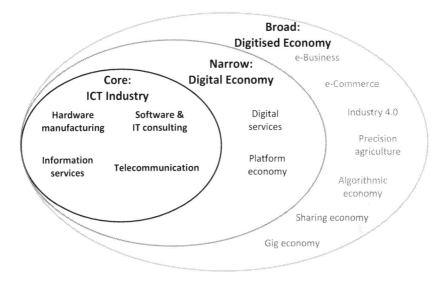

Figure 3.1: Scope of the digital economy (*Source*: Adopted from Bukht and Heeks 2018)

data are part of the digital economy: in modern economies, the entire economy" (International Monetary Fund, Statistics Department. 2018). Economists have conceptualised the digital economy in terms of industry classification codes to measure its size and to facilitate cross-country comparisons. Building on previous research by Bukht and Heeks (2018), the Organisation for Economic Co-operation and Development (OECD) has proposed a Roadmap Toward a Common Framework for Measuring the Digital Economy (Hatem, Ker, and Mitchell 2020). The roadmap proposed a tiered definition of the digital economy as seen in Figure 3.1, where the digital economy can be divided into a core, narrow, and broad definition. We will use this definition to explain what a digital economy is.

The core definition of the digital economy is limited to only the information and communications technology (ICT) industry. For measurement purposes, this is a useful definition since data on the national size of the ICT industry is often available through national statistical agencies. The national accounts show that the Singaporean ICT industry grew on average 5.9% per year over the last two decades, outpacing the overall economy by 1.2 percentage points and increasing its share of the total GDP from 2.9% in 2000 to 4.7% in 2021. This could be compared with 3.8% in the European Union (EU) and 5.6% in the United States, but the relative size of the ICT industry could be misleading if the size of the rest of the economy is small (Eurostat 2020; Statista 2022). Furthermore, the definition does not include many important elements of digital goods and services that are bought and sold online, and it thus fails to capture much of the recent growth in digital platforms that occurred during the COVID-19 pandemic.

The second definition of the digital economy is the narrow definition, which extends beyond the core definition to also include digital services and platforms. This definition is what Bukht and Heeks (2018) refers to as the true "digital economy". In addition to the ICT industry, it includes digital services and online platforms, such as Amazon, Facebook, and Netflix, that primarily provide services over the internet. Related to the service and platform economy, the gig and sharing economy are an important and growing part of the digital economy, but they differ in the sense that most of the services are sold online but provided in the physical space. This can be exemplified by the Grab ride hailing service, where the app matches consumers with drivers, and most of the payment for the service goes to the driver and fuel costs rather than the IT service. The gig and sharing economy can thus be classified as borderline traditional services that leverage digital technology to improve matching between the consumer and provider. While the core definition was easier to define in terms of industry classifications, the digital technology associated with digital services and platforms in the narrow definition transcends industry codes. The lack of a consensus on industry codes under this definition complicates its usage and prevents accurate measurements and comparisons across countries.[1]

The broadest definition is called the "Digitised Economy" and includes all sectors of the economy that in anyway uses digital technology (Bukht and Heeks 2018). The difference between the broad and narrow definitions is that the broad definition also includes traditional businesses that previously existed offline and now have adopted digital solutions to enhance their business. If the industry exists solely because of the ICT industry, it can be thought of as part of the digital economy, while industries that would have existed without the ICT industry can be classified as outside of the digital economy. This includes retail stores, agriculture, and the manufacturing industry, which have been digitally transformed into e-commerce, precision agriculture, and industry 4.0. E-commerce had a large boom during the COVID-19 pandemic and by one estimate, the gross merchandise value of e-commerce in Singapore increased by 35% in 2021 and reached US$15 billion (Google, Temasek, and Bain & Company 2021). Whichever definition that is used, it is important to note that the digital economy has been growing over time, and this trend is likely to continue post COVID-19.

THE IMPORTANCE OF THE DIGITAL ECONOMY

To understand what the digital economy is, it is also important to know its implications for society. The transformative force of the digital economy is its cost-saving and productivity-increasing potential. Research has identified five costs that are rapidly decreasing in the digital economy: search costs, replication costs, transportation costs, tracking costs, and verification costs (Goldfarb and Tucker 2019). Lower search costs increase the search scope and makes it easier for consumers to identify niche products among a diverse set of heterogenous goods, which theoretically allows for more product variety. It also reduces the cost of comparing products that vary in quality and price, thereby increasing competition. Replication costs are close to zero for digital goods, and due to their non-rival nature, they can be consumed by multiple consumers at the same time without the consumption of one consumer affecting the experience of another. While replication costs are low, initial development costs are very high. This combination implies that copyright laws are more important in the digital economy, where high development costs need to be divided over a large number of transactions, while pirated copies that are cheap to forge undercut the price of the developer and reduce the number of transactions over which development costs can be shared. Similar to replication costs, transportation costs are close to zero when goods are digitally distributed over the internet. The reduction in tracking costs brought about by big data has made it easier for companies to monitor consumers behaviour on the internet and offer tailored products to fit the consumer. This has also altered the way traditional supply chains have been organised.[2] It has also raised questions about privacy concerns as more data is collected with limited knowledge by the user. Lastly, lower verification costs make it easier for consumers and businesses to communicate their identity and reputation. Examples include digital identities such as the Singapore Personal Access (Singpass), product reviews, and rankings on online platforms. Overall, the digital economy has a great cost-saving potential that can bring about unprecedented efficiency improvements in the economy.

Moreover, the geographical boundary within which a digital economy can be defined is increasingly blurred when goods and services are digitally produced and sold online. For a land-constrained country such as Singapore, this brings opportunities since physical activities can be transferred to the internet and thus frees up costly space. Another consequence of the zero-transportation cost is that cross-border competition increases, which presents new challenges, but also opens up new markets. International regulations surrounding the digital economy are established through Digital Economy Agreements (DEA), which are treaties that regulate digital trade rules and digital economy collaborations. Singapore has proactively sought to integrate itself with other digital markets, and in June 2020, Singapore became one of the founding members of the Digital Economic Partnership Agreement (DEPA), the world's first digital-only trade agreement.

The non-physical nature of digital goods and services and the lack of a common transaction location are defining features of the digital economy. While services can be sold by companies that are not physically present in the country where the consumer is based, the definition of the transaction location has, for tax reasons, been regulated and defined as the location of the consumer (Ministry of Finance n.d.). Some countries have fared better in this competition, and there are lessons to be learnt by studying the most successful digital economies.

WHO ARE THE LEADERS?

The geography of the world's digital economy is concentrated in two countries: the United States and China. In terms of the value added, the United States has the world's largest ICT sector. The United States plays a frontier role in many of the emerging digital technologies including Internet of Things (IoT), 5G mobile broadband, cloud computing, automation, and robotics. At the epicentre of this success is the Silicon Valley attracting Big Tech firms with ubiquitous cheap capital and tech talent supported by a tech friendly regulatory environment. Silicon Valley-based companies have been leading the development in new technology for decades, and recent advances in generative artificial intelligence (AI), such as ChatGPT from OpenAI, have sparked renewed interest in AI and technology investments in the area. For decades, cities have attempted to follow and replicate the Silicon model; but failed. Nevertheless, few superstar economies have emerged in the digital space.

In Asia Pacific, digital transformation accounts for nearly 60% of Asia Pacific's gross domestic product (Jimenez et al. 2018). The Fletcher School at Tufts University ranks Singapore as the leader in their digital evolution index, recognising Singapore as one of the "super stand-out" economies, alongside Hong Kong, South Korea, and Malaysia, for high digital advancement and momentum (Chakravorti et al. 2020, 7). Since the onset of the pandemic, Vietnam, Taiwan, Thailand, and Indonesia have become hot spots for investments due to evolving digital infrastructure and increasing digital engagement by citizens (e.g., Indonesia has the world's fourth-largest internet-user population). The pandemic has pushed online purchases to an unprecedented level, making e-commerce the star industry in the Asian digital economy. While Asia Pacific is home to many fast-growing digital economies, most European countries are considered "stall out" economies due to the existing high state of digital advancement but low momentum. Yet, they enjoy optimistic attitudes towards digitalisation because of their ability to push regulations and policies for greater digital inclusion, equity, and protection. Since these topics have taken centre stage around the future of digital economy, it is useful to look at a few countries that have pushed regulatory boundaries to enhance inclusive growth in the digital economy. The next section provides three case studies on Singapore, Sweden, and Estonia. Sweden and Estonia were selected as case studies because of their reputation for digital innovation, and they both rank within the top ten, globally, for their higher levels of digital evolution, digital trust, and sustainable digital maturity (Chakravorti *et al.* 2020). For ten consecutive years, 2010–2020, Sweden ranked as the most innovative economy in the world in the Global Innovation Index and is home to many successful IT start-ups, while Estonia is well known for its leading role in e-governance, being the first country to adopt online voting in 2005 and to offer cross-border digital identities. Both Sweden and Estonia are competitive in the digital economy, and the conditions for their success carry important lessons for Singapore. The experiences of these economies will set the stage to understand what makes a good leader in the digital economy.

SINGAPORE'S DIGITAL TRANSFORMATION

Singapore's national digitalisation efforts started as early as the 1980s with the foresight that digital disruption is a key enabler of industrial transformation. Since then, the city-state has undergone two waves of successful digital transformation. The first transformation converted Singapore into a regional hub for computer software development and services while the second, led by growth in the ICT sector, transformed Singapore into a hyper-networked, global hub for services. At present, Singapore's digital economy is valued at US$15 billion (GMV) and is expected to reach US$27 billion by 2025 (The State of SEA, 2020). The smart nation movement was introduced to push digital infrastructure in the public domain. These included e-payments (e.g., FAST, PayNow, SGQR), national digital identities, smart nation sensor platforms, digital mobility solutions, e-invoicing

(PEPPOL standard), national trade platforms, CODEX, and 5G technology, to name a few. In the race for internet speed, Singapore has secured the fastest average fixed broadband internet speed in the world (181.47 Mbps), beating Hong Kong and Iceland, while ranked fourth in the mobile internet category (The ASEAN Post team 2016). Although universal, fast, and reliable internet connection is a necessity, it is not sufficient to sustain a digital economy.

A few factors seem to have aligned due to the concerted efforts to push Singapore as a digital hub, both regionally and globally. First, Singapore has become a hot spot for global technology giants. For example, technology firms such as Microsoft and social media platforms like Facebook, Twitter, LinkedIn, and many others have anchored their regional offices and R&D labs in Singapore. Low taxation, a business-friendly environment, efficient and agile regulatory institutions, high-quality education, world-class healthcare, and a skilled workforce[3] have contributed to Singapore's success. It is home to a dynamic and thriving innovation ecosystem and a springboard for digital entrepreneurial ventures and partnerships.[4] Global geopolitics and stronger bilateral partnerships have also led many technology firms to shift to Singapore in recent years. In 2021, ByteDance, the parent company of TikTok, and American consumer electronics company Razer opened their regional offices in Singapore while Amazon, Spotify, Alibaba, Lazada, and Tencent increased their office footprint (see Chapter 2).

While these tech firms bring new economic opportunities, the city state pushes for digitalisation to overcome slow productivity growth. The public sector is a major actor and contributor to this initiative. One such example is Singapore's Housing and Development Board (HDB). In most countries, purchasing a house is an arduous task, having to deal with numerous paperwork from signing to verifying contracts or applying for housing loans. To enhance the efficiency, HDB introduced the "HDB Flat Portal", a one-stop solution to streamline buyers' and sellers' experience. This single integrated platform offers virtual tours of flats, customised self-assessment tools to assess financial credibility of buyers, estimated sale proceeds for sellers, and complete formalities related to documentation, such as submitting resale checklists, applying for valuations, and managing loan applications by both HDB and other financial institutions. The portal guides buyers and sellers on the schedule of transactions and formalities without having to rely on property agents. This has helped reduce balloting time for new build-to-order (BTO) flats from 6 to 3 weeks while time to resale flat transactions have decreased from 16 to 8 weeks. HDB continues to deliver digital services through augmented reality tools such as the mobile@HDB app, which uses camera images to search for the latest transaction prices of flats, and the "e-lobby" concept (self-help kiosk machines) to access HDB e-services around the clock.

On the commercial side, the government continues to deepen digital engagement through e-commerce and e-payment systems to help businesses automate and digitalise their products and services, to overcome declining productivity and labour constraints faced by many industries. As noted by Prime Minister Lee Hsien Loong in his 2021 APEC CEO speech: "Small and mid-sized enterprises (SMEs) account for 97% of all businesses and employ more than half of the combined workforce in APEC economies. But most SMEs are not as digitally prepared, and risk being left behind" (Chen 2021). Singapore had its share of SMEs vulnerable to digitalisation and introduced government programs to support their transition to the digital economy. For instance, the "Go Digital" programme supports small- and medium-sized enterprises (SMEs) to embark on digitalisation by guiding firms to self-assess their digital readiness, deploy curated digital solutions, and participate in industry-wide pilot programmes. In 2019, 39% of the enterprises invested in various digital infrastructure. In 2019, the share of enterprises that participated in e-commerce activities and adopted e-payment systems rose by 19% and 81% respectively from the previous year (Statista 2022).

The nature of the digital economy has enabled Singapore's small and large enterprises to access the region with similar market conditions at lower costs. In the wake of the pandemic, the transition of businesses and enterprises to the digital space have been relatively smooth due to Singapore's extensive connectivity and efficient supply chain ecosystem. This is reflected by Singapore's position in many of the global rankings related to e-trade. Among many others, Singapore is ranked first for its efficiency in customs procedures, third in global logistics competence, sixth in the timeliness of international shipments, and eighth in the tracking and tracing of shipments (Table 3.1). These have helped the city state to position itself as an intermediary hub for e-trade.

THE SWEDISH DIGITAL ECONOMY

Both Sweden and Singapore have achieved a high standard of living, but they differ considerably on other economic indicators that pose different challenges for the development of a digital economy, such as income and wealth inequality, levels of taxation, cost of labour, and population density. These are factors that have generated different outcomes in the adoption of digital solutions and digital competitiveness between the two countries.

Sweden is the third most advanced digital economy in the European Union, according to the Digital Economy and Society Index (DESI) and the second most innovative country in the world, according to the Global Innovation Index. It is also home to well-known start-ups such as Spotify, Klarna, King, Mojang, iZettle, Kry, Trustly, Truecaller, and Yubico, to name a few. Apart from being a global hub for tech start-ups, having a world-class educated labour force has been crucial for Swedish success. As stipulated in the digital economy and social index (European Commission 2021), over 70% of the Swedish population have basic digital and software skills. Furthermore, Sweden has invested heavily in digital infrastructure. In terms of connectivity, Sweden is ranked fifth, with 80% of the households connected to the very high-capacity network (VHCN). Although the quality of the services provided differs greatly between urban and rural areas in Sweden, 87% of the rural households have access to broadband internet. Sweden is also an early adopter of digital technologies in the public sector. For example, in 2020, the Swedish postal service (Postnord) reduced its mail delivery service in some areas from 5 to 2–3 days a week due to increasing operational costs caused by high wages and declining volumes of mail. This

Table 3.1: Global ranking of Singapore in e-trade indicators

Indicators of e-trade	Year	Leader	SG	MY	ID	PH	VN	TH	HK	KR	CN	IN
ICT use for business-to-business transactions (Global rank)	2016	Japan	13	21	53	58	55	52	20	34	57	108
Business-to-consumer Internet use (Global rank)	2016	United Kingdom	24	6	28	51	47	39	27	10	32	77
Burden of customs procedures (Global rank)	2018	Singapore	1	25	63	125	95	78	3	48	44	47
Fixed broadband Internet tariffs, PPP $/month (Global rank)	2016	Vietnam	99	110	46	104	1	89	54	73	68	36
Active mobile-broadband subscript per 100 inhabits (value)	2015	Macao	142	90	42	42	39	75	107	110	56	9
Credit card ownership (% age 15+)	2017	Canada	49	21	2	2	4	10	65	64	21	3
Debit card ownership (% age 15+)	2017	Netherland	92	74	31	21	27	60	83	75	67	33
Postal Reliability Index (1–100)	2014	South Korea	98.2	84.3	65.6	48	70.3	90	97.7	100	83.4	68.1
Logistics competence (Global Rank)	2018	Germany	3	36	44	69	33	32	12	28	27	42
Timeliness of international shipments (Global rank)	2018	Belgium	6	53	41	100	40	28	15	25	27	52
Tracking and tracing of shipments (Global ranking)	2018	Finland	8	47	39	57	34	33	15	22	27	38

Notes: The table provides the global ranking of Singapore (SG), Malaysia (MY), Indonesia (ID), Philippines (PH), Vietnam (VN), Thailand (TH), Hong Kong (HK), South Korea (KR), China (CN), and India (IN) in various indicators related to e-trade. The year refers to the latest year in which the rankings are available. The Leader refers to the country that received the top ranking in each indicator.

Source: World Bank 2021

development was partly driven by increased usage of digital mailboxes to replace physical mail. A digital mailbox is a personal mailbox that replaces regular mail with pdf files. The Swedish government is one of the main drivers of this technology, and most government agencies send digital mail instead of regular mail once a person has acquired a digital mailbox.

Sweden leads in their efforts to integrate digital solutions into business activities. Among many things, it has largely done away with physical currency. Payment by credit/debit card is accepted more often than cash, and in the ten years between 2010 and 2020, transactions by cash decreased from 40% to 10%. Cash is still considered legal tender, which means that the Swedish government guarantees its usability, but this is not always the case in practice. For example, most buses do not accept cash to reduce delays in traffic and the risk of robberies. Today, payment by card is universally accepted everywhere, with 98% of the population between 18 and 67 years using the Swedish electronic identification BankID for transactions (European Commission 2021). Another technology that simplifies transactions is digital receipts. Some companies send digital receipts by email, but a growing number of firms have started to provide receipts through third-party apps, which store receipts from multiple companies on a shared platform. While digital receipts existed before the pandemic, the adoption was accelerated by the pandemic to make transactions contactless. The digital receipts have many advantages. Receipts can be stored in one location without the risk of losing or destroying them; it speeds up transactions when customers no longer need to wait for the receipts to be printed, and it reduces the climate impact caused by the four billion receipts printed in Sweden each year.

While Sweden scores high on many measures of the digital economy, it is less competitive in attracting tech talent due to its high levels of taxation. The marginal tax rates in Sweden, Estonia, and Singapore are shown in Figure 3.2 for comparison. In Sweden, most tech talent pay taxes in the highest tax bracket, with a marginal tax rate of 66.1%, compared with a marginal tax rate of 18–20% in Singapore (Torstensson n.d.; Inland Revenue Authority of Singapore (IRAS) n.d.). The tax on income, capital gains, restaurants, and

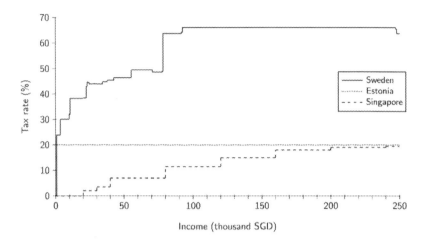

Figure 3.2: Marginal income tax rates in Sweden and Singapore in 2022 (*Sources*: Ekonomifakta.se and IRAS n.d.)

consumption, all contribute to high living costs. The comparison does not consider the difference in welfare services. However, for most tech talent, welfare services are of smaller importance since they often receive generous healthcare benefits from their employer and are not eligible for subsidised education or other welfare services.

e-ESTONIA

Estonia is a small Baltic country of 1.3 million residents that gained its independence from the Soviet Union in 1991. Since its independence, digitalisation was seen as a cost-saving and productivity-enhancing project which led Estonia to leapfrog to become a frontrunner in the digital economy race. During the COVID-19 crisis, Estonia managed to offer 99% of its public services online and a seamless transition to online education through digital classrooms (virtual classrooms), educational tools, and materials already in place, while other countries grappled to function and keep schools and higher education institutions open. It is the first country in the EU to introduce digital COVID-19 vaccine certificates and has since then partnered with the

World Health Organization (WHO) to introduce universally accepted vaccine certificates.

The ambitious digitalisation efforts started in the 1990s with the reimaging and redesigning of the public sector to improve citizen-government interactions. Instead of a traditional approach, the Estonian government introduced "life/business-event-based services" for people and enterprises where services are triggered automatically online by anticipated events without having to follow up (e.g., childbirth, business registration etc.). This greatly reduced administrative burdens for citizens, businesses, as well as for the public sector. The "once-only" principle — that no information should be entered twice — was adopted to ensure seamless integration across public services. The high-tech digital ID enables Estonians to pay taxes, vote (or revote), do online banking, access health services including e-ambulances, search exam results, and even keep track of their pet's vaccine registry. In a time when citizens are becoming extremely sceptical over state use of public data, Estonians have shown greater public trust towards e-governance because of the transparency, security, and reliability of their digital infrastructure. For instance, Estonians own their data, and public officials have no access to personal data without authorisation. They can easily backtrack who has retrieved or used their personal data and even block access to their health data (Silaškova and Takahashi 2020). Furthermore, Estonia keeps business and land registry data public to maintain transparency and openness. For example, the public has access to land/house ownership data, even of those considered elite (Heller 2017).

Another bold effort that caught international attention is the e-residency which allows non-citizens of Estonia to get a digital signature, access financial services, and do business remotely. The e-residency program redefines the population. It is proposed as a solution to the ageing and declining population without having to restrain their resources. It is aimed to attract digital nomads, especially the young talents who increasingly prefer to work remotely. Further, Estonia has become attractive to IT companies because of its corporate tax policy and liberal regulations around tech research. Companies

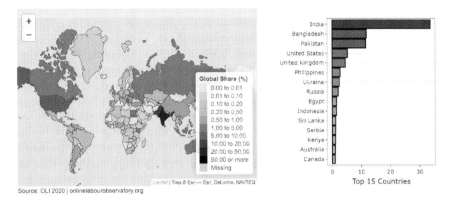

Figure 3.3: Supply of gig talent by country (*Source*: Online Labour Observatory 2020)

that reinvest their capital gains pay zero corporate taxes in Estonia. The Tax Foundation lists the corporate tax as the main reason why it ranks Estonia as number one on the International Tax Competitive Index (Bunn 2022). Furthermore, income is taxed at a flat rate of 20%, as seen in Figure 3.3. While salaries in the tech industry are typically lower in Estonia, the relatively low income tax implies a high disposable income in relation to living costs compared to high-tax counties such as Sweden. All these factors have contributed to create a vibrant start-up culture in Estonia. Today, Estonia is home to approximately 1,300 start-ups and have the highest number of unicorns per capita in the world (Work in Estonia n.d.).

Estonia should continue to improve integration of digital technologies to businesses, especially SMEs. Estonia's e-commerce sector is not as developed as the other Nordic countries. E-commerce penetration among SMEs is only 16% and less than 10% globally (Publications Office of the European Union 2022). The digitalisation effort is largely spearheaded by the Estonian government with heavy investments into e-government services. However, more public-private partnerships should be forged to encourage the uptake of digital solutions to increase the competitiveness of the business ecosystem.

The three case studies on Singapore, Sweden, and Estonia reveal a common fact: digitalisation of the public sector is crucial to ensure equitable growth in the digital economy. The case studies show a variety of roles and strategies the states could play to facilitate and enhance a digital economy. These include nurturing a national digital transformation strategy that pioneers digital innovation and adoption, developing policies and institutions that support a digital ecosystem, playing an entrepreneurial role to foster private-public partnerships, investing in digital infrastructure and R&D, and taking a lead role in strengthening relationships among various actors of the digital economy.

Beyond the uncovered strategies, the next section discusses what governments and cities should do to ensure a thriving digital ecosystem. We identify attracting talent, capital, digital governance, reconfiguration of supply chains, sustainability, and digital inclusiveness as important enablers of a digital economy. They are discussed through the lenses of different actors — countries, governments, firms, and society — that participate in the digital economy.

THE CONDITIONS TO SUPPORT A DIGITAL ECOSYSTEM — LESSONS LEARNT

Talent

Singapore is ranked as the most digitally prepared nation in Southeast Asia in the 2021 ASEAN Digital Integration Index Report (USAID, ASEAN, and US-ASEAN Connect 2021). The report estimated scores on a scale of 0 to 100 on various measures of the digital preparedness, and Singapore came out on top on almost all measures, with high scores on Institutions and Infrastructure (90.4), Data Protection and Cybersecurity (89.7), Digital Payments and Identities (86.6), Digital Trade and Logistics (82.6), and Innovation and Entrepreneurship (71.1). However, Singapore scored relatively low in absolute terms on Digital Skills and Talent (63.8). Anecdotal evidence from our interactions with the tech industry has also identified "talent, talent, and talent" as the three most important conditions for sustaining a successful digital economy. For these reasons, we listed talent as the first and most important factor in sustaining a digital economy.

For the longest time, economists have debated over Richard Florida's creative capital versus human capital theory; whether cities should invest in creative labour or skilled labour (measured by education attainment) for economic growth. Here, we go beyond this debate to look at labour in the form of talent required for knowledge creation. Any economy will benefit from a talented workforce. However, the talent required for the development of a digital economy is relatively specialised, recent, and evolving. The technological complexity surrounding digitalisation makes it a necessity to talk about talent with both hard and soft digital skills. The APAC Digital Skills Index 2021 set out eight digital competencies required for a digital economy. These include harnessing "hard digital skills" on device and software operations, information and data literacy, digital content and product creation, and cloud computing, while "soft digital skills" include digital communication and collaboration, problem-solving, security and ethics, and digital project management (Amazon Web Services 2021). In addition to the technical talent around IoT, the new economy demands "digital leadership", to help next-generation technology firms and start-ups identify growth opportunities and create jobs. This type of digital leadership includes chief technology officers, chief information officers, ICT managers, and professional services managers, to name a few.

Although digital talent predominantly encompasses highly skilled knowledge workers and managers with fixed contracts, there are other forms of talent demanded by a digital economy. One such group is the gig talent. A rise in the adoption of productivity tools like telecommuting has made remote working convenient. Virtual work platforms have brought together avatars of real people, allowing them to easily transition between multiple locations. This has made gig work or crowd working economical, convenient, and popular among younger populations. Although they are being ushered in by the digital economy, they are also an important source of digital talent. This also makes the geography of talent less relevant. For instance, India,

Bangladesh, and Pakistan are the world's largest suppliers of gig talent (Figure 3.3) in software development and technology, while regionally, Indonesia, Malaysia, and the Philippines also offer low-cost gig talent, posing a threat to countries like Singapore with high labour costs. On the flip side, geographical proximity to neighbouring talent makes it attractive for tech companies to co-locate in Singapore, enjoying a world-class business environment while reaching out to low-cost labour that can be readily sourced regionally. This has socio-spatial consequences for the labour market, allows for labour to be employed abroad, and could reduce the need for foreign labour in Singapore, and thus the demand for Singapore's limited land resources.

Although there is no contestation that talent — both technical and managerial, with fixed or flexible contracts — is important for the growth of a digital economy, a recent surge in so-called "social media influencers" and "YouTubers" who have made millions of dollars out of digital platforms make us question whether technical skills alone are sufficient to be competitive and thrive in the digital ecosystem. Besides, those who consume digital platforms for free are also "prosumers" that indirectly provide labour to produce valuable data and knowledge to the digital economy. Seemingly, the material and discursive boundaries between different types of talent or labour are increasingly blurred in the digital economy. The enormity of digital technologies and their evolving nature make it difficult to pre-define talent required for a digital economy.

Attracting talent

While the workforce is getting more specialised to meet the needs of the digital economy, the labour market becomes increasingly international and competitive. Younger generations will be more mobile, have social networks abroad, wait longer before getting married, and have fewer possessions that tie them to one place. This will broaden their search scope for jobs, and employers and cities will have to compete harder for their attention. As noted by urban scholars, the decision on where to live has become one of our most important life choices (Glaeser 2012), and politicians and urban planners will thus need to support businesses in attracting talent by building desirable cities to live in (Florida 2002). In order to assist businesses, cities need to understand the preferences of talent and provide talent-attracting urban amenities, and evidence suggests that young talent are particularly concerned about social values, physical activity, and their mental well-being.

It is important to note that talent, for the most part, desires the same things as everyone else: good education, affordable housing, healthcare, rule of law, culture, restaurants, a clean environment, and other urban amenities. However, due to differences in demographics, values and work conditions, talent will have needs and preferences that stand out. One aspect in which talented workers differ is that they will be younger and more likely to belong to Generation Z (born in the mid 1990s to early 2010s). Generation Z will thus be a key group of talent that policymakers and planners will need to attract. Evidence suggests that young tech talent desire individualism, meritocracy, diversity, and openness, and that they wish to live in cities, and work at companies that promote these values. According to Richard Florida's (2002) book, *The Creative Class*, cities could attract talent by promoting these values. Florida also makes the argument that tolerance is important in the creative process, since innovation requires collaboration, critical thinking, and openness to new ideas. In this regard, Singapore can continue to attract talent by promoting tolerance and harmony.

Young talent also demands for greater flexibility in work. They appreciate work-life balance and opt for work arrangements that allow them to work from home. As a result, demand for affordable and quality housing has increased post COVID-19. While many countries have dismally failed to provide affordable housing, Singapore's public housing model has been a success for the longest time, with nearly 90% of the total population living in public housing through public rental and subsidised ownership. The housing affordability issue is not unique to Singapore. The Smart City Observatory survey asked respondents in more than one hundred of the world's most global cities about social issues in the city where they live, and respondents in almost all developed countries listed housing affordability as the number one issue. In Singapore, 76.2% of the respondents answered that housing affordability was a social problem, higher than any other social issue in the survey (Smart City Observatory Report, 2023). However, among all developed countries, Singapore had the highest share of respondents that agrees with the statement that it is easy to find an apartment or room with a rent not exceeding 30% of their income. This reflects the fact that Singapore has a liberal and flexible rental market where many HDB owners sublet rooms in their homes. The housing policy not only targets the quantity through the supply of housing but also recognises that the quality of housing is important for the well-being of the people. "Singapore's housing policy is a social policy that impacts society and people's lives, rather than just focusing on infrastructure development," said the Minister of National Development, Desmond Lee, at a public engagement session at the URA Centre in September 2022 (Lee n.d.). With the HDB as the main regulator of housing market, both public and private housing have been relatively affordable, compared to other developed cities.

While younger generations and tech talent are more likely to work from home, they are also likely to suffer from anxiety. For this reason, they find it more difficult to physically and mentally sign off from work. While stress at work can have a positive effect on work performance by momentarily increasing focus when faced by immediate challenges, anxiety hurts productivity by creating a constant feeling of unease due to a fear of future stress, or a sense of guilt for not working. This is a growing problem that was exacerbated when companies adopted hybrid work as a new norm post COVID-19.

Besides anxiety, mental well-being is a growing concern among younger generations. Much research has documented the therapeutic effects of sunlight and green environments. The "Garden City" programme was first introduced in 1967 by Lee Kuan Yew as a concept aimed to promote Singapore to investors as a clean and green city in a garden (National Library Board 1967). Today, it also serves to attract talent and provides a highly cherished urban amenity for Singapore citizens. Since its inception, the Garden City has developed into a City in a Garden, with a Park Connector Network (PCN) that creates corridors of greenways around the city. Therapeutic gardens have been established to promote mental well-being, and efforts are underway to create parks and green spaces within a 10-minute walk from all households by 2030 (Tham 2021). Through its abundance of sunlight and green spaces, Singapore continues to offer mental support for hardworking talent.

Relating to the observation that talent tends to have more flexible work hours is the fact that work hours also tend to be longer, and most of that time is spent sitting down in front of a computer screen. For this reason, talent tends to engage in light exercises throughout the day, such as walking or biking to and from work instead of driving or walking up the stairs instead of taking the lift. Outside of work, talent optimise their time usage by engaging in intensive physical activities, like jogging or going to the gym, rather than watching a lengthy movie or baseball game. One such activity enjoyed by talented individuals is biking. This is an activity that has increased in popularity during the pandemic, as evidenced by the 50% increase in bike sales during the pandemic (Abdullah 2020). Singapore has historically not been a bike-friendly city, but this is rapidly changing, and Tampines was named Singapore's first cycling town in 2009. In March 2020, it was announced that the Ministry of Transport is investing S$1 billion on tripling Singapore's cycling path network to a total of 1,320 kilometres over the next decade (*Channel News Asia* 2020). By prioritising and building more infrastructure for pedestrians and cyclists, the socio-spatial organisation of the city improves to better fit the needs of young talent.

Overall, Singapore has been successful in attracting talent to the city state. As of June 2022, 338 thousand foreign workers hold Employment Pass and S Pass work permits allocated to attract skilled labour (Ministry of Manpower 2022). During the pandemic, the skilled foreign workforce to resident population ratio dropped from 10% to 8% between 2019 and 2022. Although globally, the tech sector is facing massive layoffs, the recent spree of tech hiring by tech giants, Tiktok, Wise, Binance, Grab, and Lazada signals that Singapore remains a hot spot for tech talent (Sivakumar 2022). However, the city state must be cautious about rising property and rental prices that may deter young talent from choosing Singapore.

VENTURE-BACKED START-UPS

A vibrant start-up ecosystem is central to idea creation. What attracts start-ups beyond talent is money and power. New York City (NYC) is an example for attracting venture-backed start-ups and technology companies, second only to Silicon Valley. According to NYC's Economic Development Corporation (NYCEDC), the start-up ecosystem comprises approximately 7,000 companies valued at over US$71 billion (NYCEDC 2018). Much of this success owes to the sheer amount of venture capital (VC) the city's innovation ecosystem has attracted in the past 20 years. In recent years, fintech, e-commerce, digital media, enterprise software, and telemedicine have been the prominent recipients of venture capital investments.

While NYC continues to lead in venture capital activity, the global distribution of venture capital has slowly shifted towards other parts of the world. With Southeast Asia's digital transformation just beginning, it is not a surprise that venture capital firms eye the Southeast Asian market. According to Anand (2021), Southeast Asian tech companies should reach a valuation of US$1 trillion by 2025, with 30% of that attributed to start-ups and tech firms directly operating in the digital space. Some of the prominent fundraisings came from the merger of Singapore's ride-hailing app, Grab, with US SPAC Altimeter; the merger of Gojek, a ride-hailing app, with Tokopedia, an e-commerce platform, to form GoTo; courier start-up J&T Express; and the AI-driven car marketplace — Carro (Greeven and Feng 2021; Ang 2021). E-commerce and digital financial services attracted 60% of the venture funds raised in 2021 while nascent sectors such as health tech and edtech saw a steep uptick in funding. Singapore based e-commerce unicorns, Lazada and Sea group, have been key enablers of the e-commerce boom in the region. Despite the pandemic, tech companies in Singapore have shown growth and resilience, with 9 out of 12 start-ups receiving unicorn status in 2021. Most of these tech firms fall under the digital economy (Table 3.2).

Table 3.2: Singapore-based unicorn companies

Company	Approximate valuation ($ billion)	Industry
Grab	$14.3	Auto & transportation
Lazada	$4.2	E-commerce
HyalRoute	$3.5	Mobile & telecommunications
Advance Intelligence Group	$2	Artificial Intelligence
Trax	$1.3	Internet Software & Services
Carousell	$1.1	E-commerce & direct-to-consumer
PatSnap	$1	Internet software & services
Moglix	$1	E-commerce & direct-to-consumer
Matrixport	$1	Fintech
Carro	$1	E-commerce & direct-to-consumer
Bolttech	$1	Fintech
NIUM	$1	Fintech
Ninja Van	$1	Supply chain, logistics, & delivery

Source: CB Insights 2021

CROSS-BORDER PARTNERSHIPS IN DIGITAL GOVERNANCE

The nature of digital economies complicates the legislature and regulation of digital activities since rules, regulations, and even public choices vary between jurisdictions. However, greater openness to data, data privacy, transparency, and accountability are warranted to ensure fair competition across borders. Our aim is not to discuss the legal frameworks or the lack thereof, as it goes beyond the intended scope of this chapter, but rather emphasise the merits of institutionalising the rules governing data mobility, user privacy, and regulation of digital/tech companies to encourage fair competition, and discuss issues faced by digital workers who do not fall under standard labour laws, as it fundamentally affects the growth and ease of doing business in the digital economy.

First, data protectionism or data localisation laws can diminish growth, competitiveness, and innovation as it raises the cost of entry and doing business for start-ups. It encourages rent-seeking behaviour and eventually reduce competition. To support smooth data transfer across borders, countries must ensure data privacy, protection, transparency, and accountability. One good example of this is Estonia, which has shown the world a new form of data internationalisation with X-road, a unified data exchange platform that allows secured data exchange between organisations. It is the backbone of e-Estonia. In 2014, neighbouring Finland adopted X-road to facilitate secure connectivity, searches, and data transfers between governments and private databases between the two nations. Now, Estonian and Finnish citizens can seamlessly access e-services, letting go of geographical and bureaucratic barriers. Synchronised information between the two countries also means that, for example, an Estonian could easily reach out to a pharmacy in Finland using prescriptions integrated into his or her digital ID by the doctor; pharmacists in Finland can verify the prescriptions digitally and deliver medicine, vis-à-vis. In 2018, Iceland become a member of the X-road family. The APAC economies are also pushing for their own Cross-border Privacy Rules (CBPR) system to build consumer, business, and regulator trust within the region.

Second, every functionality of a digital enterprise has implications for cybersecurity. Companies need to constantly reinvent and update their IT systems, software, and user interfaces for fraud prevention, data protection, security, and product enhancement to ensure a better user experience (e.g., authentication). Since these enterprises gather large customer-centric personal and sensitive data, the lack of integrated and advanced security systems makes them vulnerable to constant cyber-attacks. A recent attack on social media giant, Twitter, shows that not only does the complex security environment matter, but also the "lack of leadership, vulnerability to social engineering, and a failure to address the new vulnerabilities caused by the pandemic-driven shift to mass remote working" increases the risks of cyber-attacks (Department of Financial Services (New York State)

2020). In the wake of the pandemic, countries have experienced a rise in cyber threats with hefty extortion demands. In 2019 alone, the average organisational cost from a data breach was estimated at U$2.62 million in Southeast Asia (IBM Security 2019). Therefore, becoming digitally safe is one of the most sought-after discussions today. Even the most advanced digital economies are becoming increasingly vulnerable to cyber-attacks. In Singapore, 96% of businesses reported some sort of data breach between 2018 and 2019 (Lago 2020). The city state has also suffered a few major cyber-attacks on government agencies and enterprises which included the 2018 attack that compromised 1.5 million patient data from the SingHealth database, including Prime Minister Lee Hsien Loong's and several other ministers' (Sim 2018). In 2007, Estonia suffered a massive cyber-attack that brought down most of its digital infrastructure. Many argue that their e-citizenship program was responsible for many of the sanction breaches. However, the outgrowth of the 2007 attack led to Estonia becoming home to NATO's Cyber Defense Centre of Excellence, the first of its kind to conduct massive cyber drills. Further, Estonia introduced the concept of "data embassy" to store copies of their data in Luxemburg. These examples show that cyber threats are inevitable; they evolve quickly, and we must be nimble to solve them. Usually, data breaches take up to 206 days on average to be discovered but blockchain technology can be a useful solution. According to experts, blockchain systems make every footprint immediately noticeable, allowing cyber threats and data breaches to be identified and resolved immediately. For example, the Estonian X-road data platform uses cryptographic hash functions in blockchain to link data items securely. The blockchain architecture stores data in blocks serving as a distributed ledger that decentralises the way data is stored, verified, and secured. This also means that in the event of a data breach, the system could quickly locate where the data breach has taken place.

Third, competitive market conditions encourage innovation, the formation of new businesses through early-stage funding, increase entrepreneurship rate, and job creation. In the United States, venture capitalists appear to avoid funding start-ups and other enterprises that directly compete with dominant firms in the digital economy, leading to a sharp decline in the share of start-ups and young firms in the industry. According to the Antitrust Subcommittee report, monopolistic firms with weak privacy protections creates a "kill zone" for those newer firms and market products that offer greater privacy protection for user data and information. Hence, tech moguls like Apple, Google, Amazon, and Facebook have received constant scrutiny for exercising entrenchment powers and monopolistic control over the digital economy (Nadler and Cicilline 2022). Therefore, more regulatory efforts are needed to encourage fair competition, to create a vibrant ecosystem for start-ups and newer firms to blossom. Across the borders, fair competition can be promoted through the interoperability of standards and systems to support businesses engaging in digital trade and e-commerce on the same grounds. To establish common digital trade rules, Singapore has entered four digital economy agreements (DEAs) with (1) Chile–New Zealand — a first of its kind, (2) Australia, (3) the UK, and (4) South Korea. The aim is to align digital rules and standards across partner countries, support cross-border data flows, protect personal data and consumer rights, increase economic partnerships between countries through the use of digital IDs, artificial intelligence, e-invoicing, fintech and e-payments, data protection trust-mark certification, and data innovation.

Lastly, regulating the "gig economy" is an integral part of the digital ecosystem, specifically when the economic security of gig workers and freelancers are at risk when they do not fall under the historical standard occupation classifications. Some corporations classify their gig employees as independent contractors to avoid payroll taxes, minimum wages, overtime, healthcare (Medicare), unemployment insurance (social security), and other worker compensation benefits. Western economies are progressive towards protecting the rights of actors in the digital economy. For instance, a long-standing legal battle between app-based drivers and delivery companies such as Uber, Lyft, DoorDash, Instacart, and Postmates led to California legislature ruling in favour of classifying drivers as "employees" rather than self-employed independent contractors, paving the way for gig-workers to enjoy state labour laws (Associated Press 2021). In Singapore, legal entitlement to labour laws is still a question for such gig-workers. Fair earning is also a burgeoning issue faced by many gig workers as most platforms lack transparency to their incentive structures.

RECONFIGURING GLOBAL SUPPLY CHAINS

The COVID-19 pandemic and the subsequent lockdowns caused enormous disruptions, and permanent and structural changes to global supply chains. Labour constraints in production, disruptions to logistics, and a sudden drop in demand led to a sharp increase in the cost of world trade. During this time, we saw supply chain resilience from regionalisation, localisation, and diversification of production networks. In any case, the nature of the supply chain is changing with technology. Digital technologies have brought services closer to the consumers (e.g, virtualisation of services). Smart manufacturing, automation, big data, cloud technology, blockchain, and artificial intelligence are revolutionising traditional manufacturing and services sectors. For example, SAIC Motor — China's largest automaker — provides digital solutions to help buyers customise their orders via 3D digital car simulations that can help reduce the time to market by 35% (Bu *et al.* n.d.). Virtual showrooms through augmented reality already shortens the business to consumer supply chain and could in the long run impact the spatial organisation of cities when car dealerships, furniture, interior design, and clothing stores offer a more customisable experience online while removing the middleman. On the commercial side, the supply chain of low-cost labour is gradually ending. Relocation of operations to low-wage countries is no longer economical with decreasing costs of digital and smart solutions through AI that can easily replace low-skilled labour. Therefore, the rising popularity of virtual or remote work is consistent with the restructuring of value chains in the international division of labour. Virtual environments also reduce the business-to-business interaction cost. New products are often reviled at big exhibitions, but the COVID-19 pandemic forced many industries to reorganise their annual events online. Examples include the world's largest annual consumer electronics and video game exhibitions, CES and E3, which are usually held in convention centres in Las Vegas, but went online-exclusive in 2021 due to the pandemic. The 2021 CES and E3 had free admission due to the close-to-zero marginal cost of additional online attendants, and were thus able to set new attendance records. Singapore has some of the largest convention centres in Asia, and future development in augmented reality could greatly affect the demand for exhibition space.

Further, global supply chains are reorganising around data. Although digital trade may involve the physical movement of products bought through online marketplaces, the underlying digital product is the data, and hence, the movement of data is another form in which supply chains can be organised. The previous section discussed the fundamentals of regulating digital data and the importance of redefining trade rules in an era where data is traded as a "digital good" across borders. Instead, here we discuss how digital transformations can reconfigure the way traditional supply chains are organised and delivered using Singapore's experiences.

For the longest time, Singapore's strength has been its connectivity to the rest of the world; it is a major maritime and airport hub, a global financial centre, and a global centre for arbitrage. Singapore is moving towards seamless integration between these pillars to provide unified and secure trade services through digitalisation. For instance, the Port of Singapore Authority (PSA) combines both digital and analog flows (physical shipment of goods) through 'Portnet', a world's first B2B system created to connect PSA with the shipping industry — shipping lines, hauliers, freight forwarders, and government agencies — to manage information better and synchronise complex operational processes. 'Portnet' integrates with Singapore's customs system (tradenet), the government's networked trade platform (NTP), and banks' trade financing systems to offer seamless connection between import, export, and trans-shipment related regulations, trade financing, reconciliation of payments, invoicing of bills permitting not only business–to–business (B2B) but also business–to–business–government (B2B2G) transactions. Further, 'Calista' — an AI-powered trade and supply chain platform, allows shippers and cargo owners to track shipments in real time, streamline processes, documents, and data in the flow of trade goods across borders.

Overall, Singapore has provided valuable lessons as to how the traditional hub approach to supply chains can be improved and reconfigured through digital connections.

SUSTAINABILITY — GREEN DIGITAL INFRASTRUCTURE

With ongoing climate changes, the green agenda is inevitable and irreversible. The 'energy star' program that started in the 1990s in the United States led to the development of sleep mode electronics that significantly reduced the electricity consumption of devices and computer hardware. Countries are now shifting away from copper-based network infrastructure to fibre networks. Technology firms are switching to green computing, green electronics, green energy, and e-waste management as a commitment towards a zero carbon footprint.[5] The newest wave of green IT is led by cloud solutions. It revolutionised the way resources are shared and utilised in the digital economy. Data centres form an important part of this architecture. However, they produce massive heat. Countries with cold temperatures are experimenting with the idea of reusing waste heat to keep communities warm.[6]

Although this is not feasible for tropical countries like Singapore, redesigning efficient data centres is important to reduce the burden on energy sources. At present, Singapore supplies 60% of the data centres required by the Southeast Asian region. These data centres consume 7% of the total electricity generated, and approximately 40% of it feeds into cooling systems. This puts enormous stress on energy grids. Further, the land scarcity of Singapore limits its ability to tap into renewable energy sources. This led Singapore to push back the approval of new data centres in 2019. However, public-private partnerships (e.g., Facebook–NUS–NTU–NRF) are forged to push for innovative and energy-efficient cooling systems to suit the tropical climates of Singapore. Further, solar power generated in HDB rooftops and government buildings is used to power digital infrastructure. Despite these efforts, small actors must also actively participate in the green digital economy movement. There is an explosion in device usage and data generation, especially post-pandemic. Globally, the average number of connected devices per person is expected to increase up to 9 by 2025. This calls for scalable and sustainable digital infrastructure. However, green technologies are also capital intensive. Yet, they provide low risks and steady returns. Another aspect of sustainability is digital waste management. The United States and China produced 16 million tons of e-waste (electronic equipment that has reached the end of its useful life) in 2019 alone, which accounts for 18% of global e-waste (Statista n.d.-a). While e-waste management is a relatively new concept to Singapore, citizens must be actively educated about e-waste recycling programmes offered by industry partners and available e-waste collection centres throughout the island. Overall, countries must push towards aligning their digitalisation efforts to meet climate goals.

DIGITAL INCLUSIVITY

Lastly, countries must move towards digital inclusivity. Lack of capital and technology know-how are the main reasons for the modern digital divide. As of 2021, only 20% of the least developing economies have access to the internet, and 50% of the world's students and women population are offline (United Nations Conference on Trade and Development 2021; Tyers-Chowdhury and Binder 2021). Besides, there are language barriers to internet access as most of the internet content is available only in 10 languages (Sitsanis 2021). During the pandemic, even advanced economies like NYC found over a hundred thousand students unable to access the internet and Wi-Fi enabled devices (New York City Comptroller 2020). Further, Singapore's Household Expenditure Survey in 2019 revealed that only 45% of the households living in 1-room and 2-room public housing have internet access, compared to 96% living in private housing (Tan, n.d.). This is despite initiating national digital inclusive programs such as the "Silver Infocomm Initiative" and the "NEU PC Plus Programme" to help seniors, needy students, low-income households, and people with disabilities to acquire computers, get access to internet, and improve digital competencies.

While the evidence from different countries suggest that the nature of digital inequalities is different in various jurisdictions, narrowing the digital divide is crucial to ensure equitable growth among all segments of society. Digital services must be made affordable and accessible to all, including the vulnerable and marginalised. This could be achieved through cost-effective technologies that flatten the architecture such as open-source software development, scalable infrastructure, and easy device financing. Further, technology firms must create user-centric technologies rather than design-centric technologies. Overall, even advance economies like Singapore who are at the top of Digital Economy must work towards digital inclusivity to ensure all segments of the society can reap the benefits of a digital economy. Another aspect of digital inclusiveness is its ability to enhance social capital.

CONCLUSION

The COVID-19 pandemic has shifted economic activity to the internet and generated a growing need to understand the digital economy. Digitalisation is not a new phenomenon, but it has been accelerated by the pandemic and recent advancements in information technology and data science. While many workers were displaced by the pandemic, traditional jobs were being replaced by jobs in the new digital economy. This has created a need for upskilling and reskilling workers to meet the growing need for digital skills. Many tech companies have relocated their headquarters to Singapore due to its strategic location, talented labour, and economic and political stability. This has generated many new jobs and helped to position Singapore as a standout economy in the new digital economy. The rapid expansion of Singapore as a digital hub has created new challenges to its continued growth, and we have identified key conditions that need to be met to sustain a growing digital economy.

First, the most immediate challenge facing the expansion of the Singaporean tech industry is the growing global demand for talented labour. The competition for talent is growing as demand for tech skills increase, and newly graduated students become more mobile. A particular focus should thus be directed to identifying the needs of talent to build a city that supports businesses in attracting talent. Singapore is well-known for its iconic architecture, abundance of green spaces, and high-quality amenities, and our analysis suggests that it can continue to attract talent by building its reputation as a tolerant and loving city, while offering a high standard of living.

Second, many of the new jobs will be generated by global digital companies that establish headquarters in Singapore to gain access to the growing Southeast Asian market, but a growing number of jobs will also be generated by start-ups. Therefore, tech start-ups are important for a vibrant digital hub, help fuel digital innovation through network effects with existing tech companies, and work as incubators for new tech talent. A thriving tech start-ups ecosystem is reliant on high risk-taking venture capital and financial backing. So far, Singapore has been successful in securing capital for new start-ups. However, Singapore must also be cautious about the spatial implications of attracting digital firms, as tech firms no longer require traditional office spaces to operate their businesses.

Third, the presence of multinational companies has created a need for data governance agreements to ensure data protection and cybersecurity. As a small island nation with a growing digital economy, Singapore stands particularly vulnerable to disruptions in data flows and data protectionism in much the same way as in trade with physical goods. Fortunately, Singapore has already made leaps in data governance by securing the world's first digital economy agreements with countries such as Australia, Chile, New Zealand, and the UK, and more agreements are currently being negotiated to secure smooth cross-border data flows for the future.

Lastly, a high digital literacy rate and access to digital infrastructure is needed not only to supply digital goods and services, but also to decrease the digital divide and create support for digital solutions among the public.

ENDNOTES

1. See for example the appendix of the United Nations' (2019) Digital Economy Report for a brief summary of alternative definitions.
2. For goods and services produced through the participation of multiple countries, digital technologies are reducing product costs and time to market through greater visibility and connectivity of the supply chain. Further, supply chains are reconfiguring with declining demand for low-cost labour brought by digitalisation.
3. According to AWS (2021), 63% of Singaporean workers apply digital skills in their daily work, while 22% of the workforce apply advanced digital skills. Relevant to advanced technical skills, Singapore's capabilities in general programming (for example, expertise in Python or JavaScript programming) is twice the average capability of Southeast Asia, while big data and statistical computing capabilities (e.g., R programming) are four times the regional average (Asia Partners, 2021).
4. Some of the prominent public-private partnerships includes the Grab and Infocomm Media Development Authority (IMDA) venture capital program (GVI); the Facebook–NRF–NUS–NTU research partnership for sustainable green data centres and innovative cooling systems; the NRF–Keppel–Huawei partnership for multistorey data centres; and the National Cybersecurity R&D Programme (NCR) between universities and industry to improve the trustworthiness of cyber infrastructures.
5. Apple powers its global facilities through 100% clean energy, including retail stores, offices, data centres, and co-located facilities in 43 countries. The company is also pushing its additional manufacturing partners and suppliers to commit to 100% clean energy.
6. Denmark and Sweden feed excess heat generated from data centres back into their district heating systems.

REFERENCES

Abdullah, Ahmad Zhaki. 2020. "Singapore Sees Cycling Boom Amid COVID-19, With Increased Ridership and Bicycle Sales." *Channel News Asia*. August 25, 2020. https://www.channelnewsasia.com/singapore/covid-19-cycling-popularity-bicycle-sales-shared-bikes-631621.

Amazon Web Services. 2021. "Unlocking APAC's Digital Potential: Changing Digital Skill Needs and Policy Approaches." https://access partnership.com/changing-digital-skill-needs-policy/.

Anand, Amit. 2021. "The Rise of Southeast Asia's $1trn Tech Economy." Content-marketing. *Venture Capital Journal* (blog). August 23, 2021. https://www.venturecapitaljournal.com/the-rise-of-southeast-asias-1trn-tech-economy/.

Ang, Jolene. 2021. "Internet Economy Investments in South-East Asia at All-Time High in 2021: Report." *The Straits Times*, November 10, 2021. https://www.straitstimes.com/business/economy/internet-economy-investments-in-south-east-asia-at-all-time-high-in-2021.

Asia Partners. 2021. "Southeast Asia's Golden Age: Resilience and Recovery". https://www.asiapartners.com/wp-content/uploads/2022/04/Asia-Partners-2021-Southeast-Asia-Internet-Report.pdf.

Associated Press. 2021. "Blow for Uber as Judge Finds California's Gig-Worker Law Unconstitutional." *The Guardian*, August 21, 2021, sec. Technology. https://www.theguardian.com/technology/2021/aug/20/california-gig-worker-law-proposition-22-unconstitutional.

Baig, Aamer, Bryce Hall, Paul Jenkins, Eric Lamarre, and Brian McCarthy. 2020. "The COVID-19 recovery will be digital: a plan for the first 90 days" McKinsey. Accessed October 25, 2023. https://www.mckinsey.com/capabilities/mckinsey-digital/our-insights/the-covid-19-recovery-will-be-digital-a-plan-for-the-first-90-days.

Bu, Lambert, Violet Chung, Kevin Leung, Kevin Wei Wang, Bruce Xia, and Chenan Xia. n.d. "The Future of Digital Innovation in China: Megatrends Shaping One of the World's Fastest Evolving Digital Ecosystems." McKinsey. Accessed June 27, 2023. https://www.mckinsey.com/featured-insights/china/the-future-of-digital-innovation-in-china-megatrends-shaping-one-of-the-worlds-fastest-evolving-digital-ecosystems?cid=app.

Bukht, Rumana, and Richard Heeks. 2018. "Defining, Conceptualising, and Measuring the Digital Economy." *International Organisations Research Journal* 13 (2): 143–172. https://doi.org/10.17323/1996-7845-2018-02-07.

Bunn, Daniel. 2022. "International Tax Competitiveness Index 2022." Centre for Global Tax Policy. https://files.taxfoundation.org/20221013150933/International-Tax-Competitiveness-Index-2022.pdf.

CB Insights. 2021. "State of Venture 2021 Report". https://www.cbinsights.com/research/report/venture-trends-2021/.

Chakravorti, Bhaskar, Ravi Shankar Chaturvedi, Christina Filipovic, and Griffin Brewer. 2020. "Digital in the Time of COVIDL: Trust in the Digital Economy and Its Evolution Across 90 Economies as the Planet Paused for a Pandemic." The Fletcher School at Tufts University.

December 2020. https://sites.tufts.edu/digitalplanet/files/2021/03/digital-intelligence-index.pdf.

Channel News Asia. 2020. "Expansion of Cycling Path Network to Be Sped up, Will Cost More Than S$1 Billion: Lam Pin Min." Head Topics. March 5, 2020. https://headtopics.com/sg/expansion-of-cycling-path-network-to-be-sped-up-will-cost-more-than-s-1-billion-lam-pin-min-11683700.

Chen, Katherine. 2021. "PMO | PM Lee Hsien Loong at the APEC CEO Summit 2021." Text. Prime Minister's Office Singapore. November 12, 2021. https://www.pmo.gov.sg/Newsroom/PM-Lee-Hsien-Loong-at-the-APEC-CEO-Summit.

Chia, Osmond. 2022. "99% of Government Transactions with Citizens Can Now Be Done Digitally: Josephine Teo." *The Straits Times*. November 15, 2022. https://www.straitstimes.com/tech/99-of-government-transactions-with-citizens-can-now-be-done-digitally-josephine-teo.

Department of Financial Services (New York State). 2020. "Twitter Investigation Report." July 2020. https://www.dfs.ny.gov/Twitter_Report.

European Commission. 2021. "Digital Economy and Society Index (DESI) 2021." 2021. https://digital-strategy.ec.europa.eu/en/library/digital-economy-and-society-index-desi-2021.

Eurostat. 2020. "ICT Sector — Value Added, Employment and R&D." 2020. February 2022. https://ec.europa.eu/eurostat/statistics-explained/index.php?title=ICT_sector_-_value_added,_employment_and_R%26D.

Florida, Richard L. 2002. *The Rise of the Creative Class: And How It's Transforming Work, Leisure, Community and Everyday Life*. New York: Basic Books.

Glaeser, Edward L. 2012. *Triumph of the City: How Our Greatest Invention Makes Us Richer, Smarter, Greener, Healthier, and Happier*. New York: Penguin Books.

Goldfarb, Avi, and Catherine Tucker. 2019. "Digital Economics." *Journal of Economic Literature* 57 (1): 3–43. https://doi.org/10.1257/jel.2017 1452.

Google, Temasek, and Bain & Company, E-conomy SEA 2021. 2021. "Roaring 20s: The SEA Digital Decade." https://www.thinkwithgoogle.com/_qs/documents/12741/economy_sea_2021_report.pdf.

Greeven, Mark, and Yufei Feng. 2021. "Commentary: With Tokopedia Merger, Gojek Will Take Indonesia by Storm." *Channel News Asia*. June 30, 2021. https://www.channelnewsasia.com/commentary/gojek-tokopedia-goto-indonesia-app-food-ride-payment-tech-grab-2003531.

Hatem, Louise, Daniel Ker, and John Mitchell. 2020. "A Roadmap Toward a Common Framework for Measuring the Digital Economy." Report for the G20 Digital Economy Task Force. Saudi Arabia. https://www.oecd.org/sti/roadmap-toward-a-common-framework-for-measuring-the-digital-economy.pdf.

Heller, Nathan. 2017. "Estonia, the Digital Republic." *The New Yorker*, December 11, 2017. https://www.newyorker.com/magazine/2017/12/18/estonia-the-digital-republic.

IBM Security. 2019. "IBM: Cost of a Data Breach Report 2019." *Computer Fraud & Security* 2019 (8): 4–4. https://doi.org/10.1016/S1361-3723(19)30081-8.

International Monetary Fund, Statistics Department. 2018. "Measuring the Digital Economy." *Policy Papers* 18 (016): 7. https://doi.org/10.5089/9781498307369.007.

"IRAS | Individual Income Tax Rates." n.d. Default. Accessed June 27, 2023. https://www.iras.gov.sg/taxes/individual-income-tax/basics-of-individual-income-tax/tax-residency-and-tax-rates/individual-income-tax-rates.

Jimenez, Daniel-Zoe, Victor Lim, Lawrence Cheok, and Huimin Ng. 2018. "Unlocking the Economic Impact of Digital Transformation in Asia Pacific." IDC White Paper. https://news.microsoft.com/wp-content/uploads/prod/sites/43/2018/11/Unlocking-the-economic-impact-of-digital-transformation.pdf.

Lago, Cristina. 2020. "The Biggest Data Breaches in Southeast Asia." CSO Online. January 18, 2020. https://www.csoonline.com/article/3532816/the-biggest-data-breaches-in-southeast-asia.html.

Lee, Desmond. n.d. "Opening Address by Mr Desmond Lee, Minister for National Development." Accessed June 27, 2023. https://www.forwardsingapore.gov.sg/news/speech-by-minister-desmond-lee-at-mnd-forward-singapore-engagement-session-on-public-housing.

Ministry of Finance. n.d. "BEPS Explainer." Accessed June 26, 2023. https://www.mof.gov.sg/policies/taxes/beps-explainer.

Ministry of Manpower. 2020. https://stats.mom.gov.sg/Statistics/Pages/Statistics.aspx.

Nadler, Jerrold, and David N. Cicilline. 2022. "Investigation of Competition in Digital Markets." Subcommittee on Antitrust, Commercial, and Administrative Law of the Committee on the Judiciary of the House of representatives. https://www.govinfo.gov/content/pkg/CPRT-117HPRT47832/pdf/CPRT-117HPRT47832.pdf.

National Library Board. "'Garden City' Vision is Introduced — Singapore History." May 11, 1967. https://eresources.nlb.gov.sg/history/events/a7fac49f-9c96-4030-8709-ce160c58d15c.

New York City Comptroller. 2020. "Comptroller Stringer Calls on DOE to Provide Internet Passports to All Low-Income Families to Guarantee Equal Internet Access for All Students." November 2, 2020. https://comptroller.nyc.gov/newsroom/comptroller-stringer-calls-on-doe-to-provide-internet-passports-to-all-low-income-families-to-guarantee-equal-internet-access-for-all-students/.

NYCEDC. "Global Startup Ecosystem Report: NYC Home to Over 7,000 Startups, $71B Ecosystem." NYCEDC Press Release. April 17, 2018. https://edc.nyc/press-release/global-startup-ecosystem-report-nyc-home-over-7000-startups-71b-ecosystem.

ONline Labour Observatory. 2020. "Online Labour Supply". http://onlinelabourobservatory.org/oli-supply/.

Publications Office of the European Union. 2022. *International Digital Economy and Society Index 2022: Final Report*. Estonia: Publications Office of the European Union.

Segmanta. 2020. "Gen Z-Ers: Pet Ownership Redefined." September 8, 2020. https://segmanta.com/blog/gen-z-ers-pet-ownership-redefined/.

Silaškova, Jana, and Masao Takahashi. 2020. "How Estonia's Digital Society Became a Lifeline during COVID-19." World Economic Forum. July 1, 2020. https://www.weforum.org/agenda/2020/07/estonia-advanced-digital-society-here-s-how-that-helped-it-during-covid-19/.

Sim, Royston. 2018. "SingHealth Cyber Attack: PM Lee Says Nothing Alarming in His Data That Was Stolen, No 'Dark State Secret.'" *The Straits Times*. July 20, 2018. https://www.straitstimes.com/singapore/singhealth-cyber-attack-pm-lee-says-nothing-alarming-in-his-data-that-was-stolen-no-dark.

Sitsanis, Nikolaos. 2021. "Top 10 Languages Used on the Internet for 2023." *Speakt.Com* (blog). January 17, 2021. https://speakt.com/top-10-languages-used-internet/.

Sivakumar, Yoganeetha. 2022. "Grab to TikTok: Despite the Rampant Layoffs, These 7 Tech Firms in S'pore Are Still Hiring." *Vulcan Post* (blog). November 24, 2022. https://vulcanpost.com/809664/tech-firms-still-hiring-despite-layoffs-singapore/.

Tan, Xi Yuan. n.d. "The Silver Generation in the Age of Digital Disruptions." Centre for Liveable Cities, https://www.clc.gov.sg/docs/default-source/urban-solutions/urbsol17pdf/11_casestudy_sg_thesilvergeneration.pdf.

Tham, Yuen-C. 2021. "COVID-19 Pandemic Presents Rare Opportunity to Reinvent Cities, Says Heng Swee Keat." *The Straits Times*, June 21, 2021. https://www.straitstimes.com/singapore/politics/covid-19-pandemic-presents-rare-opportunity-to-reinvent-cities-says-heng-swee.

The ASEAN Post Team. 2016. "Singapore Wins Internet Speed Race." 2016. *The ASEAN Post*. December 29, 2016. https://theaseanpost.com/article/singapore-wins-internet-speed-race.

The Smart City Observatory Report. 2023. "What makes a city liveable and smart?", IMD. https://www.imd.org/wp-content/uploads/2023/04/smartcityindex-2023-v7.pdf.

The State of Southeast Asia Report. 2020. https://www.iseas.edu.sg/centres/asean-studies-centre/aseanfocus/the-state-of-southeast-asia-2020-survey-report/.

The World Bank. 2021. "E-Trade Indicator". https://databank.worldbank.org/source/world-development-indicators.

Torstensson, Simon. n.d. "Marginalskatt i Sverige och internationellt." Ekonomifakta. Accessed July 3, 2023. https://www.ekonomifakta.se/Fakta/skatt/Skatt-pa-arbete/Marginalskatt/.

Tyers-Chowdhury, Alexandra, and Gerda Binder. 2021. "What We Know About the Gender Digital Divide for Girls: A Literature Review." Evidence Brief. UNICEF. https://www.unicef.org/eap/media/8311/file/What%20we%20know%20about%20the%20gender%20digital%20divide%20for%20girls:%20A%20literature%20review.pdf.

UNCTAD. 2021. "Inequalities Threaten Wider Divide as Digital Economy Data Flows Surge." September 29, 2021. https://unctad.org/news/inequalities-threaten-wider-divide-digital-economy-data-flows-surge.

United Nations. 2019. *Digital Economy Report 2019: Value Creation and Capture: Implications for Developing Countries*. Geneva: United Nations.

USAID, ASEAN, and US-ASEAN Connect. 2021. "ASEAN Digital Integration Index." https://asean.org/wp-content/uploads/2021/09/ADII-Report-2021.pdf.

Wong, Lester. 2020. "Parliament: Spike in Internet Usage During Circuit Breaker Well Within Operators' Ability to Cope, Says Iswaran." *The*

Straits Times. May 5, 2020. https://www.straitstimes.com/politics/parliament-spike-in-internet-usage-during-circuit-breaker-well-within-operators-ability-to.

Work in Estonia. n.d. "Start-up Scene." Work in Estonia. Accessed July 3, 2023. https://workinestonia.com/start-up-scene/.

Yong, Clement. 2021. "PayNow Transactions Doubled to $22 Billion in 2020, on Track to Set Higher Record This Year." *The Straits Times.* October 4, 2021. https://www.straitstimes.com/singapore/paynow-transactions-doubled-to-22-million-in-2020-on-track-to-set-higher-record-this-year.

The Future of Office

© 2024 World Scientific Publishing Company
https://doi.org/10.1142/9789811287848_0004

The Spatial Antifragile Nature of Work in the Age of New Normal

Sam Conrad Joyce

In their highly provocative book, *The Age of Earthquakes: A Guide to the Extreme Present* (2015), Douglas Coupland, Hans Ulrich Obrist, and Shumon Basar explored the impact of the internet and social media on our world. In their work, technology is viewed as transformative, and in many cases, destructive. These effects happen gradually, almost imperceptibly at a tectonic level, only to demonstrate their full impact when major shifts happen, highlighting the resultant aggregate societal change — hence the "earthquake" metaphor. They write, "The unintended side effects of technology dictate our future." (Basar, Coupland, and Obrist 2015, 174). The trope of technology as a malevolent transformer has been widely echoed by the subsequent profound change in society over the last two decades across the gamut of social, political, and cultural lives.

Between 2020–2022, we experienced a new transformative "earthquake", catalysed by COVID-19. This period saw relatively latent technology being widely and rapidly embraced to maintain work productivity. However, did this move highlight the fragility of the office or ultimately uncover a new "post-office" resilience though new working paradigms? And what now, as we move into the "new normal" in the long run?

As the COVID-19 virus demonstrated its global transmissibility and lethality, something forewarned by Bill Gates in a 2014 TED Talk (Gates 2015), many were forced to quarantine at home. During 2020 and 2021, this led to widespread uncertainty about many things, especially global trade, geopolitics, commercial productivity, and work, adding fire to the already proposed "end of globalisation" (K.N.C. 2019; Insights 2021). Unsurprisingly, this fuelled further concerns over famines, economic ruin, and mass unemployment, with some claiming that the over-optimised and globalised modern world would fall fast. However, contrary to predictions of a catastrophic "earthquake", COVID-19 proved to be a relatively dull period for many. Over the two years that COVID-19 dominated global news, economies continued, and work productivity was shown to be maintained and even improved, all of which is not to undermine the significant and real human cost of the COVID-19 epidemic (International Labour Organization 2021).

Ironically, tools like Gates' Microsoft Office and online teleworking enabled the continuation of office and economic activity, reducing the societal damage, suggesting that technology can be a stabilising factor in society. It would be inconceivable to imagine this event situation without these technologies. We would need to look to the 1918 Spanish Flu to understand a similar-sized epidemic pre-internet. The present relative working stability was realised though rapid and profound transformation, enabled by existing technology rapidly being adopted and scaled up, most notably teleconferencing, cloud working, and online delivery. The physical office was replaced with "virtual" tools — Zoom for meetings, Slack for messaging, Google Docs, Miro, Microsoft Teams, and Dropbox for collective file sharing and collaboration (Figure 4.1). These systems became ubiquitous ways of working from home, accelerating the continuing digitalisation William Mitchell predicted in *City of Bits* (1995). Importantly, these tools were not completely new, and most adapted comparatively smoothly relative to the level of change. Critically not least, the companies delivering the services were able to scale seemingly without issue. For example, Zoom hosted an increase of 3,300% more meeting minutes in October of 2019 versus October 2020 (Dean 2023).

For many, this mass pivot to a fully digital way of working was positive, at least in the short term. In this way, this societal "stress test" of COVID-19 was shown not only to achieve a pass, but to pass

The Spatial Antifragile Nature of Work in the Age of New Normal 109

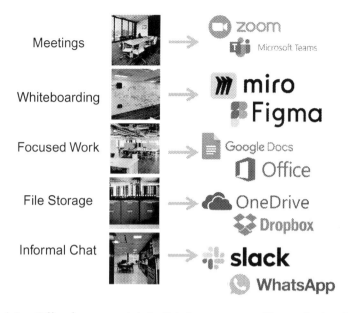

Figure 4.1: Office features and their digital counterparts (*Source*: Author 2023)

with flying colours. Working at home under low supervision and with flexible work hours, people were able to intertwine and personalise their work lives unlike ever before, disrupting power structures and office norms. Understandably, many people, especially those not in traditional positions of power or individual agency, showed a preference for Working from Home (WFH). Converse to the "earthquakes" of Obrist, the mass move to WFH instead demonstrated "Antifragility", which, defined by Nassim Talab, is the ability for a system to benefit in response to change (Taleb 2014). Although the long-term impact of COVID-19 on working is still being calculated, work has been shown to be "robust" and fundamentally, productivity seemed unaffected despite the great change.

Off the back of the "success" of this mass-enforced virtualising of the physical office, questions are being raised about the future of work and the office, as well as the long-term impact of these practices on less measurable aspects of office life. As vaccines reduced the spread and mortality of COVID-19, there has been a push by governments, institutions, and industry to go back to work as "normal". But the global situation has fundamentally changed, as indicated by the widely used concept of the "new normal", a phrase which emphasises the impossibility of life ever being the same through its oxymoronic nature. This condition of reconsideration is acute in the workplace, where many have vocally fought to maintain this new level of flexibility (Nolan 2022). Due to many reconsidering their work-life balance and personal values, many people have become more selective over their employers, exacerbated by government aid for retrenched/unemployed individuals by many developed countries over 2020 and 2021, leading to what has been called the "great resignation" (Dua et al. 2022; Ellerbeck 2022). This had led to mixed levels of acquiescence on the part of companies, with some committing to support WFH into the future, and in some cases even allowing full-time WFH (Agence France-Presse 2021).

Globally, there has been a questioning of how we work, practically leading to rethinking where we work, and existentially, why we work and how it enriches our lives. The continuum of change in the nature of work over the last two centuries has led to more office buildings being constructed all over the world. Could this perhaps mark the beginning of a new epoch? Or perhaps it is just a blip in a continuum? For this analysis, we differentiate between:

1. the individual and social activity of work [verb]
2. the space of the office [noun]

where the office space is an enabler of the activity of work. However, in both contexts, we now see both traditional and virtual iterations of them. The implications of the new normal of working on spatial conditions also lead us to ponder if the working space we call the office will change or not.

TRACING THE PAST AND PRESENT OF THE ORGANISATION AND THE OFFICE

To understand the WFH phenomenon and put the future of the office in context, it is worth considering the developmental history of

The Spatial Antifragile Nature of Work in the Age of New Normal 111

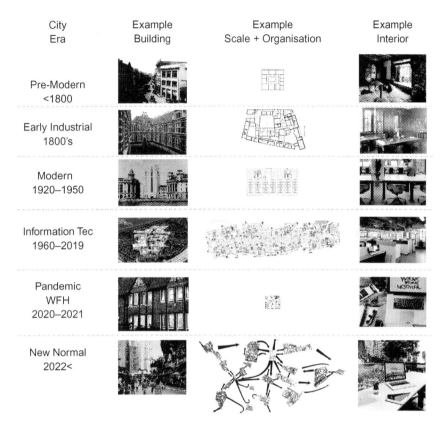

Figure 4.2: A summary of office typology during different eras (*Source*: Author 2023)

the office and the kind of work that was undertaken there. Here, we will make some generalisations about a number of historical eras, at each step looking towards the more globally progressive of each working type (Figure 4.2).

Collective work in a shared location has been integral to human productivity and progress since humans organised. It accelerated with the advent of writing and the resultant bureaucracies of ancient cultures like the Egyptians, the Sumerians, and the Chinese. Quickly, cultures formalised working structures. For example, in early England, a group of people could "incorporate" to become a "company", needing to register and address its members. The word "company" originates from the French "compagnie", implying a social group first recorded in 1150, which dates back further to the Latin word "companion", meaning "one who breaks bread with you", a legal term since 500AD.

In the premodern era, most work was small-scale and family-run, and similarly offices were typically an extension of the home. Wealthier households might have had a dedicated space to do business in the front room, bottom floor, or building entrance. Some examples include the Siheyuan, the 1st millennium Chinese courtyard, Roman houses, or multi-level structures like the 16th century Harvard House, or the 19th century Singapore shophouse. The urban condition was that offices were distributed and spatially interwoven with spaces used for other purposes. Even larger "organisations" like aristocrats or royalty residences were combined with work, as seen from vast palaces dedicating similar space for work and living, such as the Forbidden Palace or the Palace of Versailles.

By the 1600s (pre- and early industrial era), larger and more differentiated scales of business activity existed. Early multinational organisations like the United East India Company, or The British East India Company, developed corporate hierarchies to maintain their complex colonial trade activities, thus relying on substantial administrative effort. Consequently, this led to centralised, specialised office infrastructures, situated in non-residential zones and focused on trade and business. These organisations were sufficiently big to require dedicated working spaces separate from living quarters. Internally, newly complex offices became spatially structured to replicate the organisational hierarchies and enable efficient interaction within the large organisation. Hence, this led to buildings being designed not just for function, but also to strategically project power and wealth in new territories.

By the end of the 1800s and 1900s, the workplace, for most, had become distinct from living space. This was enabled by a range of technologies and ideas — clocks unifying people's times, public transport enabling longer distance commuting, and Taylorism identifying and measuring the productive value of specially designed workspaces. These city and building innovations started with the industrialisation of fabric mills and factories. Following the zeitgeist of the period, specialised office budlings copied suit, becoming technologically advanced, using gas then electric lighting, central heating, and air-conditioning to ease and streamline work. For the first time, the city was functionally segregated into the central business district (CBD), industrial, and residential areas. The industrial, then later modernist, buildings that functioned as "machines for living" (and working), were perfected by architects like Mies van der Rohe. But at the same time, they also possessed mono-functional, hermetic, and boring forms, breaking the programmatic-mix and historical continuity of the city, as argued by Jane Jacobs or mocked by film maker Jaques Tati.

With the shift to the office, which became the de facto location where many spent most of their working and also waking time, new identities built up. This social impact was explored by William Whyte, in *The Organization Man* (2002). In his book, he identified how workers now embedded in larger dehumanising spaces and organisations conflated their companies' goals as their own, creating a so-called "group think" (Whyte 2002). And while this builds up commercially useful collectivist behaviour, these corporate identities also reduce creativity and innovation. The same author, in a later work called *The Social Life of Small Urban Spaces* (2010), then went on to show how the city landscape could be designed to be more animated though careful consideration of public spaces on informal urban inter-actions (Whyte 2010).

By the 1960s, the office environment began to pivot from the Industrial Age to the Information Age, prioritising data and commu-nication over focused desk activity. This coincided with new ideas of office organisation that moved away from the established hierarchical external ring of private executive offices with windows and an internal typing pool with rows of communal desks, and moved towards more egalitarian open plans to encourage less siloed interaction. With inno-vative furniture design like Charles And Ray Eames, most notably the "action office" by Robert Propst, this led to activity-differentiated spaces that encouraged group work beyond ridged spaces. In the 1950s, room-sized computers moved into offices, and by the 1970s, personal computers arrived on desks. The 1980s saw them networked via local intranets, and in the 1990s, globally via the internet. As computers became more connected, the office, conversely, became more isolated, with collaborative spaces of the "office landscape" corrupted into rigid cubicles, promoting focused work and interaction over emails.

With the rise of software companies in the 1990s and 2000s building on technology and expertise borne at universities, corporate working mutated into a more individualistic, collegiate, and "start-up" type of format. Driven by the 'dotcom' and internet boom, office buildings were driven by individualistic and campus-style headquarters like Pixar, Google, or Facebook. Such companies boasted designs that project decentralised innovative and social goals, including shared and informal spaces, office canteens, and playful elements. This pushed employees to spend more of their time there at these intellectual property (IP)-intensive companies, whilst promoting internal movement and collaboration.

Simultaneously, these companies reversed trends of centralising offices in high-rise branded towers located in CBDs. Offices were now decentralised and distributed across residential areas, with low-rise low-density forms more akin to out-of-town shopping malls. These spaces were surrounded by ample parking, with space for quick growth, and expansion for R&D-intensive companies.

By the 2010s, the use of technology became ubiquitous but also more inconspicuous. Large desktops with cathode-ray tube (CRT) screens and wired Local Area Network (LAN) connections were replaced with portable wireless laptops. This allowed people to work more flexibly, reducing the need to be in the office. The reduced office occupancy prompted the introduction of "hot desking", invented by IBM in order to maintain high space utilisation and reduce cost, which became increasingly popular after the 2008 economic downturn. At the same time, technology was enabling this move — the proliferation of cloud services like Google Docs allowing collaborative work, teleconferencing which once required dedicated rooms and expensive commercial connectivity now made accessible with built-in laptop webcams, and free hosting like Skype and Zoom. Similarly, a generation of workers who grew up with the internet transferred their proficiency in phone messaging into more corporate collaboration tools like Microsoft Teams or Slack. Similarly, with the development of many key office systems (payroll, accounting, and HR processing etc.) into web services by companies like Oracle and others, the need to be in the same workspace was removed, at least for purely practical functional reasons.

This locational freedom saw companies decentralise their offices, move out of single high-cost locations, diversify to get new talent, expand their company reach, obtain more office space etc., or otherwise known as the hub-and-spoke model. The vanguard is the aforementioned tech campuses, but taken further with building real-estate companies like WeWork.

This disrupted businesses centred around allowing companies to freely use one of many distributed offices internationally, eschewing centrally branded spaces for flexibility. This work flexibility also supported the invasion of work into "third places" — like cafes and libraries — areas discussed by Robert Putnam in *Bowling Alone* (2000).

COVID-19 AND THE "DISCOVERY" OF ANTIFRAGILE WORK AND THE "NEW NORMAL" OFFICE

All of this arguably created a perfect mitigating solution for the seemingly black swan of COVID-19. Ironically, the technologies initially built to encourage fast scaling, travel, and globalisation of companies and employees became of critical value in dealing with the imposed lockdowns needed to control the spread of the epidemic in the initial two years. During this time, ways of working heretofore viewed as extreme or solely of relevance to novel, leading-edge companies became normalised.

COIVD-19 working, although different across nations and individuals, might be broadly said to fit into a few specific phases:

1. Full Lockdown: People forced to stay at home
2. Partial Lockdown: Limited permission to access office and cafes, small gatherings

3. Limited Restrictions: Offices allowed to open, no large gatherings, limited travel
4. New Normal: Most restrictions removed, social adjustment.

Many countries imposed full lockdowns when the pandemic began in early 2020, easing them to partial lockdowns or limited restrictions, in response to lower perceived risk. In some cases, there was a return to full lockdown but most eventually eased into states of New Normal by the end of 2022. The initial and direct impact on workers in the first phase was to fuse their living and working. For many, this lockdown resulted in using home offices, family dining tables, and even bedroom dressing tables to work, forcing these worlds together. The physical space diminished incredibly. People were forced to stay where they lived, the commute becoming the act of moving from one room to another.

The potential of the previous digital services was fully unlocked, with workers relying on the services mentioned in Figure 4.1. This way of working was shown to be largely effective and productive and will be discussed later in the temporal section. As a result, the lockdowns uncovered not only the full-scale reliability of modern digital systems, as an effective "digital twin" for the physical office, but also the viable possibility of using the home and other "remote" spaces in place of the office for both focused isolated work and group activities.

In the age of a "New Normal", we now have three spaces (office, remote, and virtual) which, mediated though the virtual, are mutually compatible; you can meet in person and include someone online usually, or you can work in a virtual space/online whilst on a real/virtual meeting etc. This allows for significantly more flexibility and possibility, most notably in the spatial realm. This is also an example of anti-fragile behaviour such that even under significant pressure of the COVID-19 restrictions, work has been further strengthened and enabled, rather than just maintained (robust) or weakened (fragile). Importantly, however, the power balance of spaces has been changed. With the digital being the store of data and connector between the physical and remote office, it has arguably become centralised, despite not being tangible (Figure 4.3).

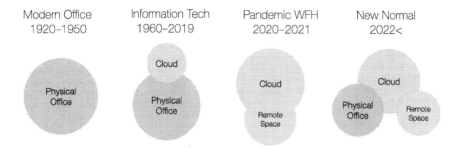

Figure 4.3: The evolution of the three main workspaces (*Source*: Author 2023)

This new level of multiplicity in spatial possibility for the office, proven by the pandemic, now promises a new type of antifragility, namely that of adaptive capacity. Previously, a company would have to change and respond to needs such as growing, re-organisation, relocation, or diversification of locations etc. with the physical office as the first priority. Nevertheless, services like WeWork have lowered the complexity of such undertakings, albeit at a high cost. Now, with both a digital space and employees open to using their own spaces to work, there are significantly more degrees of freedom. For example, a new city "office" can be deployed by simply having an internet connection and relying on third spaces for client meetings, before a physical premise is acquired. This has led to architects to push for more ideas of buildings that can spatially adapt to these variable needs, such as the "Elastic Office" and similar concepts (Davis n.d.).

The impact of these new social-technical-building developments on the city is still to be understood. Cities have oscillated between centralising and dispersing factors — the centralisation of the modern building and public transport, and the decentralisation into the suburbs, enabled by the car and campus-type offices enabled by the cloud. Rather than forcing one type of city, this adaptive capacity will likely de-risk reconfigurations of the city that are the negotiated balance between citizens' and commercial needs. As compared to previously more formal modern cities, this new "three-space office" (physical, digital, and remote) will allow for more fluid cities. This

118 The City Rebooted: Networks, Connectivity and Place Identities in Singapore

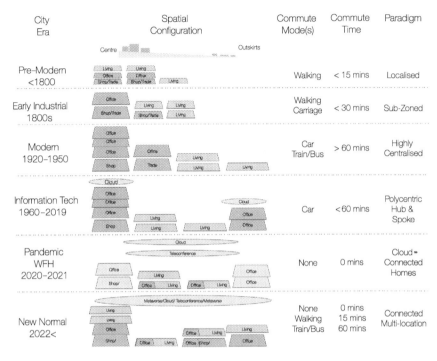

Figure 4.4: Spatial-temporal relationships of the office in the city (*Source*: Author 2023)

will allow work and the office to spread away from the CBD, and also residential and other programmes to move into the city (Figure 4.4).

This is pointing to the fact that cities that will be more mixed, most obviously through inserting residential spaces into the CBD (Mukherjee 2019), but also likely through weaving work and offices into more residential areas, such as WeWork's "hub-and-spoke model" (WeWork 2020), which has arguably already been implemented in Singapore as many banks separate different office actives across locations (Singapore Business Review 2023; CapitaL and n.d.). This means that at both a city and a building level, we will be spatially and temporally integrating work and play more. However, this still opens up design questions about which types of these combinations are preferable.

THE ANTIFRAGILE WORKER — SURVEYING THE SENTIMENT BEHIND THE CHANGING OFFICE

Much of what has practically changed the office in the last decade has been socio-technical. In earlier decades, practical improvements to the office environment, and technological advances like software, drove productivity and efficiency. But what is left after this automation, which is likely to accelerate due to Artificial Intelligence? As we reduce the need for doing dull, repetitive tasks, the future focuses on enabling workers to leverage their strengths as humans. Tasks which cannot be automated, like complex negotiation, persuasion, perceptiveness, originality, and decision making under creative, qualitative, and contextually sensitive situations (Osborne and Rose 1999) and roles which require professional application of social interaction, emotional intelligence, and intellectual engagement would be reserved for humans.

Thus, modernist changes to the office environment which have previously been aimed towards efficiency, scalability, and productivity, have instead focused on improving the human aspects of work, resulting in a new social-technical working environment. There is value in considering the impact of this interaction and their outcomes, using this as a lens to consider what the resultant steady state New Normal might be.

For example, during industrialisation, the use of large-scale machines improved productivity (technical], reducing hard labour, and encaging it for maintaining machines. This led many rural people to urbanise with the infrastructural and material benefits. This technical shift impacted people through Taylorism management, removing people's flexibility, resulting in a regimented lifestyle (technical → social). There was resistance initially, expressing itself as efforts to stop the use of technology which was taking away traditional work and disrupting existing artisan labour practices, such as the Luddites (social → technical). However, this resistance through protectionism was ultimately not sustainable as the skills being protected were already obsolete and uneconomic (Bailey 1998). However, this modernist centralised model was socially embraced by the workers, leading to collective action in newly formed unions and other working associations, which lobbied to improve working conditions, including the formalisation of the weekend (Beaven 2020). The success of this is predicated on its capacity to be mutually beneficial, that is, to improve the outcome of the work and worker, through better worker conditions, often referred to as Fordism. This end outcome is realised over iterated negation and experimentation of a stable mediated equilibrium between commercial and workers' interests (technical ↔ social).

More recently, software and digital tools have been widely adopted, initially due to their ability to improve efficiency of typical white-collar activities (technical). These changed the nature of work, quickly expanding from just document editing to encompass social activities like messaging meetings (technical → social). This has added new pressures, with many reporting that this expands their working hours, due to the expectation that people can be online constantly. Whilst the pandemic intensified the ubiquity of connection technology, this led to greater "constantly online" behaviours (Horowitz and Parker 2023). Remote work, however, allowed new modes for employees to take back their time, such as "quiet quitting" (Klotz and Bolino 2022) and "lying flat" (Ji and Hu 2021), something that is possible as people WFH away from scrutiny or group pressure (people → technology). This results in retaliatory activities like companies banning or recalling WFH privileges (Milmo and Hern 2022), using considerable worker surveillance (Skopeliti 2023), or undertaking mass layoffs of those they deem not to be contributing, focusing on those not physically present in the office (Meta 2023). This is believed to be a major contributing factor for the "Great Resignation" (Ellerbeck 2022), as people reconsider their priorities and values, creating new issues of finding willing workers. For those seeking a balance (technology ↔ people), however, many companies are now working towards being attractive places to work by building a good work-life balance, realising that this is the way to sustainable new conditions.

SURVEY ON WORK LOCATION PREFERENCES

Whilst much of the data is focused on the US, there is value in understanding the situation in other countries, specifically, Singapore.

The Spatial Antifragile Nature of Work in the Age of New Normal   121

To this end, we have worked on an office survey to understand more. In our survey, we got feedback from 512 individuals, all based in Singapore and working in a range of industries including Tech, Law, Engineering, Education, and Creative, with 95% of the workers ranging from ages 25 to 65. This survey data was obtained in 2022, when there were still restrictions in place preventing people going back to the office full time. However, in 2021, there had already been periods where workers could fully go back to the office.

The focus on this survey was to understand what people preferred in terms of office and WFH duration, but also understand the relationship between time spent in the office on social interaction, and exploring the technology used. During the survey, most people were working remotely, with over 50% working either fully WFH or one day a week in the office (Figure 4.5). Younger members were more keen to return and already working full time in the office than older members. Those between 25 and 45 were working fully at home (Figure 4.6). When asked, younger members identified less ideal home working conditions and social interaction as a "push" back to the office, whereas in the middle demographic, the trend was for full WFH or one day a week, citing reasons such as the ease of focussing

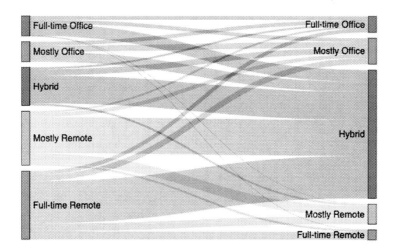

Figure 4.5: Sankey diagram showing current work situation during survey on the left and desired situation on the right (*Source*: Author 2023)

122 The City Rebooted: Networks, Connectivity and Place Identities in Singapore

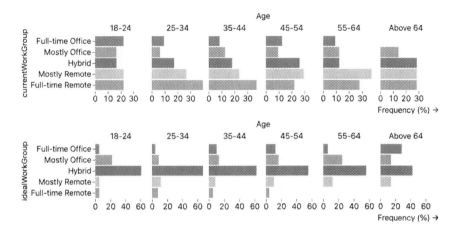

Figure 4.6: Distribution of work type by age group, with situation at time of survey above and ideal situation reported below (*Source*: Author 2023)

on tasks, the ability to manage other aspects of life, and reduced commute as reasons for this change.

When asked what their ideal would be going forward, respondents in senior positions indicated that they wanted to work hybrid in the long term. Just under 60% of all Singapore-based respondents indicated that 2–3 days in the office (hybrid) is ideal, with 9% of workers wanting full WFH, 7% full back to office. Those who indicated 'hybrid-lite' (one day WFH) came up to 12% and 'office-lite' (one day in office) 10%.

Across all age groups, the average was unanimous in preferring 3 days a week (Figure 4.6). However, we saw a 'U' type distribution in age for those who preferred more time in the office, with both older workers (45+) and those younger than 25 years indicating their wish to spend more time in the office as compared to middle-aged peers.

Combined with feedback and informal interviews from junior and senior (C-Suite) office workers, this finding suggests that younger workers desire more interaction time, mentorship, hence desiring more time in the office. Similarly, the more managerial senior members of an office desire this face-to-face time to disseminate their ideas and work on strategy. Whereas established workers in the middle,

The Spatial Antifragile Nature of Work in the Age of New Normal 123

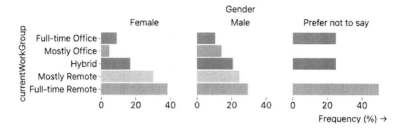

Figure 4.7: Distribution of current work type at time of survey by gender (*Source*: Author 2023)

who are likely to be already productive are less reliant on decision making, prefer more focused time at home.

Consistent with other surveys of this kind, fully WFH or mostly remote workers skewed somewhat towards females (Figure 4.7). However, the difference is not that great, implying a roughly similar desire to work form the office for both sexes which is different from more European and US-based studies.

SURVEY ON COMMUNICATION METHODS AND SOCIAL SENTIMENTS

What was interesting in relation to how communication and interaction quickly evolved during lockdown and easing measures was how quickly workers adapted to different mediums of interaction and socialising at work. We can differentiate between synchronous mediums like Zoom and asynchronous mediums like Messaging and Email. Typically, WFH people rely more on asynchronous means.

In the same interview, we asked about communication methods. During a period of significant WFH, most reported spending the most time interacting though email (20% of total daily working time), with video calls second at over 13% of total daily working time. However, the quartile range skews quicky, up to as much as 25% of a working day, indicating many spent more time on this mode of communication (Figure 4.8). Singapore reports a significant amount of time (12%) spent interacting for work on mobile messaging, like WhatsApp. This is independent from more focused work instant messaging, like

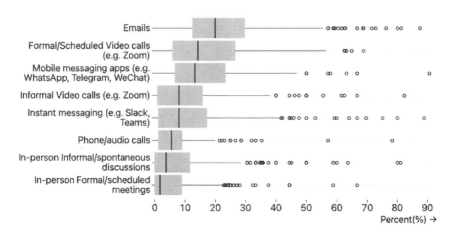

Figure 4.8: Boxplot of workers' time spent on interaction platforms by percentage of overall day (0.0–1.0). The central line indicates the arithmetic mean; the grey box indicates the range of the 25th and 75th percentile; line whiskers indicate the 1.5th interquartile range; and the dots indicate the outliers (*Source*: Author 2023)

Slack (around 8%). Often, the total time spent on these platforms exceeds the regular 8 hours working day. This is consistent with increased communication "off the clock", shown by other higher income workers elsewhere in the world (Horowitz and Parker 2023). Women spent statistically more time on asynchronous communication like email and messaging over a day than men. However, this difference does not extend to video calling or synchronous mediums.

For synchronous WFH interaction, in total, people appeared to spend 22% of their time on video messaging like Zoom. But this splits into approximately 8.5% of their day on informal unscheduled meetings, and 13.5% on formal scheduled meetings.

When looking at the experience in the office, however, a similar 'U' shape emerges if we consider WFH video calls. In our survey, those with ten or more years of experience in a company spent approximately twice as much time on video calls than those with a moderate 5–10 years' experience. However, for those with less than five years' experience, it went up again, to a similar amount as the "less than 10 years of working experience" group; implying that Zoom was less required for non-management experienced workers but more for relatively new and management level employees. This also links to the desire for those undertaking lots of calls to also desire to be in the office more.

The Spatial Antifragile Nature of Work in the Age of New Normal 125

Moving the focus towards sentiment, we found some weak but statistically significant correlations that linked social interaction with more positive outlooks on the office. People who spent less time in the office generally felt that interactions were less personal compared to those who spent more time in the office. Those who felt a greater sense of community, on average, had more informal discussions than those who felt less or no change. We also saw that those who felt a greater sense of community had more informal discussions than those who felt no change.

The overall difference in social interaction is statistically significantly higher for those who spent more time in the office. The latter include, obviously, those who are in the office full time as well as those who are in a hybrid work mode but ended up spending more time working in office than from home. However, there is still a lot of variability in the other modes. This all points to a link between opportunity for face-to-face still being a valuable and important means to drive social interaction, especially informal social interaction, which is an important activity linked to team creativity and decision making (Pentland 2015).

It can be argued that workers typically are trying to find quality interactions and balance deep, focused work with work interactions. But post-COVID-19, they have a relatively higher amount of flexibility. Across all ages, there is a desire to mix WFH and WFO, and this is mirrored by companies. At the time of writing, we found that most companies supported two to three days of WFH (Figure 4.9).

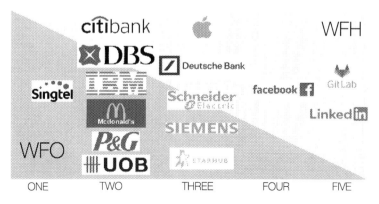

Figure 4.9: Various large companies with offices in Singapore and their public policies on the number of days of WFH (*Source*: Author 2023)

However, our data suggests that there is a balance to be made both to support different age groups, especially the many 'U' shapes, where older and younger workers align better with middle-aged workers and ensure that social interactions are kept regular enough such that connectivity, sociability, and good sentiment are maintained. As our data indicates, WFH does not fully fulfil this, leading to reduced cohesion in the long run. This supports our idea that a social debt has been incurred and needs to be compensated in the office through design and planning.

REFERENCES

AFP. 2021. "Facebook Makes Remote Work Option Permanent as Offices Reopen." *The Straits Times*, June 10, 2021. https://www.straitstimes.com/business/companies-markets/facebook-remote-work-made-permanent-as-offices-re-open.

Bailey, Brian. 1998. *The Luddite Rebellion*. Sutton.

Basar, Shumon, Douglas Coupland, and Hans Ulrich Obrist. 2015. *The Age of Earthquakes: A Guide to the Extreme Present*. Blue Rider Press.

Beaven, Brad. 2020. "The Modern Phenomenon of the Weekend." *The Conversation*. January 21, 2020. https://www.bbc.com/worklife/article/20200117-the-modern-phenomenon-of-the-weekend.

CapitaLand. n.d. "Time to Flex Those Space Muscles." CapitaLand. Accessed June 30, 2023. https://www.capitaland.com/sg/en/lease/businesspark-industrial-logistics/workspace-content-studio/time-to-flex-those-space-muscles.html.

Davis, Daniel. n.d. "The Elastic Office Building." Hassell. Accessed June 30, 2023. https://www.hassellstudio.com/research/the-elastic-office-building.

Dean, Brian. 2023. "Zoom User Stats: How Many People Use Zoom in 2023?" Backlinko. March 28, 2023. https://backlinko.com/zoom-users.

Dua, André, Kweilin Ellingrud, Phil Kirschner, Adrian Kwok, Ryan Luby, Rob Palter, and Sarah Pemberton. 2022. "Is Remote Work Effective: We Finally Have the Data." McKinsey & Company. June 23, 2022. https://www.mckinsey.com/industries/real-estate/our-insights/americans-are-embracing-flexible-work-and-they-want-more-of-it.

Ellerbeck, Stefan. 2022. "The Great Resignation is Not over: Here's What Employees Say Matters Most at the Workplace." World Economic Forum. June 24, 2022. https://www.weforum.org/agenda/2022/06/the-great-resignation-is-not-over/.

Gates, Bill. 2015. "Bill Gates: The Next Outbreak? We're Not Ready | TED Talk." TED. 2015. https://www.ted.com/talks/bill_gates_the_next_outbreak_we_re_not_ready.

Horowitz, Juliana, and Kim Parker. 2023. "How Americans View Their Jobs." Pew Research Center. https://www.pewresearch.org/social-trends/2023/03/30/how-americans-view-their-jobs/.

Insights, Imperial Business. 2021. "Does COVID-19 Mean the End for Globalization?" *Forbes*. January 8, 2021. https://www.forbes.com/sites/imperialinsights/2021/01/08/does-covid-19-mean-the-end-for-globalization/.

International Labour Organization. 2021. "Why Would Labour Productivity Surge During a Pandemic?" International Labour Organization. December 14, 2021. https://ilostat.ilo.org/why-would-labour-productivity-surge-during-a-pandemic/.

Ji, Siqi, and Huifeng Hu. 2021. "What is 'Lying Flat', and Why Are Chinese Officials Standing up to It?" *South China Morning Post*. October 24, 2021. https://www.scmp.com/economy/china-economy/article/3153362/what-lying-flat-and-why-are-chinese-officials-standing-it.

Klotz, Anthony C., and Mark C. Bolino. 2022. "When Quiet Quitting is Worse Than the Real Thing." *Harvard Business Review*. September 15, 2022. https://hbr.org/2022/09/when-quiet-quitting-is-worse-than-the-real-thing.

K.N.C. 2019. "Globalisation is Dead and We Need to Invent a New World Order." *The Economist*. June 28, 2019. https://www.economist.com/open-future/2019/06/28/globalisation-is-dead-and-we-need-to-invent-a-new-world-order.

Meta. 2023. "Update on Meta's Year of Efficiency." *Meta* (blog). March 14, 2023. https://about.fb.com/news/2023/03/mark-zuckerberg-meta-year-of-efficiency/.

Milmo, Dan, and Alex Hern. 2022. "Elon Musk Scraps Twitter's Work from Home Policy." *The Guardian*, November 10, 2022, sec. Technology. https://www.theguardian.com/technology/2022/nov/10/elon-musk-scraps-twitter-work-home-staff.

Mitchell, William. 1995. "City of Bits: Space, Place and the Infobahn." MIT Press.

Mukherjee, Andy. 2019. "Downtown Singapore is a New Property Playground." *Bloomberg*. September 29, 2019. https://www.bloomberg.com/opinion/articles/2019-09-29/redevelopment-of-singapore-s-downtown-is-a-boon-to-developers?leadSource=uverify%20wall#xj4y7vzkg.

Nolan, Beatrice. 2022. "Apple Workers Hit Back Against the Company's Return-to-Office Plans, Saying They Have Carried out 'Exceptional Work' from Home." *Business Insider*. August 22, 2022. https://www.businessinsider.com/apple-employees-remote-work-office-three-days-2022-8.

Osborne, Thomas, and Nikolas Rose. 1999. "Do the Social Sciences Create Phenomena? The Example of Public Opinion Research." *The British Journal of Sociology* 50 (3): 367–396. https://doi.org/10.1111/j.1468-4446.1999.00367.x.

Pentland, Alex. 2015. *Social Physics: How Social Networks Can Make Us Smarter*. Penguin.

Putnam, Robert. 2000. *Bowling Alone*. Simon and Schuster.

Singapore Business Review. 2023. "'Hub-and-Spoke' Office Model Gains Traction in APAC." *Singapore Business Review*. January 20, 2023. https://sbr.com.sg/economy/news/hub-and-spoke-office-model-gains-traction-in-apac.

Skopeliti, Clea. 2023. "'I Feel Constantly Watched': The Employees Working Under Surveillance." *The Guardian*. May 30, 2023. https://amp.theguardian.com/money/2023/may/30/i-feel-constantly-watched-employees-working-under-surveillance-monitorig-software-productivity.

Taleb, Nassim Nicholas. 2014. *Antifragile: Things That Gain from Disorder*. Random House Trade Paperback edition. New York: Random House Trade Paperbacks.

WeWork. 2020. "The Hub-and-Spoke Model, as Demonstrated by WeWork." WeWork Ideas. August 26, 2020. https://www.wework.com/en-GB/ideas/workspace-solutions/flexible-products/the-hub-and-spoke-model-as-demonstrated-by-wework.

Whyte, William Hollingsworth. 2002. *The Organization Man*. University of Pennsylvania Press.

———. 2010. *The Social Life of Small Urban Spaces*. 7. print. Project for Public Spaces.

© 2024 World Scientific Publishing Company
https://doi.org/10.1142/9789811287848_0005

Future of Work is Hybrid, but How?

Sam Conrad Joyce & Nazim Ibrahim

INTRODUCTION

The office plays a critical role in the functioning of most companies and organisations. It is the social and spatial nexus of connectivity and activity. In addition to providing a dedicated space for employees to carry out their work, it facilitates the flow of information and knowledge through formal and informal interactions, making it central to the productivity and culture of an organisation. Prior to COVID-19, most organisations operated from centralised offices with daily synchronised schedules (Choudhury *et al.* 2020). However, when the pandemic struck, many were forced to work remotely from home. This impacted our work habits as much as it changed our social lives. But as we slowly returned to our social routines, our expectations of work seemed to have been permanently affected and the role and future of offices critically questioned.

Although working remotely was initially a challenge for employees and organisations, many seemed to quickly adapt to its challenges and some even "thrived" in this new mode of working (Kaufman *et al.* 2020), to the extent that many employees preferred to work remotely or in a hybrid mode even after the restrictions were removed. Some employers were keen to oblige as this had some immediate advantages on an organisational level.

For employees, remote working removed the need for potentially expensive and lengthy commutes, and provided more flexibility for how, when, and where they worked. As a result, many employees reported to have less stress, more personal well-being, and better work-life balance. For employers, this translated into higher employee job satisfaction, leading to increased productivity, reduced effective absenteeism, and lower turnovers (Kaufman et al. 2020). Additionally, remote working lowered companies' costs in renting office space and reduced the use of general resources as well as enabled them to expand their talent pool away from traditional locations (GitLab n.d.). These are clear and direct benefits from remote working.

At the same time, however, remote working fundamentally changed the way we communicated and socialised with our co-workers. These social links and the resultant larger networks are integral to human behaviour and have a significant impact on commercial information, accuracy of decision making, and consequently, corporate productivity and competitivity (Travers and Milgram 1969; Pentland 2014). The potential impacts of remote working in this regard are less certain.

Studies on the impact of remote working on office connections reported long-term impacts on our ability to maintain or form new relationships with our colleagues (Work Trend Index Annual Report 2021; Lund et al. 2021). While many studies have proposed hybrid working as a compromise to balance personal preferences and organisational values, few have discussed how this could look like spatially or temporally. Most do not focus on the complex communication and social aspects of different configurations in relation to the wider organisation connectivity.

To fundamentally understand this better, we employed an agent-based model using proxemic distances to explore the impact of number of days (temporal) and office configuration (spatial) on frequency and quality of communication (social). We examined the performance of the agents under different scenarios and organisation sizes and evaluated the resulting network using network metrics. In this chapter, we discuss our findings that suggest that the number of days in the office and seating configurations have an important and complex impact on the connectivity of an organisation, and result in varying levels of intra- and inter-team communication among employees.

We also discuss how these findings can be used to identify the most effective temporal and spatial work arrangements depending on the characteristics of an organisation.

SOCIAL INTERACTIONS AND THE WORKPLACE

Communication and Co-location

Beyond productivity, the office, typically portrayed as a place for focused work, plays an important role in providing a common space for the employees of an organisation to come together and function as a connected entity. The office layout and the organisational structure create a network of individuals and teams based on their co-location, collaboration, and communications. Multiple studies previously have demonstrated the importance of the structure of this network as well as the strength of its connections, or "ties", for the success of both the individuals and the organisation (Granovetter 1973; Burt 2004; Yang et al. 2021). Strength of ties and the level of interconnectivity within and across teams can indicate how easily information flows through the organisation and can result in different configurations of networks that impact a team or organisation's performance in terms of productivity, creativity, and innovation (Reagans and McEvily 2003).

In a key study on communication and team performances across different industries, patterns of communication were identified as the most important predictor of a team's success and were more crucial than things like the intelligence, personality, skills of individuals, or even the substance of discussions (Kim et al. 2012). By monitoring physical interactions between employees, Pentland's team identified three key predictors — one, energy which refers to a member's contribution to a team, two, engagement which refers to communication among team members, and finally, exploration which refers to communication with members outside the team. They found that successful teams had equal contributions of high-energy and high engagement with periodic explorations outside the team, with exploration being more important for teams requiring innovation and creativity.

By comparing these physical interactions with other communication, they concluded that the most valuable form of communication is face-to-face, which accounts for 35% of the variation in a team's performance. This is followed by phone/video conferencing which is far less effective with more people. The least valuable are email and texting. They identified that electronic communication does not create the same levels of energy and engagement that face-to-face interactions do. They also found that social time outside of formal meetings played a critical role in a team's performance and accounted for more than 50% of successful communication patterns.

Prior to COVID-19, as most employees worked from a centralised location, a lot of this communication happened physically in and around the office (Figure 5.1). Formal scheduled meetings happened in dedicated meeting rooms, while more informal and impromptu discussions took place around the desk or other common areas such as pantries or lifts, leading some like Steve Jobs to design offices expressly to force people together (Stone 2015). During weekdays, these informal discussions and social interactions spilled over to spaces outside the office, such as cafés or bars in the area, referred to as third spaces (Oldenburg 1989). These informal interactions allowed for a lot more social connections to emerge spontaneously. Online meetings were generally used for external meetings, often with parties in different geographic locations, and home was reserved for family

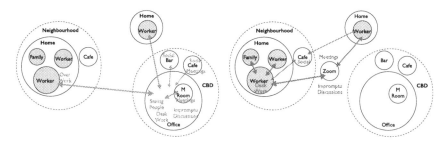

Figure 5.1: Spatial use before and during COVID-19 (*Source*: Authors 2023)

time, with occasional weekend work done from home limited to individual tasks.

Impact of COVID-19

During COVID-19, most knowledge workers worked from home (WFH), which served as both an office and a personal family space. Our study that covered pre- and post-COVID-19 activity in the legal, tech, education, and creative industries in Singapore found that most, if not all, communication was conducted digitally through video conferencing, phone calls, emails, and chat (see Chapter 3). According to a study by Microsoft (2021) on their online collaborative tools, during COVID-19, people spent 2.5 times longer on Teams meetings, 45% more on chat and sent 40 billion more emails compared to pre-COVID-19 numbers. They reported that more than 60% of these calls and meetings were unscheduled, indicating a substitute for the impromptu discussions that typically happen in an office environment.

However, the study reported a trend towards diminishing networks, leading to more siloed companies and organisations, which can hinder the productivity and innovation of a company. This typically results in decreased interaction with people in distant networks, or "weak" ties, as well as a reduction in participation and messaging in group chats and channels. These weak ties are ties formed outside of an immediate group, often with people whom one meets infrequently but are considered important in acquiring new information and bridging different groups (Granovetter 1973). Although there was a significant increase in digital communication with an immediate network, or "strong ties" in the beginning, these were also found to be diminishing with time, further demonstrating that it is difficult to maintain or create new social relationships outside of one's own teams primarily through these types of communication.

Similar findings were reported by Carmody *et al.* (2022) where they studied the email network of over 2,800 MIT researchers within an 18-month period. They found that the removal of co-location due to the pandemic resulted in an immediate and persistent drop in the number of weak ties between distant networks, as employees who are not co-located are less likely to form ties. This affected both existing and new ties, with more than 5,100 weak ties, approximately 1.8 ties per person, estimated to be lost during the period of full remote work, indicating a long-term impact of continuous remote working (Carmody *et al.* 2022).

At the same time, both studies reported an improvement in these networks once restrictions were eased, especially between employees who were co-located. Although the lost connections cannot be immediately restored by going back to the office, these findings suggest that a balance of both WFH and work-from-office (WFO) can be achieved through a combination or hybrid of in-person and remote interactions.

HYBRID: ALTERNATIVE WORKPLACE MODELS AND "GOLDILOCKS" SOLUTIONS

Although many studies have suggested hybrid working as the way forward, the discussions around how exactly to do that have been quite limited and mainly focussed on hybrid working as a single working model comparable to full WFH or full WFO. However, as one key study done on Australian companies suggests, organisations are adopting different hybrid models for the workplace (Davis n.d.). They categorise these based on how employees use the office spaces and identify five key types, including the traditional centralised office as well as the fully remote working model.

The three "hybrid" models identified include:

1. Turbocharged Activity-Based Work (ABW) model: where employees use the office as a shared workspace without dedicated desks.
2. Clubhouse model: where employees use the office only for collaborative work with focussed work done at home or third spaces.
3. Hub-and-Spoke model: where employees work from satellite offices.

Future of Work is Hybrid, but How? 135

These high-level models provide a practical starting point to think about the physical distribution of spaces that can be most suitable for a specific organisation as they are being actively applied in real organisations. However, they do not provide guidance on how the number of days or synchronicity of use can be considered, or how that might impact co-location and resulting social interactions, specifically through informal and in-person communication within the space.

In this study, we explore how these parameters might impact the social network of an office based on spatial and temporal synchronicity and provide guidance on determining the "right" combination(s) of hybrid working to match different organisational needs (Figure 5.2).

Figure 5.2: Examples of office configurations differentiated by the ability for workers to vary their seating locations (vertical axis) or vary their working from office dates (horizontal axis) (*Source*: Authors 2023)

136 The City Rebooted: Networks, Connectivity and Place Identities in Singapore

MEASURING OFFICE NETWORKS

Social networks

A social network, such as an office network, is the social structure made up of all the individuals in an organisation and the ties between them. Like most networks, they can be represented in different ways, most common of which is a graph (Figure 5.3). In a graphical representation, the individuals of the network are represented as nodes, while their ties are represented as edges/links. Generally, the length and/or thickness of the links represent the strength of ties between pairs of nodes. One of the most useful aspects of this representation is that it allows us to examine and evaluate the networks using graph metrics (Figure 5.4).

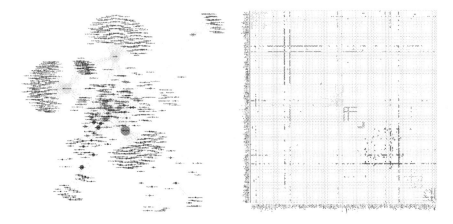

Figure 5.3: Two representations of the same social network, graph (left) and adjacency matrix (right) (*Source*: Authors 2023)

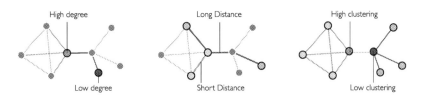

Figure 5.4: Key metrics used to evaluate the performance of a network (*Source*: Authors 2023)

Three of the key network metrics used in social networks are:

1. Degree Centrality: It measures the number of other nodes a node is directly connected to. Within a social network, this represents the number of direct contacts of an individual.
2. Shortest Path Length: It measures the distance between a pair of nodes as the number of individual nodes in their shortest path. In a social network, this represents the degrees of separation between two individuals and impacts how easily information can flow through a network.
3. Clustering Coefficient: It measures how connected a node's neighbours are to each other. It ranges from 0, no connections, to 1, all nodes connected to each other. In a social network, this measures how closely knit a group is.

These metrics can help us to understand the connectivity and grouping of different network configurations (Figure 5.5). A

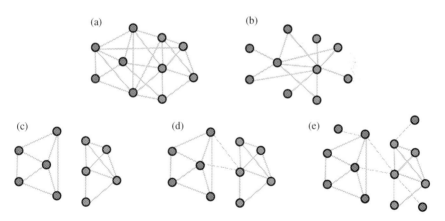

Figure 5.5: Indicative network configurations. The numbers indicate the degree or number of connections of each node:

(a) A highly connected network, with no clear subgroups
(b) A highly centralised network with two highly connected nodes
(c) A highly siloed network with isolated subgroups that are highly connected within
(d) Same network with two separate subgroups connected by bridges
(e) Same network with some nodes linked to nodes outside the network
(*Source*: Authors 2023)

network with high degree centrality will generate a highly connected network where many people are directly connected to many others. A network with fewer nodes having high degree centrality will result in centralised networks where a small pool of people become "gatekeepers" in information distribution. When networks have high clustering coefficients, distinct groups start to emerge; but when there are no edges or "bridges" between such groups, they become siloed and disconnected from each other.

Analysing social networks

To generate and analyse social networks, interaction data of the individuals in the network is required. Although social sciences relied heavily on observation and self-reporting in the past (Whyte 2010), new tools and technologies have operationalised such research, simultaneously making it easier to collect such data. Social media platforms such as Facebook or LinkedIn are a good example of this. By recording the millions of interactions people perform on their platforms, they can generate a network of users and their interactions with each other and their content. Depending on how they assign weight to different interactions, they can then use network analysis to determine which individuals belong to the same or similar groups and use this to recommend new people and content to the users.

In the case of office interactions, a similar approach is commonly used by analysing records of digital communication such as emails or messaging apps (Davis n.d.). Here, each email or message can be considered an interaction between two or more people and can be aggregated to determine the strength of connection between them. This is especially useful in the context of COVID-19, where most people were communicating through emails and other forms of messaging.

This was done in the aforementioned MIT study, where they collected emails of over 2,800 in an academic setting during an 18-month period, using the daily number of emails between pairs as the edge weights or a proxy for the strength of connection. By keeping track of which research groups each participant belonged to, they were able to determine communication within and across different groups pre- and post-COVID-19. Additionally, by comparing these connections with the location of the offices, they were able to determine the impact of co-location and proximity of offices on the strength of ties between the individuals.

However, despite research demonstrating that e-mail communication is often a good proxy for physical encounters (Spiliopoulou and Penn 1999; Baym, Zhang, and Lin 2004), they were found to overemphasise organisational hierarchy and therefore might not fully capture interpersonal ties between organisationally distant colleagues (Sevtsuk *et al.* 2022).

Alternatively, data on physical interactions can be captured using sensors. In Kim *et al.*'s study (2012), data on how people physically interact with each other was captured using sociometric badges — wearable electronic sensors that capture people's tone of voice and body language (Kim *et al.* 2012). These badges do not record their actual words but collected more than 100 data points a minute, including their tone and voice, their body positions relative to each other, body languages and gestures, and how much they talk, listen, or interrupt. They identified communication patterns of teams and individuals within teams and outside of the team. By comparing these communication data with team performances, they were able to determine the communication patterns that make for the most successful teamwork.

Where such data on actual physical interactions are unavailable, studies on socio-spatial relationships often model these interactions using detailed spatial data such as location of workspaces, shared physical spaces (elevators, canteens, restrooms, and hallways) and circulation networks (Kabo *et al.* 2015; Sevtsuk *et al.* 2022). The movement of people as "agents" in the spatial model are then simulated, and their interactions used as a proxy for physical interactions in combination with digital communication to understand the impact of spatial characteristics on social ties. Such agent-based modelling is commonly used in fields such as social epidemiology to simulate the impact of dynamic social behaviour on the spread and outcome of a disease, and has been widely used during the COVID-19 pandemic to forecast the spread under different circumstances (El-Sayed *et al.* 2012; Shamil *et al.* 2021). This is especially useful for decision making prior to the availability of data, as it provides a more nuanced understanding of how different parameters and their variations might impact the outcome in a dynamic social environment where individual agents are involved.

As hybrid working has only gained universal attention in recent times, there is a lack of data on communication and collaboration under different hybrid scenarios. Most empirical studies on hybrid working to date has primarily focussed on understanding employee preferences and experience in terms of number of days at home versus office and therefore does not provide any insights into how these scenarios and variations in co-location, schedule, or number of days might impact social connections. In the absence of such data, we believe that an agent-based model can be used to understand these better, and gain preliminary insights to help determine the right hybrid working configuration for organisations.

MODELLING HYBRID WORKING

Agent-based model

Our model environment is set up as two spatial zones for home and office. The office space is assumed to have seating in groups of 10, relatively positioned at uniformed distances from each other. The distance between the seats and groups of seats is controlled using a force-based physical simulation. All distances in the model are based off Hall *et al.* (1968) definition of proxemics, which categorises physical distances into intimate, personal, social, and public distances, based on different levels of comfortable interpersonal communication (Figure 5.6) (Hall *et al.* 1968).

The seats are placed at "personal" distance while groups are placed at "social" distance. The total number of seat groups is equal

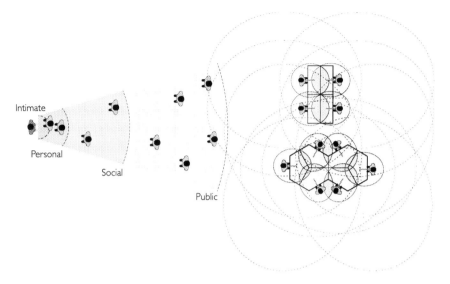

Figure 5.6: Hall's proxemic distance (left) and its application in a given office configuration (right) (*Source*: Hall et al. 1968)

to the number of teams in the population. The organisation and its employees are modelled as agents are distributed into teams of 10. This was the most common team size found in our survey. To avoid complexities arising from varying team sizes, we decided on a common size for all teams. Different population sizes, representing organisation sizes, were modelled by varying the number of teams into 5, 10, 20, or 50.

For any day, agents are assigned to either home or office. For those in the office, a seating group is allocated, based on the scenario parameters. The proximity of the agents inside the office space each day is measured and categorised using Hall's proxemics. Agents record a connection with each of the agents within their "social" proxemic. This is repeated for the duration of the simulation, which is set in number of weeks, where each week is considered 5 working days (Figure 5.7).

142   The City Rebooted: Networks, Connectivity and Place Identities in Singapore

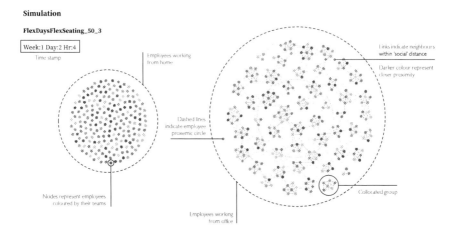

Figure 5.7: Day 2 snapshot of the simulation environment under flexible seating and schedule with 50 teams. The left-hand side shows all isolated WFH people on a given day, and the right-hand side is all those in office with different levels of connectivity (*Source*: Authors 2023)

Scenarios and simulation parameters

For our study, we were most interested in understanding the general comparative relationships between the different hybrid working parameters and social connections. So rather than modelling discrete hybrid working configurations, we designed four key office models based on a combination of either Fixed or Flexible seating with Fixed or Flexible schedule (Figure 5.2) and generated different scenarios for each using a range of 1–5 for the number of days workers are required in the office. The four key office models are:

1. Fixed Seating and Fixed Schedule
2. Fixed Seating and Flexible Schedule
3. Flexible Seating and Fixed Schedule
4. Flexible Seating and Flexible Schedule.

    We make the following assumptions:

1. Fixed schedule: same days at office each week, synchronised with the team

Future of Work is Hybrid, but How? 143

2. Fixed seating: seating assigned and fixed based on team co-location
3. Flexible schedule: days at the office randomly assigned for each person
4. Flexible seating: individual seats assigned randomly each day.

Whilst this is simplistic it enables us to most clearly infer the social impact of the effect of enforced co-location and scheduling. For each model, different scenarios were generated for number of days at office (1, 2, 3, 4, or 5) and organisation size represented by number of teams (5, 10, 20, 50), resulting in a total of 80 (4 × 4 × 5) individual scenarios (Figure 5.8). This represents high-level factors that an office manager or company in general could decide on. Each scenario is simulated for a duration of 4 weeks, with each week consisting of 5 working days starting from an initial state of no connections (Figure 5.9). Whilst it is artificial to believe that people would not know each other especially in

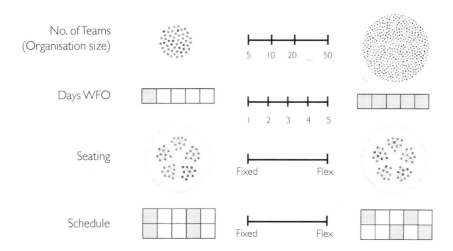

Figure 5.8: Visual representation of the independent model parameters. (Left) The combinations which define the scenarios, (right) the sub-plot visual format for the complex situations. The order of the sub-plots follows Figure 5.2, with the number of days in the office on the *x* axis. In this example, the constant seating is shown in the *y* axis. The darker colour lines demonstrate larger team sizes. This plot organisation will be used for subsequent dependent social network variables on the *y* axis (*Source*: Authors 2023)

144 The City Rebooted: Networks, Connectivity and Place Identities in Singapore

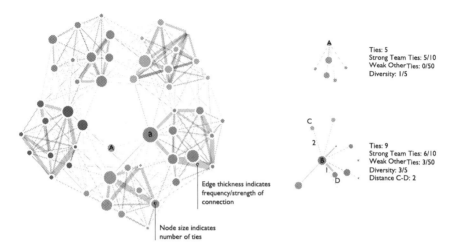

Figure 5.9: Snapshots of the spatial simulation and resulting network model of 5 teams of companies in different scenarios. The dots represent individuals coloured by team with lines showing social connection. Each scenario is shown on a different row, with the starting situation on the left, and the end result after a few iterations on the right. Both the spatial and social network model are shown for both the start and end. The social network is displayed using a force density approach where social strength between people pulls them together (*Source*: Authors 2023)

a pre-existing company, this measurement from zero also enables us to measure the upkeep of existent relationships.

ANALYSIS AND METRICS

Based on the previously mentioned studies and network metrics, we identified the following as useful/important metrics for our analysis (Figure 5.10). It's important to note that these can be computed for each individual, but we will be showing the average and range of these values over the whole network.

1. Strong ties: The number of direct connections of an employee as a percentage of overall connections. This is equal to the degree centrality of the node in the network. We also differentiate between strong team ties and strong other ties to indicate the quantity of connections within and outside the team.

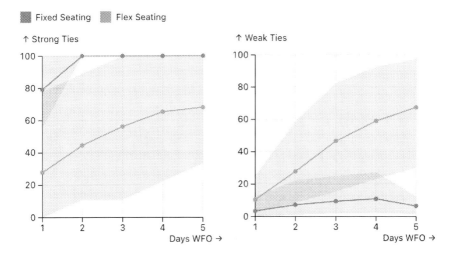

Figure 5.10: An example of individual social metrics as calculated in a team-based network. (Left) for two people 'A' and 'B', (right) for their own networks and numbers (*Source*: Authors 2023)

2. Frequency: The number of days connected as a percentage of total days. This indicates how often people connect and is used as the edge weight/strength indicator of the network.
3. Diversity: The number of different teams connected to a person as a percentage of total groups. This indicates how many different groups a person interacts with.
4. Distance: The degrees of separation between people in the network. This is equal to the shortest path lengths of the network and indicates how connected the network is.
5. Clustering: The degree of connectivity among a person's strong ties. This is equal to the clustering coefficient of the network.

RESULTS

The results below explore the influence of the given dependent variables shown in Figure 5.8 on the above metrics. The intent is to examine how various office configurations and organisations might affect the social interactions.

Strong ties

Strong ties indicate the total number of direct connections or close working colleagues the average worker might have. Seating impacts the number of strong or direct ties more than any other parameter. With fixed seating, employees can connect with all their team members with only two or more days in the office, regardless of team size or schedule. This, however, is significantly harder with flexible seating arrangements (such as hot desking), especially in larger companies. Although it can be improved by fixing the schedules to specific days, this limits ties to only those with same schedule. Nevertheless, flexible seating appears to work most effectively to grow the number of ties with other teams and is not much affected by schedule flexibility likely owing to the inherently more haphazard nature of connecting beyond the regular team (Figure 5.11). For the days of the week, building strong ties in teams is quite optimal, with 3 days or more time in the office having less improved (asymptotic) impact as the time increases to 4 or 5 days. However, for between-team links, the influence of time in the office on links is quite linear, meaning that those who spend twice as much time will likely gain twice as many connections. Furthermore, this keeps increasing even up to 5 days. However, this is only true for flexible seating.

Frequency of connections

Predictably, fixed seating is the most important for more frequent connections, for ties not just within but also across teams. It further improves with fixed schedules as the same people can connect with each other more frequently and is unaffected by the size of organisation. However, company-wide flexible seating affects larger organisations more as the chances of the same people being neighbours decreases significantly (Figure 5.12). The frequency of interactions is affected much more significantly by a low number of office visits and hot desk practices than the number of people connected with, meaning that for building deep connections, and not just wide connections, having people co-located is key. So, the traditional

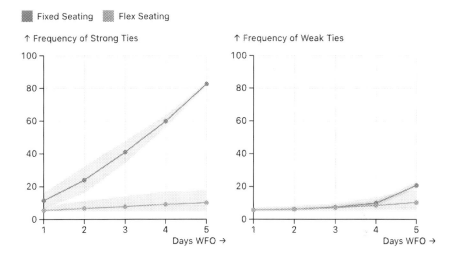

Figure 5.11: Strong ties ratio within teams (left), and among teams (right). The sub plots are organised by schedule flexibility and seating allocation in the columns and rows respectively. With the individual plots, the *x* axis is number of days in the office and the *y* axis is the number of connections as a percentage of the total, with 100 being fully connected and 0 being no connections at all. The top left of the figure shows that fixed seating results in full team connectivity (100%) with 2 days in the office. The coloured line is the average, and the area is the variation within a company. The coloured lines are darker for larger number of teams (*Source*: Authors 2023)

approach of co-locating teams near each other is very valid for close collaboration. Furthermore, for inter-team collaboration, we see exponential improvement in the frequency with increased office time, meaning that having 5 days a week pays off much more than 2 or 3 days for between-team interactions.

Diversity ratio

Diversity measures how many different teams an individual interacts with. Flexible seating impacts the diversity ratio the most, with flexible seating and schedules being the best. For both, individuals can interact with at least one person from every group with about three days at

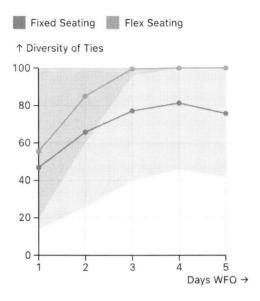

Figure 5.12: Mean ties (frequency) within teams (left) and among teams (right) (*Source*: Authors 2023)

office, regardless of team size. With fixed seating, this is not possible for larger organisations (Figure 5.13), and interestingly, whilst more time increases interaction and thus diversity generally, if 5 days a week is spent in fixed seating, it actually has a negative effect, whereas by enforcing random hot desking, even 50-team companies can have high team interaction diversity with only 3 days in the office.

Clustering

Fixed schedules with flexible seating are best for connectivity between mutual ties. Fixed schedules ensure that the same people are in the office at the same time, while flexible seating ensures those people mingle with each other over time, which makes possible a high clustering coefficient with increased number of days. With fixed seating, there is a limit to this intermingling, so there is a plateau effect even with flexible schedules, as compared to flexible seating and schedules, which improve over time with a greater number of days at the office (Figure 5.14).

Future of Work is Hybrid, but How? 149

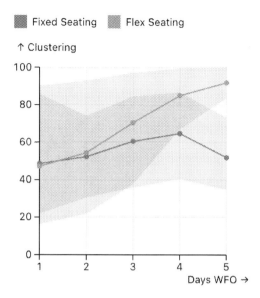

Figure 5.13: Diversity, score (left), and count (right) (*Source:* Authors 2023)

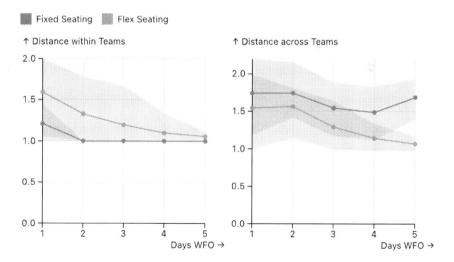

Figure 5.14: Clustering coefficient (*Source:* Authors 2023)

Distance

The distance measures the average number of people in the shortest path between all pairs in the network. A distance of 1 indicates they are

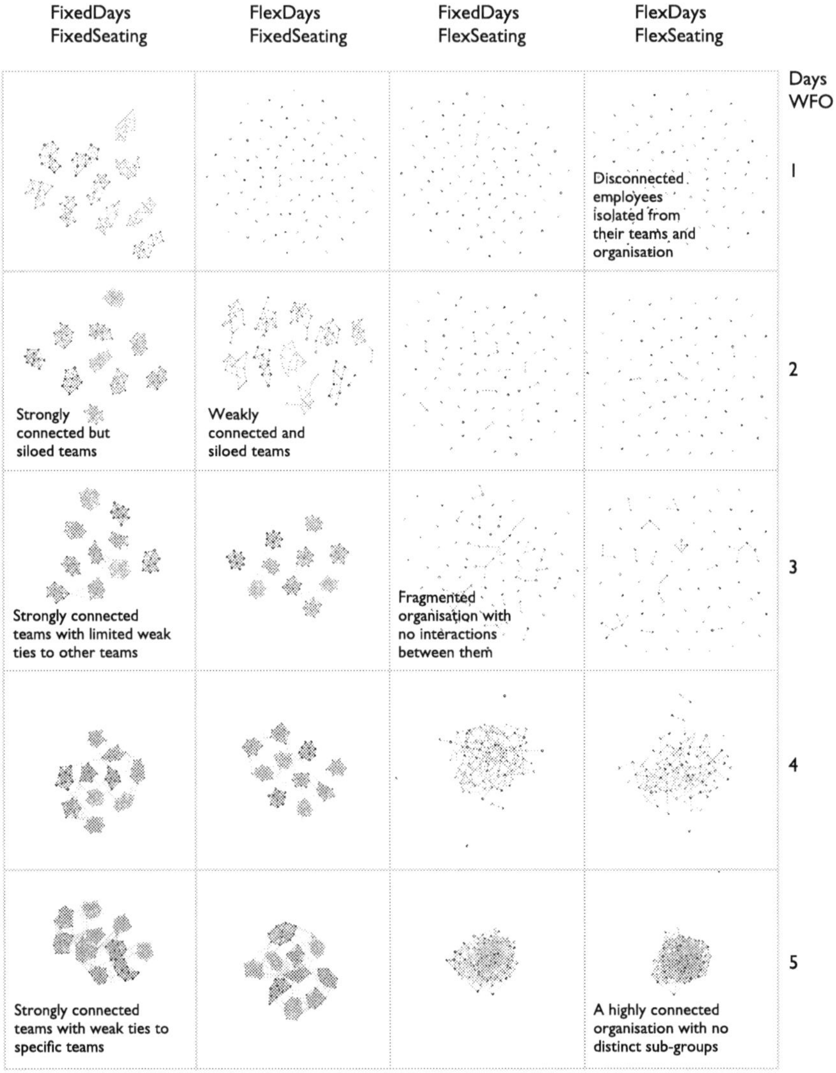

	FixedDays FixedSeating	FlexDays FixedSeating	FixedDays FlexSeating	FlexDays FlexSeating	Days WFO
				Disconnected employees isolated from their teams and organisation	1
	Strongly connected but siloed teams	Weakly connected and siloed teams			2
	Strongly connected teams with limited weak ties to other teams		Fragmented organisation with no interactions between them		3
					4
	Strongly connected teams with weak ties to specific teams			A highly connected organisation with no distinct sub-groups	5

Figure 5.15: Mean distance between people within a team (left) and with others (right) (*Source*: Authors 2023)

directly connected. For people in the same team, this is ideal or even necessary, and can be easily achieved through fixed seating and schedule. However, for overall connectivity and reduced distance across teams, flexible seating and schedules allow for shorter distances (Figure 5.15).

KEY FINDINGS

1. Seating flexibility has the biggest impact on the overall connectivity across teams: the overall number of teams, the cluster coefficient and the distance of connections.
2. Fixed schedules limit this impact as the number and diversity of connections hit a plateau.
3. Fixed seating is best for team connectivity: the number, strength, and distance of team connections as well as overall stronger connections over time.

MAPPING SCENARIOS

Goals and trade-offs

A key takeaway from the analysis is that there is no singular scenario that excels in every metric, and in fact, most scenarios experience a trade-off between "within team" and "across team" metrics. Therefore, determining the right option or combination of options depend on the overall goals and priorities of the organisation and its employees.

At a basic level, the scenario should fit the work style of the organisation. This requires an understanding of the different work activities carried out by its employees and an identification of those that might not be supported when working at home or third spaces. At the same time, the degree of collaboration or individual work requirement might also vary among teams. Depending on how diverse these activities are within the organisation, the range of options needed might also vary.

At an organisational level, there is a need to also consider its overall culture and demographics. For organisations that want to promote a culture of research and innovation, an increased exchange of ideas and collaboration between different teams would be important. However, this might be harder to do in companies that attract a younger talent pool since younger employees are more likely to prefer working fully or mostly remotely (Leesman Index 2022).

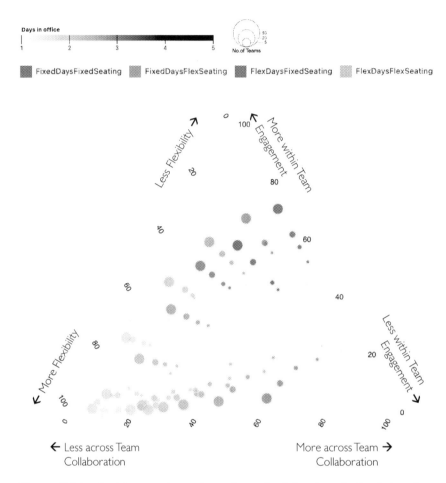

Figure 5.16: Social network result at the end of the 4-week simulation for a 10-team scenario. The columns corresponding to the seating and timetable scenario, and the rows the number of days spent in the office. For highly flexible configurations with low days, we see disconnected people shown as team-coloured dots. Fixed seating always maintains a high team structure whereas flexible seating can result in highly connected networks if sufficient time is spent in the office (*Source*: Authors 2023)

Future of Work is Hybrid, but How? 153

To capture these complexities, we broadly grouped our metrics into the following objectives and evaluate the scenarios as trade-offs between them (Figure 5.17):

1. Flexibility: This represents the level of flexibility available to employees in terms of the number of days at the office, synchronicity of schedules, and seating arrangements. We measure flexibility using a combination of flexibility of seating, schedule, and the number of days in the office. Scenarios with both flexible schedule and seating as well as minimum days at the office will have a higher flexibility score. For the employees, higher

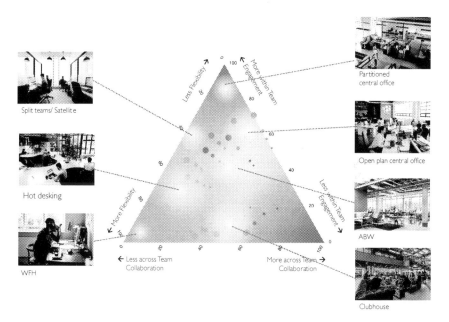

Figure 5.17: Trade-offs compared against competing scales of individuals flexibility, intra-team interactions and between-team interactions. The closer to one corner, the more singular that scenario is, the more in the centre, the more balanced it is. The dot colour indicates the scenario; the dot size is the company size, and the dot colour intensity indicates the number of days in office. Smaller offices (small dots) and more time in the office (brighter dots) generally help between-team (or inter-team) interactions. Fixed seating scenarios (blue and red) drive higher intra-team interactions (*Source*: Authors 2023)

flexibility provides more freedom over how, when, and where they work. This allows them to live further from centralised locations with reduced days of commute as well as provides them with more opportunities for family time and work-life balance. For the organisation, this provides access to a bigger talent pool as more workers seek higher flexibility from their employers.
2. Intra-team engagement: Like the measure of team engagement by Pentland, this represents the level of engagement between team members as well the strength of connection between them. We measure this using the number of ties within team members as well as the mean frequency of connection. As demonstrated by previous studies, physical interaction between team members is a good indicator of team performance and productivity of the organisation.
3. Inter-team collaboration: Like the measure of exploration outside their own teams by Pentland, this represents the encounters between members of different teams. It is measured by the diversity of these connections and their strength, based on the frequency of encounters. Physical interactions with people outside of their own teams have been shown to not only improve the performance of a team, but also enhance the degree of innovation in an organisation.

RECOMMENDATIONS

Overall flexibility results in low connectivity if not tempered with other means of connecting people. Less time in the same place invariably led to a lower chance to connect. Thus, to enable flexibility, offices must try to create opportunities for interaction. Organisations that want to provide flexibility of remote working while maintaining existing assigned seating offices can opt for a 1–2 days per week synchronised schedule for teams. This would ensure that teams can maximise engagement by being in the office for a minimum time. As fixed seating and fixed schedules limit physical interaction across teams, teams that often collaborate with each other can have overlapping schedules so that they have enough physical interactions to maintain their connections. At the same time, the schedules can be shifted routinely to allow different teams to meet over a longer duration, to achieve formation of new ties and improved overall connectivity.

Organisations that require good team engagement but want to minimise cost of space and resources may opt for smaller offices with non-dedicated desks catering to a smaller percentage of the staff each day, followed by synchronised scheduling and co-location of people in the same team so that they are in the office at the same time and in close proximity. Additionally, spaces for discussions and brainstorming can be provided to make up for the lack of shared team spaces. A flexible seating will also allow teams to sit close to different

Figure 5.18: Popular office configurations mapped onto the trade-off diagram (*Source*: Authors 2023)

teams across days, which can facilitate more opportunities for diverse connections.

Organisations that require diversity of connections and more interaction across teams can opt for more flexible seating and schedules. This allows for a consistent intermingling among people in the office. However, to improve interactivity within this environment, repeated encounters are important. This can be facilitated through more common areas, internal and external third spaces, where people are able to interact informally. Within this configuration, team engagement needs to be improved through dedicated meeting spaces and schedules.

CONCLUSIONS

While WFH was successful in terms of productivity and collaboration within teams in the short term, their long-term impact on individual relationships and connectivity across teams have been found to be largely detrimental. Multiple studies have identified these ties to be significantly important to produce successful teams and innovative organisations, with informal physical interactions playing a key role in promoting them. Many discussions around the future of the office and potential alternatives to existing office configurations have lacked a focus on the negative social impacts of those options. Our analysis of different office scenarios, based on various spatial and temporal flexibility using an agent-based simulation, reveals that these choices have varying degrees of impact on intra-team and inter-team connectivitym and in most cases, favour one over the other.

The right choice of office configuration therefore should be a combination of different options to ensure a balance of flexibility, team engagement and collaboration across teams. This can only be realised through a robust understanding of the culture, the working style of the organisation, and profiles of employees. There must be a clear idea of the target culture and interaction, and what should be implemented to achieve this. Furthermore, our work, like those of others, indicate that developing metrics to understand how well such a change is really happening is critical, as changes can have surprising nonlinear consequences.

REFERENCES

Baym, Nancy K., Yan Bing Zhang, and Mei-Chen Lin. 2004. "Social Interactions Across Media: Interpersonal Communication on the Internet, Telephone and Face-to-Face." *New Media & Society* 6 (3): 299–318. https://doi.org/10.1177/1461444804041438.

Burt, Ronald S. 2004. "Structural Holes and Good Ideas." *American Journal of Sociology* 110 (2): 349–399. https://doi.org/10.1086/421787.

Carmody, Daniel, Martina Mazzarello, Paolo Santi, Trevor Harris, Sune Lehmann, Timur Abbiasov, Robin Dunbar, and Carlo Ratti. 2022. "The Effect of Co-Location on Human Communication Networks." *Nature Computational Science* 2 (8): 494–503. https://doi.org/10.1038/s43588-022-00296-z.

Choudhury, Prithwiraj, Kevin Crowston, Linus Dahlander, Marco S. Minervini, and Sumita Raghuram. 2020. "GitLab: Work Where You Want, When You Want." *Journal of Organization Design* 9 (1): 23. https://doi.org/10.1186/s41469-020-00087-8.

Davis, Daniel. n.d. "How to Structure the Workplace after COVID-19." Hassell Studio. Accessed July 2, 2023. https://www.hassellstudio.com/research/how-to-structure-the-workplace-after-covid-19.

El-Sayed, Abdulrahman M, Peter Scarborough, Lars Seemann, and Sandro Galea. 2012. "Social Network Analysis and Agent-Based Modeling in Social Epidemiology." *Epidemiologic Perspectives & Innovations* 9 (1): 1. https://doi.org/10.1186/1742-5573-9-1.

GitLab. n.d. "A Complete Guide to the Benefits of an All-Remote Company." GitLab. Accessed July 2, 2023. https://about.gitlab.com/company/culture/all-remote/benefits/.

Granovetter, Mark S. 1973. "The Strength of Weak Ties." *American Journal of Sociology* 78 (6): 1360–1380.

Hall, Edward T., Ray L. Birdwhistell, Bernhard Bock, Paul Bohannan, Diebold A. Richard, Marshall Durbin, Munro S. Edmonson, *et al.* 1968. "Proxemics [and Comments and Replies]." *Current Anthropology* 9 (2/3): 83–108. https://doi.org/10.1086/200975.

Hobbs, Lee. n.d. "Your Workplace of the Future." Leesman. Accessed July 2, 2023. https://www.leesmanindex.com/your-workplace-of-the-future/.

Kabo, Felichism, Yongha Hwang, Margaret Levenstein, and Jason Owen-Smith. 2015. "Shared Paths to the Lab: A Sociospatial Network Analysis of Collaboration." *Environment and Behavior* 47 (1): 57–84. https://doi.org/10.1177/0013916513493909.

Kaufman, Kenneth R., Eva Petkova, Kamaldeep S. Bhui, and Thomas G. Schulze. 2020. "A Global Needs Assessment in Times of a Global Crisis: World Psychiatry Response to the COVID-19 Pandemic." *BJPsych Open* 6 (3): e48. https://doi.org/10.1192/bjo.2020.25.

Kim, Taemie, Erin McFee, Daniel Olguin Olguin, Ben Waber, and Alex "Sandy" Pentland. 2012. "Sociometric Badges: Using Sensor Technology to Capture New Forms of Collaboration: Sensor Technology and Collaboration in Teams." *Journal of Organizational Behavior* 33 (3): 412–427. https://doi.org/10.1002/job.1776.

Leesman Index. 2022. "Hybrid: Where Are the Risks Hidden in the Hype?" https://accesscre.net/wp-content/uploads/2022/04/Leesman-Hybrid-Risks.pdf.

Lund, Susan, Anu Madgavkar, James Manyika, Sven Smit, Kwelin Ellingrud, and Olivea Robinson. 2021. "The Future of Work after COVID-19." McKinsey & Company. February 18, 2021. https://www.mckinsey.com/featured-insights/future-of-work/the-future-of-work-after-covid-19.

Oldenburg, Ray. 1989. *The Great Good Place: Cafés, Coffee Shops, Community Centers, Beauty Parlors, General Stores, Bars, Hangouts, and How They Get You through the Day.* 1st ed. Paragon House.

Pentland, Alex. 2014. *Social Physics: How Good Ideas Spread-the Lessons from a New Science.* The Penguin Press.

Reagans, Ray, and Bill McEvily. 2003. "Network Structure and Knowledge Transfer: The Effects of Cohesion and Range." *Administrative Science Quarterly* 48 (2): 240–267. https://doi.org/10.2307/3556658.

Sevtsuk, Andres, Bahij Chancey, Rounaq Basu, and Martina Mazzarello. 2022. "Spatial Structure of Workplace and Communication between Colleagues: A Study of E-Mail Exchange and Spatial Relatedness on the MIT Campus." *Social Networks* 70 (July): 295–305. https://doi.org/10.1016/j.socnet.2022.03.001.

Shamil, Md. Salman, Farhanaz Farheen, Nabil Ibtehaz, Irtesam Mahmud Khan, and M. Sohel Rahman. 2021. "An Agent-Based Modeling of COVID-19:

Validation, Analysis, and Recommendations." *Cognitive Computation*, February. https://doi.org/10.1007/s12559-020-09801-w.

Spiliopoulou, Georgia, and Alex Penn. 1999. "Organizations as Multi-Layered Networks." *Proceedings, 2nd International Space Syntax Symposium* 11: 1–24.

Stone, Brad. 2015. "'Becoming Steve Jobs,' by Brent Schlender and Rick Tetzeli." *The New York Times*. March 31, 2015. https://www.nytimes.com/2015/04/05/books/review/becoming-steve-jobs-by-brent-schlender-and-rick-tetzeli.html.

Travers, Jeffrey, and Stanley Milgram. 1969. "An Experimental Study of the Small World Problem." *Sociometry* 32 (4): 425. https://doi.org/10.2307/2786545.

Whyte, William Hollingsworth. 2010. *The Social Life of Small Urban Spaces*. 7. print. New York, NY: Project for Public Spaces.

Work Trend Index Annual Report. 2021. "The Next Great Disruption is Hybrid Work — Are We Ready?" Microsoft Work Lab. March 22, 2021. https://www.microsoft.com/en-us/worklab/work-trend-index/hybrid-work.

Yang, Longqi, David Holtz, Sonia Jaffe, Siddharth Suri, Shilpi Sinha, Jeffrey Weston, Connor Joyce, *et al.* 2021. "The Effects of Remote Work on Collaboration among Information Workers." *Nature Human Behaviour* 6 (1): 43–54. https://doi.org/10.1038/s41562-021-01196-4.

The Future of Polycentres

© 2024 World Scientific Publishing Company
https://doi.org/10.1142/9789811287848_0006

Polycentricity in a City State? Regional Centres as Singapore's Exceptional Socio-Spatial Development Project

Harvey Neo & Li Bayi

INTRODUCTION

The appeal of "polycentricity" is obvious for planners and policymakers. At its simplest, polycentricity refers to the spatial clustering of human activities. The concept, however, has wide applicability in urban and developmental studies and underpins many theories which seek to explain the changing spatial structures of urban systems. These include von Thünen's Ring Theory and Christaller's Central Place Theory (both of which were formulated in the early 1900s), as well as Gottman's Megalopolis concept in the 1960s. Polycentricity manifests in the works of von Thünen, Christaller, and Gottman at an increasingly higher spatial scale, ranging from regional to national to supranational.

Importantly, our understandings of polycentricity shift — in terms of its objective, how it can be achieved and its relative costs/benefits — as its scalar foci changes. Although such variations meant that polycentricity is an inherently complex concept (Kloosterman and Musterd 2001; Meijers 2008), its defining traits can still be surmised as follows (Meijers 2007):

1. Polycentricity is a means to achieve a more balanced spatial pattern of development.
2. Polycentricity ameliorates the problems resulting from an over-centralisation of functions and services in a central location.
3. Polycentricity may emerge organically or deliberately, planned through a reallocation of resources.
4. Related to Point 3, polycentricity can be understood in a socio-spatial sense or a functional-morphological sense. The former refers to different centres which form a network of complementary services and intra-city cooperation, while the latter refers to different centres which perform similar roles with each supporting a given threshold population.
5. Polycentricity aims to produce multiple centres with a similar degree of "importance".
6. Places that exhibit polycentricity are believed to be more competitive.

In practical terms, polycentricity tends to reduce the travel distances of residents taken for work and leisure, as well as their access to essential administrative services. In redistributing people, resources, and housing, polycentricity also pre-empts overcrowding. The importance of such reduction in travel distances and moderation of overcrowding is valorised in the wake of the COVID-19 pandemic, as these positive benefits afforded by polycentricity are likely to slow down the spread of the virus. For this reason, the discussion for polycentricity in Singapore, as encapsulated in the development of "regional centres", has been revigorated — just when it appeared that interest for regional centres had waned previously. At first glance though, even as polycentricity can be operationalised across various spatial scales, it still seems odd for Singapore to be keen to develop polycentricity. This is partly because the extant research on polycentricity by far analysed it at a supranational scale (Derudder *et al.* 2022). One might argue that developing multiple centres in a small city-state like Singapore may result in a duplicity of resources. However, this is less likely to happen if polycentricity is developed in a socio-spatial sense — i.e., polycentres which provide complementary services to other polycentres or the core city. A more robust challenge against polycentricity in Singapore relates to its physical size. Given that travelling between any two points in the city state is rarely onerous, polycentricity in Singapore may not demonstrate key traits such as reduction of travel (especially from home to office and back) and significant cost savings due to agglomerative effects. Yet, one must not forget that the concept is both an analytical frame for research (Taubenböck *et al.* 2017) and a normative development goal (Rauhut 2017). The latter suggests that polycentricity can be the means towards a larger desired urban form. As will be discussed later, of relevance for this chapter is the relationship between polycentricity and place identity (van Houtum and Lagendijk 2001). The concept of regional centres was first proposed in early 1990s, and the recent pandemic has generated fresh debates on how one might live, work, and play in Singapore — it is an opportune time to take stock of Singapore's experimentation with polycentricity. Specifically, this chapter aims to:

1. Evaluate the development of polycentricity in Singapore, focusing on the evolution of the three regional centres of Jurong, Woodlands, and Tampines.
2. Analyse the extent to which Singapore's regional centres exhibit traits of polycentricity, particularly during the pandemic.
3. Discuss how the pandemic has further affirmed the importance of Singapore's regional centre concept and sharpened its vision therein.

The chapter will conclude with some consideration of other positive externalities of polycentricity in a city state.

SINGAPORE'S REGIONAL CENTRE CONCEPT

The idea for regional centres in Singapore was first mooted in 1991, as part of an overall shift in national urban development policy towards decentralisation. Prior to 1991, the strain experienced by Singapore's city core (especially the Central Business District or

CBD) has long been known to planners. Various measures to alleviate congestion in the CBD, such as the Area Licensing Scheme which restricts vehicular movement into the CBD, have been implemented with some success. Decentralisation was touted as a more decisive and impactful solution to counter congestion by not only spreading out services more widely across the country but also to redistribute jobs away from the CBD.

The latter point is an explicit goal in pushing for polycentricity in Singapore. The landmark Urban Redevelopment Authority (URA) 1991 Concept Plan, for instance, was a bold attempt to comprehensively address a litany of issues faced by the working population because of rapid urbanisation. It specifically sought to identify new centres to "achieve a higher degree of employment decentralisation" (Sim *et al.* 2001, 401) to improve individuals' work-home balance.

Regional centres are envisioned to be 15 times the size of a typical town centre in HDB towns and expected to support a threshold population of at least 800,000 people. With these general guidelines, the 1991 Master Plan identified four regional centres, including Tampines Regional Centre (East), Seletar (North-East), Woodlands (North), and Jurong East Regional Centre (West). In part built upon the Concept Plan of 1971, they were also chosen as Singapore's regional centres due to their relative distance from the city centre/core, with Jurong, Woodlands, and Tampines located furthest in the western, northern, and eastern ends of the island respectively. An immediate task to ensure the success of regional centres is the development of new public transport systems that will balance between residential and occupational spaces and facilitate the decrease in overall congestion in the city centre (Sim *et al.* 2001, 401). Evidently, without a comprehensive transport network linking the regional centres to other parts of the country, polycentricity would not be easily achieved. The next section will look at the nexus of polycentricity and connectivity in greater detail.

TRANSPORT NETWORKS, CONNECTIVITY AND TRAVEL PATTERNS IN REGIONAL CENTRES

The reorganising of transport networks and flows of people are symbiotic to polycentricity, where such reorganising is essential to drive polycentricity in the first instance, but as polycentricity takes shape, it further prompts denser transport networks (Louf and Barthelemy 2013). Beyond transport networks per se, since the late 1990s, the Land Transport Authority has also built Integrated Transport Hubs (ITHs) at major housing estates, with Jurong East and Tampines being two of the largest. Integrated Transport Hubs not only offer seamless connectivity for commuters between buses and trains, but also have malls located onsite. Where shopping malls were largely concentrated in the city core as recent as the 1980s, with numerous malls co-located within ITHs, consumers need not travel far to visit a shopping mall. Tampines ITH, for instance, comprises three malls and several office buildings.

In September 2019, the 10th ITH was completed at Yishun. Along with the already established Woodlands ITH, the northern part of Singapore now has two major transport connectors, greatly improving connectivity in a region which was long perceived to be not as accessible compared to other regions. Furthermore, in a study by Chow *et al.* (2018), the Woodlands, Jurong East, and Tampines ITHs have been found to promote and accelerate secondary developments in their respective estates. To further cement the regional centre status of Tampines and Jurong East, the Land Transport Authority (LTA) (2019) announced plans to add another smaller-scale ITH in Tampines North and to expand the present Jurong East ITH. It is apparent that Singapore has pursued a model of transport-oriented polycentricity that works.

As stated earlier, a key objective of polycentricity (and one of the main goals for developing regional centres in Singapore) is to shorten the distances people travel for work or leisure, but a more nuanced assessment of connectivity in regional centres is needed to ensure that the high connectivity of regional centres attracts inflows of commuters without concomitantly enabling outflows of their own residents. In other words, for a highly connected place to also demonstrate high polycentricity, it should fulfil the following conditions: (1) its transport network is well-connected to all parts of the country; (2) there are more commuters who travel to the place than residents who travel out of the place (in other words there must be significant net gain in the flows of commuters into the regional centre); (3) the place draws incoming commuters from all parts of the country while outgoing residents travel to fewer locations in the country.

To allow for more granular insights into such an intricate relationship between urban polycentricity and travel connectivity, we have developed a methodology to ascertain the travel patterns of residents in the regional centres using the Global Positioning System (GPS) data provided by mobile phone users in Singapore. Cell phones regularly communicate with the signal towers of their respective mobile service providers. Such communication, commonly known as "pings", allows one to determine the location of the user to a precision of about 100 metres.

Through CityData.AI., we obtained millions of GPA data points for three months (September 2019, September 2020, and September 2021) for trips originating from the three regional centres. From these raw GPS data points, we aimed to determine which mobile phone (and by extension the individual who owns the phone) is trackable across the three September months from 2019–2021.

First, we filtered qualified tracked devices from the raw GPS data points (Figure 6.1). Then, we applied the DBSCAN (Density-Based Spatial Clustering of Applications with Noise) clustering algorithm on both spatial and temporal attributes (DBSCAN) and removed devices with less information (Figure 6.2.1). In this study, the temporal distance was set longer than normally applied because of the sparse temporal nature of the dataset. But inconsistent temporal order within same spatial cluster will be divided into different visiting frequencies

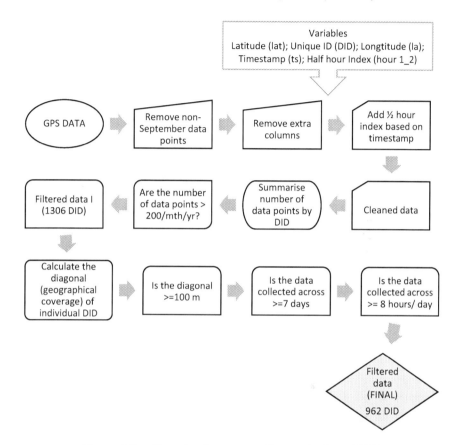

Figure 6.1: Data cleaning process (*Source*: Authors 2023)

(spatiotemporal clusters) to avoid overlarge temporal clusters (Figure 6.2(b)). Eventually, 159,783 visiting frequencies for 24,097 spatiotemporal clusters from 837 tracked devices over three years were identified (Figure 6.2(c)). Simply put, through a process of sorting, matching, and filtering, we managed to identify 837 unique devices which have "travelled" in the three months that we have selected for analysis.

Figure 6.3 summarises key information about these 837 mobile devices. In September 2019, these devices travelled to 8,419 unique places a total of 59,183 times, averaging 7.03 visits per place. The

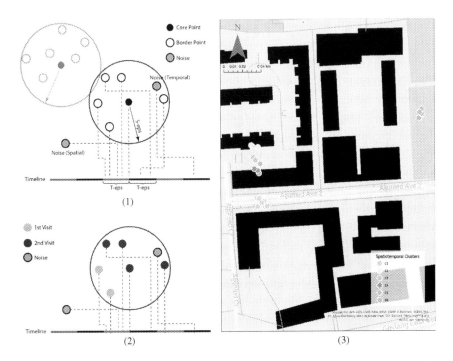

Figure 6.2: ST–DBSCAN algorithm to generate GPS points clusters for each individual device.

(spatial distance = 100 metres, temporal distance = 3,600s, minimum sample size = 2, minimum time range within cluster = 300 seconds)

(1) ST–DBSCAN diagram

(2) frequency division diagram

(3) Clustered example.

(*Source*: Authors 2023).

corresponding figures dropped dramatically in September 2020, a clear outcome of COVID-19 social distancing measures which were in place then. These figures rebounded in September 2021.

Given the data we derived in Table 6.1, we are also then able to determine the kinds of places each device travelled to by layering land use information with the geo-coordinates of places visited. This will

Polycentricity in a City State? 171

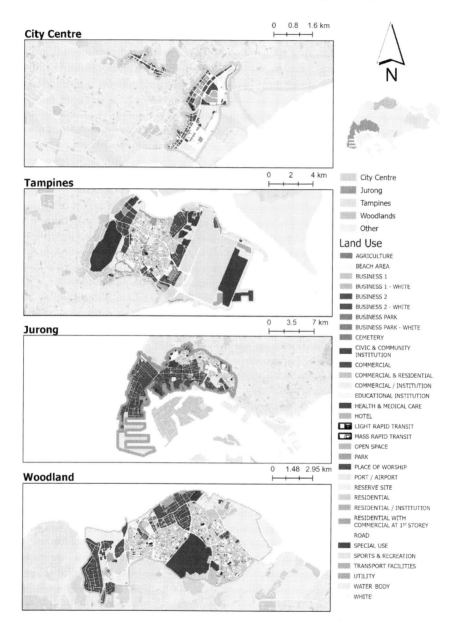

Figure 6.3: land use within centres of Singapore (*Source*: Adapted from URA database 2023)

enable us to have more granular insights of visiting frequencies for different land use (Table 6.2).

Table 6.2 below summarises the changes in frequencies of visits to a list of eight land use type places in 2020 and 2021, using 2019 as the base year. The travel data suggests that, in general, there is higher volatility (larger standard deviation and range) amongst the 837 devices/people sampled in their visits to Business 2, commercial,

Table 6.1: Visiting frequency and clusters (places) over three years

	Visiting frequency	Places	Average visiting frequency/place
2019	59,183	8,419	7.03
2020	39,233	7,010	5.60
2021	61,367	8,668	7.08

Source: Authors 2023

Table 6.2: Descriptive statistics of visiting frequency change for year 2020 and 2021 compared to 2019

Land Use	Mean 2020	Mean 2021	Std 2020	Std 2021	Min 2020	Min 2021	Max 2020	Max 2021
Business 1	−0.43	−0.27	8.77	9.11	−101	−94	75	106
Business 2	−1.36	0.21	16.19	21.43	−230	−234	118	252
Business Park	−0.38	−0.33	4.45	5.30	−66	−69	41	58
Commercial	−1.67	−0.54	16.30	25.03	−149	−232	255	449
Nature	−1.87	11.21	39.63	58.13	−1081	−1071	66	634
Recreation	−0.93	0.58	8.49	12.77	−172	−172	57	163
Services	−1.24	−0.42	13.89	18.42	−226	−380	66	76
Transport Facilities	−0.41	−0.08	6.43	7.91	−69	−113	71	68

B1: Clean and light industries are allowed; B2: General and special industries; Business Park: High-technology, research and development (R&D), and high value-added and knowledge intensive activities.

Source: Authors 2023

nature, and services. Put another way, travels to Business 1 remains constant, comparatively speaking, which indicates that commuters continue to make trips, albeit in lower frequencies, to such places despite restrictions on mobility. This affirms Sam Joyce's point (see Chapters 5 and 6) that work-from-home options must be considered in relation to industry type and nature of work.

In our third and final analysis of connectivity and travel patterns in the regional centres, we wish to determine if there are notable changes and differences in the distance travelled originating from the three regional centres. All things being equal, shorter distances travelled demonstrate a higher polycentric effect as it suggests residents do not need to commute too far beyond their regional centre for their work and leisure.

Our analysis of the sample reveals the following (Figure 6.4):

- Residents in Tampines travel the shortest average distances from their home to their destinations;
- Residents in Woodlands travel, on average, further distances, compared to residents in Jurong and Tampines;
- While residents in Jurong have a comparatively larger proportion of residents travelling the shortest average distances (5 km or less), it also sees the largest number of residents who travel the furthest. For example, only a small number of residents in Tampines travel average distances of more than 20 km and the corresponding figure for Woodlands is negligible. However, the indicative figure for Jurong is higher than both Tampines and Woodlands.
- In 2020, where social distancing measures were the strictest, Tampines recorded the most precipitous drop, suggesting that residents there were able to limit their travel range for their daily lives. This is suggestive of polycentricity at play. The reduction in average travel distances is the smallest in Jurong.

We may draw some general conclusions based on the preceding analysis on connectivity and polycentricity. First, Tampines

174 The City Rebooted: Networks, Connectivity and Place Identities in Singapore

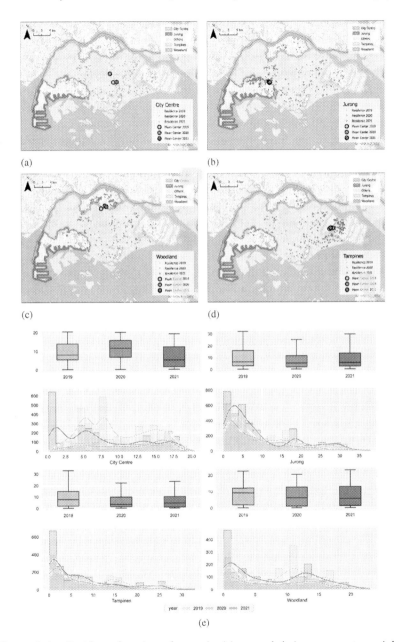

Figure 6.4: Residence location of centre's visitors and their mean centre weighted by visiting frequency
(a) City Centre. (b) Jurong. (c) Tampines. (d) Woodlands. (e) Composite plots of histogram, kernel distribution estimation line, and box plots of activities — residence trip distances to Centres from 2019 to 2021.
(*Source*: Authors 2023)

Polycentricity in a City State? 175

demonstrates the most obvious polycentricity patterns, both in terms of the travel range of their residents, as well as average distances travelled. At the height of the pandemic, residents in Tampines were still able to function well with restricted mobility. Second, Woodlands arguably demonstrate the least polycentricity based on trips made by residents out of Woodlands. These trips were on average longer distances and had significantly more destination points.

The above conclusions are largely corroborated by data provided by the LTA. Figures 6.5 to 6.7 below show the number of trips made from Tampines, Woodlands, Jurong, and the city centre in the April of 2019, 2020, 2021, and 2022. Tampines again demonstrates a degree of polycentricity when we look at trips which originated in Woodlands or Jurong with Tampines as the destination. These trips have remained reasonably constant, notwithstanding the travel restrictions in the years we are surveying. In 2020, Tampines also registered the largest drop in commuter trips (compared to 2019).

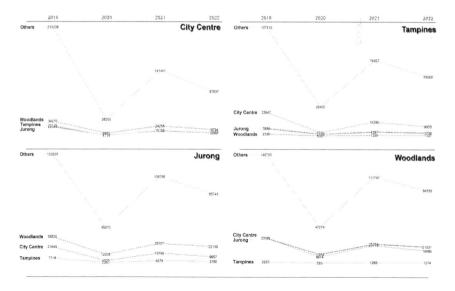

Figure 6.5: Daily average commuting number during weekdays across centres From 2019–2022 (Month: April) (Data *source*: LTA 2023)

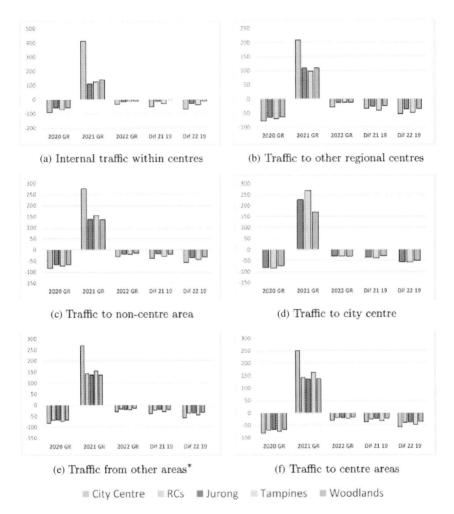

Figure 6.6: Average Trip Count During Weekdays by RTS (MRT+LRT) From April 2019–2022

*Other areas are neither city centres nor regional centres (RCs).
(*Data source*: LTA 2023).

Polycentricity in a City State? 177

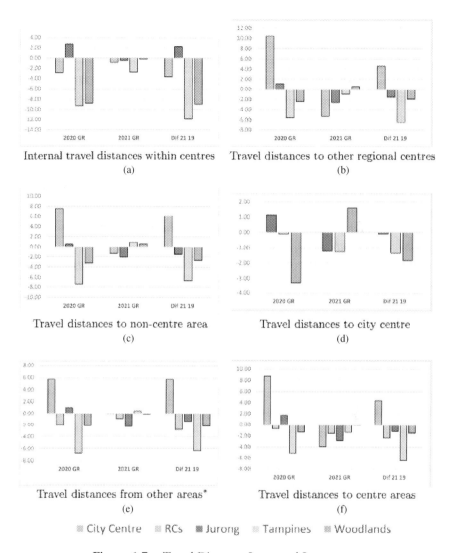

Figure 6.7: Travel Distances Intra- and Inter-towns

*Other areas are neither city centres nor regional centres.
(*Data source*: LTA 2023).

REGIONAL CENTRES BEYOND FUNCTIONALITY: PLACE IDENTITY, SOCIAL CAPITAL, AND ROOTEDNESS

Polycentricity is at the heart of an emergent interest in urban planning, and policies circle on "economies of proximity". This idea has been contextualised differently in key cities across the world. These include some variations of the 15- or 20-minute city (e.g., Melbourne's 20-minute city ascribed in its "Plan Melbourne 2017–2050" development blueprint, Ottawa's 15-minute neighbourhood as detailed in its "Draft New Official Plan" and Seoul's "100 walkable, small but strong Seouls in One Seoul") or urban densification (e.g., Hong Kong's vertical city concept).

Singapore also has various "time-referenced" strategies aligned with the concept of "economies of proximity". These include the Land Transport Authority's Master Plan 2040, which set the goal of all journeys to the nearest neighbourhood centre by "walk-cycle-ride" modes to be less than 20 minutes. For journeys from home to work, the Master Plan set a goal of 90% of such journeys to be less than 45 minutes during peak periods.

In the aftermath of the pandemic, although a hybrid working arrangement is rapidly being normalised (see Chapters 4 and 5), the key functional goal of polycentricity to bring workplaces closer to homes remains relevant, given that few workers are likely to work from home permanently. However, whether this goal continues to be compelling is subject to further study. For one, facilitating proximity between where people work and where they live has always been challenging, a task mired in complexities and uncertainties. Erstwhile, such facilitation has been affected by the creation of urban hubs which agglomerate aligned sectors of work in the hope that people who work in that sector will be drawn to live near such hubs. Moving forward, if the hybrid work model becomes the new normal, most workers will reduce the number of trips from home to work they have to make each week. To what extent will this new reality make people more willing to stay further away from their workplace? The rise of the gig economy and the tendency for younger workers to remain in any given company for a shorter length of time than older generations are additional reasons for one to rethink the link between the locations of one's work and one's home. At the very least, it will decouple the erstwhile tight conceptual link between polycentricity and commuters' work travel patterns (see Sim *et al.* 2001; Limtanakool, Schwanen, and Dijst. 2009; Lemoy, Raux, and Jensen 2017 for examples which take work travel patterns as a defining feature of polycentricity).

Setting aside this question for now, polycentricity is more than a functional urban planning strategy aimed at pre-empting or relieving congestion in urban centres. Polycentricity, as mentioned earlier, can also be understood as a normative urban goal which, for instance, aims to enable a strong place identity and accrue social capital. These positive outcomes would in turn strengthen the polycentre in question. In various parts of this volume, the importance of social capital in making cities of the future has been noted, as is the challenge of accumulating this very social capital. In what follows, the relationship between polycentricity and social capital (as well as sense of place) will be discussed. In so doing, we show why polycentricity as an urban developmental goal remains imperative.

Singapore's decades-long "experimentation" with regional centres mirrors social capital accumulation, which similarly requires time to develop. More than that, social capital has a spatial dimension (Westlund, Rutten, and Boekema 2010), and some have argued that social capital is a "spatially sticky" concept (Galaso 2018). In our discussions of the future of the office (see Chapters 4 and 5) and the magic of the city (see Chapter 10), it is apparent that even in the internet era, human beings are connected to specific places: the places where they live, work, have their family and friends, the place they call home, neighbourhoods, towns, cities, or countries. Rutten, Westlund, and Boekema (2010, 868) argue that if human beings are spatially sticky, so too are their social networks and the norms and values that are carried and developed within them. Social networks and their resulting social capital should hence not be seen as nonspatial nor assumed to have no geographical anchors (Jones *et al.* 2009, 494). This body of work provokes mainstream understandings of the

180   *The City Rebooted: Networks, Connectivity and Place Identities in Singapore*

relationship between spatiality and sociality by way of a twin critique. It argues concomitantly that proximities do not necessarily lead to social network formation (Rutten 2017) and that social networks cannot be sustained indefinitely without being anchored in space and place. For these reasons, reaping any potential benefits of the "economies of proximity" remains challenging.

For regional centres to work, merely attending to the functional needs (e.g., work, recreation, or retail) of residents might not deter them from travelling afar to meet their daily living needs. Regional centres have to exhibit a sense of place and identity that will resonate with residents such that they are rooted in place. The importance of cultivating a sense of place for residents to feed into a larger national identity formation has long been recognised in Singapore (Teo and Huang 1996; Chang and Huang 2005). At more intimate scales of interactions amongst neighbours, frequency and depth of interactions will generate social capital which feeds into the sense of belonging, character, and quality of the places they live.

The importance of cultivating a sense of "regional identity" is similarly acknowledged in Singapore where there have been efforts at placemaking which are aimed at moulding a distinct character of different regions in Singapore. The URA website prominently displays such ostensible marketing slogans (Figure 6.8, below).

While some might view these taglines as lacking in imagination, the recent launch announcement by URA of a 6.5-hectare site in Jurong East suggests that the planners are sincere in making the west

Region	Slogan/Tagline
Central	Vibrant city living, rich with heritage, close to nature
East	Our Eastern Gateway & Seaside Destination
Northeast	Heartland Living, Where the Familiar Meets the Future
North	A region with ample greenery and abundant opportunities
West	Transforming Live, Work and Play in the West

Figure 6.8:   URA marketing slogans (*Source*: URA 2023)

a place that can "transform live, work and play in the west". This is evinced by URA's decision to call for a master developer for the entire site — the second development site in Singapore to be helmed by a master developer (the first being the Marina Bay Financial Centre). Master developers are individual private developers given full rein to create a master plan, planning and design for a district, albeit subject to broad parameters set by the URA. Amongst other things, this will facilitate a robust and resonating place identity of the new site.

At the final instance, the symbiotic relationship between place identity, social capital, and polycentricity is an intricate one. As Mohan and Mohan (2002, 191–193) write:

"If social capital is created through interactions between individuals, it would seem reasonable to argue that the quality of relationships between individuals is shaped by, and itself shapes the character of, the contexts in which they live... understanding social capital is important not only because it is so pervasive and, therefore, ideologically problematic, but also because it seeks to explain different spatial patterns."

Westlund, Rutten, and Boekema (2010, 967) are even more explicit in linking social capital to where people live and play by essentially positing social capital as the proverbial glue that will hold people in place:

"Human beings may have different social networks with different kinds of social capital in the place where they live and work than in places further away. For example, local community networks are more likely to connect people from different backgrounds than professional associations that are organised on a national or continental basis."

Surmising from the preceding, all things being equal, places with high social capital are more amenable to polycentricity. Conversely, places which already exhibit polycentricity are likely to further accumulate greater social capital.

CONCLUSION

The over-congestion of the city centre so feared by policymakers and planners in the 1970s did not come to pass, having been pre-emptively solved by a broad decentralisation policy (of which the development of regional centres is a key plank). Ironically, this fear has been superseded by the worry that the city core is being hollowed out (see Chapter 2). Coupled this with the still unfolding nature of work which may upend past assumptions on how people's decision of where to live is influenced by where they work (and vice versa), does it signal an end to the polycentricity project?

Far from it. Given the positive relationship between polycentricity and social capital, as well as the importance of social capital as a key antidote against the fragmentation of future society, the polycentricity project must continue, albeit with a more explicit focus on placemaking that is authentic and that will resonate amongst residents. Chapter 10, which looks at how to reclaim the magic of the city, is instructive in this regard, but in brief, involving meaningful participation of residents in the process and imbuing them with a purpose and responsibility are some of the ways to form authentic place identities and build lasting ties (see Tan and Neo 2009; Neo and Chua 2017 for examples of green spaces and sociality in Singapore).

It is perhaps unsurprising that in the final instance, the making of regional centres in Singapore is not much different from other socio-urban developmental projects (e.g., agglomerative hubs or Tourism Singapore) in that the requisite "hardware" has been forged better and faster than the more amorphous (but no less essential) "heartware".

REFERENCES

Chang, T.C., and Shirlena Huang. 2005. "Recreating Place, Replacing Memory: Creative Destruction at the Singapore River." *Asia Pacific Viewpoint* 46 (3): 267–280. https://doi.org/10.1111/j.1467-8373.2005.00285.x.

Chow, Clarice, Jean Chia, and Mina Zhan. 2018. *Integrating Land Use & Mobility: Supporting Sustainable Growth (First edition)*. Singapore: Centre for Liveable Cities, Singapore.

Derudder, Ben, Evert Meijers, John Harrison, Michael Hoyler, and Xingjian Liu. 2022. "Polycentric Urban Regions: Conceptualization, Identification and Implications." *Regional Studies* 56 (1): 1–6. https://doi.org/10.1080/00343404.2021.1982134.

Galaso, Pablo. 2018. "Network Topologies as Collective Social Capital in Cities and Regions: A Critical Review of Empirical Studies." *European Planning Studies* 26 (3): 571–590. https://doi.org/10.1080/09654313.2017.1406898.

Jones, Nikoleta, Costas M. Sophoulis, Theodoros Iosifides, Iosif Botetzagias, and Konstantinos Evangelinos. 2009. "The Influence of Social Capital on Environmental Policy Instruments." *Environmental Politics* 18 (4): 595–611. https://doi.org/10.1080/09644010903007443.

Kloosterman, Robert C., and Sako Musterd. 2001. "The Polycentric Urban Region: Towards a Research Agenda." *Urban Studies* 38 (4): 623–633. https://doi.org/10.1080/00420980120035259.

Land Transport Authority. 2019. "Land Transport Master Plan 2040." Land Transport Authority. https://www.lta.gov.sg/content/dam/ltagov/who_we_are/our_work/land_transport_master_plan_2040/pdf/LTA%20LTMP%202040%20eReport.pdf.

Lemoy, Rémi, Charles Raux, and Pablo Jensen. 2017. "Exploring the Polycentric City with Multi-Worker Households: An Agent-Based Microeconomic Model." *Computers, Environment and Urban Systems* 62 (March): 64–73. https://doi.org/10.1016/j.compenvurbsys.2016.10.008.

Limtanakool, Narisra, Tim Schwanen, and Martin Dijst. 2009. "Developments in the Dutch Urban System on the Basis of Flows." *Regional Studies* 43 (2): 179–196. https://doi.org/10.1080/00343400701808832.

Louf, Rémi, and Marc Barthelemy. 2013. "Modeling the Polycentric Transition of Cities." *Physical Review Letters* 111 (19): 198702. https://doi.org/10.1103/PhysRevLett.111.198702.

Meijers, Evert. 2007. "From Central Place to Network Model: Theory and Evidence of a Paradigm Change." *Tijdschrift Voor Economische En Sociale Geografie* 98 (2): 245–259. https://doi.org/10.1111/j.1467-9663.2007.00394.x.

Meijers, Evert. 2008. "Measuring Polycentricity and Its Promises." *European Planning Studies* 16 (9): 1313–1323. https://doi.org/10.1080/09654310802401805.

Mohan, Giles, and John Mohan. 2002. "Placing Social Capital." *Progress in Human Geography* 26 (2): 191–210. https://doi.org/10.1191/0309132502ph364ra.

Neo, Harvey, and Chengying Chua. 2017. "Beyond Inclusion and Exclusion: Community Gardens as Spaces of Responsibility." *Annals of the American Association of Geographers* 107 (3): 666–681.

Rauhut, Daniel. 2017. "Polycentricity — One Concept or Many?" *European Planning Studies* 25 (2): 332–348. https://doi.org/10.1080/09654313.2016.1276157.

Rutten, Roel. 2017. "Beyond Proximities: The Socio-Spatial Dynamics of Knowledge Creation." *Progress in Human Geography* 41 (2): 159–177. https://doi.org/10.1177/0309132516629003.

Rutten, Roel, Hans Westlund, and Frans Boekema. 2010. "The Spatial Dimension of Social Capital." *European Planning Studies* 18 (6): 863–871. https://doi.org/10.1080/09654311003701381.

Sim, Loo Lee, Lai Choo Malone-Lee, and Kein Hoong Lawrence Chin. 2001. "Integrating Land Use and Transport Planning to Reduce Work-Related Travel: A Case Study of Tampines Regional Centre in Singapore." *Habitat International* 25 (3): 399–414. https://doi.org/10.1016/S0197-3975(01)00012-1.

Tan, Leon H.H., and Harvey Neo. 2009. "'Community in Bloom': Local Participation of Community Gardens in Urban Singapore." *Local Environment* 14 (6): 529–539. https://doi.org/10.1080/13549830902904060.

Taubenböck, H., I. Standfuß, M. Wurm, A. Krehl, and S. Siedentop. 2017. "Measuring Morphological Polycentricity — A Comparative Analysis of Urban Mass Concentrations Using Remote Sensing Data." *Computers, Environment and Urban Systems* 64 (July): 42–56. https://doi.org/10.1016/j.compenvurbsys.2017.01.005.

Teo, Peggy, and Shirlena Huang. 1996. "A Sense of Place in Public Housing: A Case Study of Pasir Ris, Singapore." *Habitat International* 20 (2): 307–325. https://doi.org/10.1016/0197-3975(95)00065-8.

Van Houtum, Henk, and Arnoud Lagendijk. 2001. "Contextualising Regional Identity and Imagination in the Construction of Polycentric Urban Regions: The Cases of the Ruhr Area and the Basque Country." *Urban Studies* 38 (4): 747–767. https://doi.org/10.1080/00420980120035321.

Westlund, Hans, Roel Rutten, and Frans Boekema. 2010. "Social Capital, Distance, Borders and Levels of Space: Conclusions and Further Issues." *European Planning Studies* 18 (6): 965–970. https://doi.org/10.1080/09654311003701506.

© 2024 World Scientific Publishing Company
https://doi.org/10.1142/9789811287848_0007

The Emerging Socio-Spatial Implications of Cloud Kitchens and Cloud Stores

Samuel Chng

Cloud kitchens and cloud stores have been popping up across Singapore in the last five years as part of the rise of on-demand food and grocery delivery services. Yet, this is taking place beyond the consciousness of many, even though these cloud operations are located near population centres, where their clienteles are. This mirrors the shift in consumer behaviour and the proliferation of cloud kitchens and cloud stores in many North American and European cities, popularised by global technology companies like Uber, Deliveroo, and DoorDash (Singh 2019). In Britain, this trend has also coincided with the gradual demise of brick-and-mortar restaurants and retail stores in their cities and high streets (Suliman 2019). Would this be repeated in Singapore?

First, what are these cloud operations? Cloud kitchens are commercial food production facilities that produce food for delivery-only food services, most often without dine-in or customer-facing areas. The delivery services are fulfilled by food delivery aggregators (e.g., Grab, Deliveroo, and foodpanda in Singapore). Cloud kitchens are also known as "dark kitchens" or "ghost kitchens" in the industry outside Singapore, but because of the potentially negative connotations of poor sanitation, working conditions, and dubious food preparation standards, the term "cloud" is generally more accepted because of its neutrality in Singapore. Because of its potential to disrupt the food and beverage industry, significant investment and funding are being made into establishing and growing cloud kitchens globally. In the United States (US), CloudKitchens was established by Uber's former CEO, Travis Kalanick, and Google Ventures has backed Kitchen United. In Asia, Swiggy and Zomato have aggressively established cloud kitchens in India. The two leading regional delivery platform companies in Southeast Asia, Grab and Gojek, have been expanding their cloud kitchens, GrabKitchen and Go Food, in the Southeast Asian region since 2019. The global cloud kitchen industry was valued at US$56.71 billion in 2021 and is expected to grow more than 12% annually and be worth about US$112.53 billion by 2027 (Statista Research Department 2022). The driving force of this growth is the Asia-Pacific region, which accounts for 60% of the market with its 4.3 billion population (Acumen Research and Consulting 2022).

The pandemic has fast-tracked the ascendancy of cloud kitchens and cloud stores in our city's everyday life and landscape. Nevertheless, the long-term implications are far from clear. Hence, the twofold goals of this chapter are to: (1) examine how cloud kitchens and cloud stores figure as the frontier in spatial materialities of platform urbanism, and (2) anticipate the socio-spatial impact of "going to the cloud" on the city. Before discussing these, we elaborate on the rise and recent developments of cloud kitchens and cloud stores in the context of the sharing economy and understand how this is the new logistical-urban frontier, as theorised by Shapiro (2023).

FOOD AND GROCERY DELIVERY: A SLICE OF THE SHARING AND DIGITAL ECONOMY

Getting food delivered to us is not new. However, food delivery services were traditionally provided by fast-food chains (such as McDonald's and Pizza Hut), whose ubiquity in the Food & Beverage (F&B) landscape enabled them to provide direct delivery services to consumers. Today, delivery services are widely available to different eateries in the food and beverage industry, ranging from hawker stalls and coffee shops to restaurants. This is made possible by food aggregators that offer food delivery services to consumers. The food aggregators are intermediaries between the eateries and consumers, and offer eateries an integrated ordering, payment, customer service, delivery, and marketing platform. The speed and ease of doing so and the wide variety of options are game-changing. More recent development has seen the rise in rapid grocery delivery services, where groceries and other products typically purchased in supermarkets and convenience stores are made available on similar aggregator platforms for on-demand deliveries.

Online food delivery services, which were fast-growing before the pandemic, are now commonplace. People have found a new convenience in having their food delivered to them. Those who can afford it do not hesitate to pay an extra fee for their food to be delivered to them, especially when you can get almost anything delivered in Singapore. For some, pandemic-induced restrictions on movements, social distancing, limits on gatherings, and work-from-home arrangements meant that food delivery became a service of necessity, not merely for convenience.

This phenomenon is bolstered by the rise of the sharing economy, which is creating new businesses and services. The main idea behind the sharing economy is optimising (excess) resources (Hamari, Sjöklint, and Ukkonen 2016). This is envisioned to generate economic impact through sharing excess assets instead of leaving them idle, while also generating social and environmental impact through fostering social interactions and more efficient use of resources. An integrated online platform is typically used for coordination. This development started earlier in the mobility (e.g., Uber, Lyft, Grab, and Gojek), hospitality (e.g., Airbnb), and commercial real estate space (e.g., WeWork), and is now in the food industry in the form of online food and grocery delivery.

Online food deliveries are typically done through a food aggregator, which uses a pool of delivery riders or drivers to deliver food from different establishments to customers. The delivery riders or drivers are typically self-employed workers using their personal vehicles (bicycles, personal mobility devices, motorbikes, cars, or vans) to make these deliveries and work on an on-demand basis. What makes it part of the sharing economy is the utilisation of excess resources in the delivery riders and drivers and their vehicles while giving the riders and drivers an additional source of income.

Though online food deliveries have been around for a while in Singapore, the pandemic spurred the adoption of online food and grocery deliveries provided by popular food aggregator platforms such as GrabFood, foodpanda, and Deliveroo. The platforms also provided consumers with options for getting food and groceries delivered to their doorstep, reducing the need to leave the comfort and safety of their homes. More importantly, these aggregator platforms have provided a crucial lifeline for the F&B industry to stay afloat amidst pandemic social distancing and activity curtailment. The economic lure was so promising that the Singapore government embarked on a campaign to help eateries get onboard on these food delivery platforms (National Environment Agency 2021).

The demand for online food and grocery delivery has grown, and customers expect a wider variety of food options in terms of brands and cuisines delivered on demand. To meet this growing demand, cloud kitchens and cloud stores started to sprout across the city. These are operated by third-party operators or by the aggregator platforms themselves. This started before the pandemic but accelerated as the demand for these facilities grew robustly since 2020. The rise of cloud kitchens and cloud stores is a global phenomenon but particularly common in high-density urban areas, such as Singapore (Rout, Dawande, and Janakiraman 2021).

This growth of cloud kitchens and cloud stores aligns with Singapore's vision to be a Smart Nation and has sped up the digitisation and digitalisation of the food and beverage services and retail sectors. Many F&B operators are Small and Medium Enterprises (SMEs) and family businesses and are among the traditionally late adopters of new technology in our push for digitalisation. However, many F&B operators have established an online presence and operations since the pandemic. This has increased the variety of food delivery options and enhanced the attractiveness of on-demand food and grocery delivery services further.

THE PANDEMIC AS A CATALYST

Singapore is a consumerist nation known for its food and shopping (Reddy and van Dam 2020). The population loves to eat, and the COVID-19 pandemic severely curtailed the national hobby of dining out as hawker centres, coffee shops, and restaurants were closed for dining in during the height of the pandemic. Nonessential retail shops were also shuttered during the height of the pandemic. These led to significant changes in food and retail consumption behaviour over a matter of months. The proportion of online transactions for retail sales in Singapore increased significantly in the early days of the pandemic compared to 2019 (Figure 7.1). The increase in online transactions for supermarkets and hypermarkets was more modest, increasing from less than 10% to about 15% (Singapore Department of Statistics 2023b). Nevertheless, this shift to shop online seems to have stabilised throughout 2021 and 2022, suggesting a new normal.

A similar shift towards online food and beverage purchases was observed. The proportion of online food and beverage sales was less than 10% in 2019 but increased almost fivefolds to nearly 50% in the early days of the pandemic in 2020 and mid-2021, when restrictions

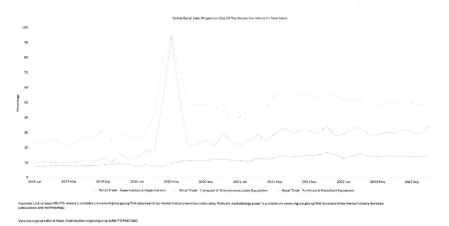

Figure 7.1: Growth of online retail sales in grocery, communication tools and electronics and household equipment in Singapore from 2019 to 2022 (*Source*: Singapore department of statistics 2023b)

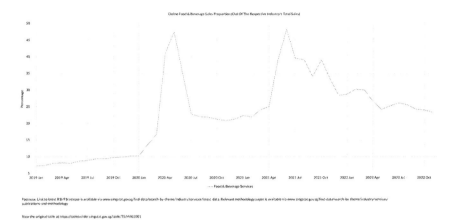

Figure 7.2: Online food and beverage sales proportion in Singapore from 2019 to 2022 (*Source*: Singapore department of statistics 2023a)

on dining in and gatherings were imposed (Figure 7.2). As some restrictions were eased in the later parts of 2021 and 2022, this proportion has decreased to 20–25%. Collectively, these figures suggest that online F&B and retail have gained in popularity following the pandemic but are still not the primary mode of consumption. Brick-and-mortar purchases, especially in F&B and grocery retail, remain the main mode of consumption.

CLOUD KITCHENS IN SINGAPORE

As of March 2022, at least 36 cloud kitchens in Singapore could be identified in an online search. However, the actual number is likely higher as we identified smaller-scale operations that were not incorporated as such. One example was found in a retail unit in a shopping mall in eastern Singapore, where seven brands operated out of the single unit (Figure 7.3).

There are different cloud kitchens in Singapore (Table 7.1). The simplest model is the independent cloud kitchen model, which is operated by one company and sells products from one brand and one kitchen. It also focuses on delivery, with no storefront for dine-in or

Figure 7.3: Cloud kitchen with seven brands occupying a retail unit in east village shopping centre (*Source*: Sara Ann Nicholas 2023)

takeaways. Jo Bakes operates this model, where customers can only order online, and their food will be delivered to them by the company (Jo Bakes n.d.).

Cloud kitchens can also take on a brand-owned model where a company uses a single kitchen to sell multiple brands with multiple cuisines. Customers would also purchase online directly with the company or through aggregators and have their orders delivered by different delivery partners. TiffinLabs uses this model in its operation globally and locally (TiffinLabs n.d.). This helps keep operation costs low through the shared use of one kitchen while still catering to different groups of customers with various cuisines and brands.

Establishments with an existing physical storefront could also open and add a delivery operation on-premises. With a storefront, they could also offer takeaway options for customers. This model gives a physical presence where customers can see the food

Table 7.1: Summary table of typology of cloud kitchens in the Singapore context

Typology of cloud kitchens in the Singapore context

Floor area	Location	Characteristics	Description	Examples in Singapore
Independent cloud kitchen model				
500–600 square feet	Lower-end rent areas on the peripheral of densely populated areas	The oldest and original model	Orders are online with a delivery-only model. Exclusive kitchen space. Highly specialised cuisine. Aggregator dependent.	Jo Bakes; Select Cloud Kitchens
Brand-owned model				
2,000+ square feet	Prime real-estate area that is densely populated	Multi-brand kitchen for multiple cuisines. A single kitchen with many child brands.	Online orders to a single kitchen with multiple brands. Different cuisine variety. Aggregator dependent, but with own platform also.	Rebel Foods; TiffinLabs; The Digital Kitchen
Shopfront franchise model				
1,200–2,000 square feet	High-rent, frequented area	Single brand in a single kitchen, with multiple outlets and a visible storefront.	Has the traits of a typical cloud kitchen with the option of takeaway. Allows physical access to end customers.	Swee Choon; Domino's Pizza; Pizza Hut

The Emerging Socio-Spatial Implications of Cloud Kitchens and Cloud Stores 193

Aggregator-owned (shell type) model				
Multiple kitchens of 100–500 square feet in a larger kitchen	Prime real-estate area that is densely populated	Multi-brand offering owned by an aggregator with rented kitchens. A shell model with only space and basic utilities. Clients bring all equipment, staff, raw materials, and menu etc.	Parent aggregator is the source of orders. Provides space for partner brands in the same kitchen. Higher vertical integration.	GrabKitchen; Deliveroo Editions; Favourites by foodpanda
Aggregator-owned (filled-shell type) model				
Multiple partners, each operating a kitchen space of 250–500 square feet	Prime real-estate area that is densely populated	Rented kitchens, but equipment provided by an aggregator. Technical details may be shared, including recipes. Has a visible storefront.	Fuller than the shell-type model, with more support from an aggregator. Customers can walk into the store for takeaway.	GrabKitchen; Deliveroo Editions; Favourites by foodpanda
Hub-and-spoke model				
NA	Centralised kitchen located in a low-rent area. Pop-up locations near densely populated areas.	A centralised kitchen (the hub) complemented by smaller pop-up locations (the spokes).	A centralised kitchen (the hub) prepares the food in advance. Smaller pop-up locations nearer to the last-mile delivery (the spokes) focuses on the finishing touches.	Not in Singapore

Source: Author 2023

preparation. Domino's Pizza and Pizza Hut have established examples of this model, while Swee Choon, a popular dim sum restaurant, is a recent adopter of this model (Swee Choon n.d.).

The dominant presence of aggregators has also led to the creation of aggregator-operated cloud kitchens. These cloud kitchens are commercial-grade kitchens with smaller units rented to individual eateries and brands. The kitchen units can come fully equipped or bare. In addition, the aggregator operators might collaborate with companies to franchise cloud dining concepts, thus providing potential franchisees with the equipment, technical know-how (e.g., recipes), and support needed to run a cloud kitchen operation. GrabKitchen, Deliveroo Editions, and Favourites by foodpanda are examples of aggregator-operated cloud kitchens, which are integrated with their respective food delivery networks.

A final operating model that has been used in overseas markets (e.g., India) but not yet in Singapore is the hub-and-spoke model. Food is prepared in a central kitchen, which functions as the hub, and delivered to smaller pop-up kitchens, which are the spokes, to be assembled and readied for delivery to the customers. The smaller pop-up kitchens can be located nearer to potential customers to reduce delivery times. Though not found in Singapore yet, it is likely to be a potential operating model as cloud kitchens and online food delivery continue to grow.

Currently, we see two distinct formats of these kitchens emerging in Singapore. The first are kitchens that house multiple brands owned and operated by the same F&B establishment (e.g., TiffinLabs). The second are kitchens that are divided into smaller units or pods rented by multiple brands owned by different F&B establishments (e.g., GrabKitchen, Smart City Kitchens). In addition, the brand owners might also choose to licence an operator to sell food under their brand instead of operating it themselves.

LOCATIONS OF CLOUD KITCHENS

For high-traffic areas like town centres and heartland malls, it is difficult to find new locations to open new food and beverage

The Emerging Socio-Spatial Implications of Cloud Kitchens and Cloud Stores

establishments, and rental rates might be too high for new entrants. Hence, cloud kitchens are usually located within the delivery radius of a high volume of food delivery customers, rather than in high foot traffic areas that are more typical of traditional F&B establishments (Table 7.2).

The cloud kitchen concept would help eateries that do not need to be in high-traffic areas to attract customers. Instead, these eateries can locate themselves in areas with lower rents and higher availabilities as cloud kitchens that focus on food delivery only. This can boost the economy of real estate prices in lower-demand areas. Notably, Grab chose to locate its first cloud kitchen, GrabKitchen, in Lam

Table 7.2: Table of the locations of key cloud kitchens in Singapore

No	Cloud kitchen name	Operator name	No. of kitchens	Locations
	Large-scale cloud kitchens in Singapore			
1	Select Cloud Kitchens	Select Group	9	Choa Chu Kang, Jurong West, Clementi, Braddell, Yio Chu Kang, Yishun, Tampines, Bedok, Toa Payoh
2	TiffinLabs Partner Kitchens	TiffinLabs	7	Hillview, Orchard, Quayside, Telok Ayer, Bedok North, Funan, Serangoon
3	Smart City Kitchens	Smart City Kitchens	8	Tampines, Clementi, Orchard, Sembawang, Telok Ayer, Bishan, Serangoon North, Bedok
4	Deliveroo Editions	Deliveroo	3	Lavender, Katong, One-North
5	Grain	Grain	3	One-North, Joo Seng, Jalan Besar
6	GrabKitchen	Grabfood	2	Hillview, Aljunied
7	Favourites by foodpanda	foodpanda	1	Woodlands
8	Kitch (closed in 2022)	Les Amis Group	1	Serangoon Garden
9	The Digital Kitchen	The Digital Kitchen	2	Bendemeer, Telok Ayer

Source: Author 2023

Soon Industrial Building, a commercial building located on the fringes of the densely populated towns of Bukit Batok, Choa Chu Kang, Hillview Avenue, and Upper Bukit Timah.

Thus, it is typical to find cloud kitchens in industrial and commercial areas on the fringes of densely populated areas rather than in town or city centres. Further, cloud kitchens run by aggregators utilise data collected from customers in their ecosystem to decide where to locate cloud kitchens and the food options to be provided by these kitchens. This is primarily done by analysing the search, travel, and purchase data and the geolocation information tagged to these searches.

THE LURE OF STARTING CLOUD KITCHEN OPERATIONS

Cost is a key driver for the adoption of cloud kitchens. Cloud kitchens offer food and beverage establishments an opportunity to expand their brand to other locations at a lower cost than opening new physical storefronts, which is significantly more costly. Operators in cloud kitchens avoid the expenditure on capital investment, rental, labour, and ongoing licencing and maintenance. Smart City Kitchens, a leading operator of cloud kitchens in Singapore, provided the following comparison between a cloud kitchen operation versus a traditional restaurant (Table 7.3).

Related to cost is the ability and flexibility afforded by cloud kitchens to allow F&B establishments to experiment with their menu and dining concepts quickly and cheaply as their brands only exist digitally. Collectively, cloud kitchens are also attractive to food and beverage entrepreneurs, who can start up new dining concepts with lesser capital and lower risk. In addition, it offers the advantage that successful cloud kitchens are easily scalable to another location or market, together with existing brands or other partners.

The proliferation of cloud kitchens also coincides with Singapore's strategic plan to increase productivity and innovation to grow the food industry. The floor area available for food factories and central kitchens in industrial zones has risen recently. These provide cloud kitchens with affordable spaces on the fringes of the customer base to set up operations.

Table 7.3: Table of comparison between operating a cloud kitchen operation and a traditional kitchen operation

Summary of comparison of cloud kitchen operations and traditional restaurant operations provided by Smart City Kitchens

Comparison	Traditional restaurant kitchen	Cloud kitchen	Advantages of cloud kitchens
Real estate	1,000 square feet	Average 165 square feet	Lower rent for a smaller space that fits the scale of operation that is equipped with commercial-grade kitchen equipment
Employees	Average 10 people	Average 3 people	Smaller team complemented by onsite support staff to ensure smooth operations
Investment	S$200,000	S$30,000	Smaller start-up cost (e.g., no fit-out costs, no front of house staff costs, no cashier, reduced overhead expenses)
Weeks to launch	24 weeks	2–4 weeks	Quick to start up as construction, permits and licences are taken care of
To break even	48 months	6 months	Projection given by Smart City Kitchen based on a 10% profit

Source: Smart City Kitchens 2023

A report by Song and Nguyen (2019) found that JTC Corporation, a statutory board under the Ministry of Trade and Industry, which manages industrial development in Singapore, added 637,115 square feet of food factory space (the equivalent of 1–2% of the food factory stock in 2020) from 2019 to 2022. This is a significant increase from 31,431 square feet the year before. It reported that an additional 3.68 million square feet (the equivalent of 9–10% of the food factory stock in 2020) would be added from 2020. The new food factory spaces are mainly located in the north, east, and west regions. This increase in supply caters to the demand for such spaces and keeps rental prices stable. Nevertheless, rental rates and prices of food factories could vary quite widely depending on location, building design, specifications, and remaining land tenure. The time sensitivity for food catering and delivery services means that locations near the central business district (CBD) area or residential neighbourhoods command higher rents and prices. Transaction data from JTC Corporation reveals that the aggregated rents and prices in major food zones proximal to the city centre (the east, northeast and central regions) are much higher than those in the west and north regions. The monthly rental in established food zones can range around S$1.50–S$2.40 per square feet in the west region (Pandan Loop, Jalan Tepong) and S$1.80–S$2.40 per square feet in the north region (Senoko Avenue, Mandai Link).

CLOUD STORES

Cloud stores work similarly to cloud kitchens but are a relatively new offering in Singapore. They are better known as "dark stores" or "dark grocers" overseas but "cloud stores" is the term chosen here to be consistent with cloud kitchens. Delivery of goods, including groceries, is not new, but a cloud provides the basis for rapid grocery delivery services. This new grocery delivery business model operates from micro-fulfilment centres located in converted retail or commercial properties near customers that are not open to the public and focuses on rapid, on-demand delivery. In addition, traditional grocers supplement the network of cloud stores. Similar to cloud kitchens, delivery here is also carried out by food delivery aggregators (e.g., Grab, Deliveroo, foodpanda). Cloud stores allow customers to use a mobile app to browse, order, and track their grocery orders on-demand, and this service is available across Singapore.

The lure of cloud stores for retailers is the ability to scale their e-commerce capacity quickly and without heavy expenditures. The physical "storefront" is now on the online platform, and the physical retail space is optimised for fulfilling delivery orders. They would have the flexibility of locating operations in more affordable logistic spaces instead of retail spaces as they rely on delivery services instead of foot traffic. Table 7.4 summarises the major cloud stores and their offerings in Singapore.

The Emerging Socio-Spatial Implications of Cloud Kitchens and Cloud Stores

Table 7.4: Summary table of comparison of major cloud stores in Singapore

Summary of the comparison of major cloud stores in Singapore

Cloud store	Operator	Aggregator-operated fulfillment centre	Delivery time	Fees	Packaged food	Fresh produce	Alcohol	Healthcare & personal care products	Gifts (e.g., flowers)	Electronics
AmazonFresh	Amazon	Unknown	Within 2 hours	$5.99 with minimum $60 purchase; free delivery for Prime members	✓	✓	✓	✓		✓
PandaMart	foodpanda	15	On-demand (target of 15 mins)	Free within delivery radius with minimum $15 purchase (otherwise distance-based fee start from around $2); $0.29 platform fee	✓	✓	✓	✓		
GrabMart	GrabMart	4	On-demand (target of 1 hour)	Distance-based fee starting from around $2; minimum $15 purchase; $0.30 platform fee	✓	✓	✓	✓	✓	
Grab-Supermarket	GrabMart in partnership with HAO	NA	Next-day		✓	✓	✓	✓		
Deliveroo Grocery	Deliveroo	NA	On-demand (target of 30 mins)	Distance-based fee starting from around $2; Varying minimum purchase, from $12; $0.30 platform fee	✓	✓	✓	✓		

Source: Author 2023

THE LOGISTICAL-URBAN FRONTIER

The introduction of cloud kitchens and cloud stores in Singapore predate the pandemic but the adaptations in lifestyles as a result of pandemic-related measures was the catalyst for its proliferation seen today. Similar phenomena are reported in other cities globally (Shapiro 2023; Rinaldi, D'Aguilar, and Egan 2022). One reason cloud kitchens and cloud stores were able to take hold in our cities is that they represent a novel convergence in the urbanisation of Amazon-style logistics and the platformisation of urban space, forming what Shapiro (2023) termed the logistical-urban frontier.

ADOPTING AMAZON-STYLE LOGISTICS

Amazon, an online retailer, is the fifth largest company in the world by market capitalisation (Statista Research Department 2023). The company pioneered a "one-click", next-day or same-day delivery service that commodifies fulfilment to gain logistical supremacy in the retail space. Amazon is an example of supply chain capitalism, a political economy in which firms compete based on the distribution of goods and services rather than merely the product themselves (Chua et al. 2018). To achieve this, Amazon experimented with cloud stores, brought their fulfilment centres nearer to consumers, and offered near-on-demand delivery services (Alimahomed-Wilson and Reese 2020). In their warehouse and fulfilment centres, work was optimised through algorithmic task allocations, personalised quotas, and elaborate tracking and surveillance systems to ensure productivity (Altenried 2019; Delfanti 2021). Further, it hires vast fleets of subcontracted delivery workers while building its global transportation and supply chain network (Alimahomed-Wilson and Reese 2020).

All these occur beyond the consciousness of consumers and Hill (2020) argues that this "engineered obscurity" is critical for soothing consumers into "a mode of unconscious consumption that dislocates buying online from the geography of fulfilment" (Hill 2020, 522). This engineered obscurity inherent in Amazon-style logistics and fulfilment is what fuels the growth of cloud kitchens and cloud stores in cities, albeit on a local scale (Alimahomed-Wilson and Reese 2020).

Fulfilment centres (both kitchens and stores) are in the neighbourhoods to reach consumers in minutes.

The Amazon model provides an earlier business and supply chain model for cloud kitchens and cloud stores. Today, more venture capital than ever is being raised to support the expansions of cloud kitchens and cloud stores as these provide good test cases for the idea that any business with the right technology and expertise could compete to become the next Amazon (Shapiro 2023). Nevertheless, there is concern about the long-term future of cloud kitchens and cloud stores and whether they would continue to thrive in the post-pandemic city.

URBANISING LOGISTICAL SPACE

It is likely that cloud kitchens and cloud stores will become permanent fixtures in our city, finding their space in the everyday food and grocery retail scene. In Singapore, cloud kitchens and cloud stores are expanding, albeit at a slower rate than during the height of the pandemic. These are aligned with Singapore's ambition to be a Smart Nation, where more economic activity will be transacted online.

To sustain the growth and operations of cloud kitchens and cloud stores, and online economic activity in general such as e-commerce, the infrastructure and logistical spaces need to support it. And this is, perhaps, where a key attraction for investors lies. Cloud kitchens and cloud stores present investors with the potential to wrest logistical value from under-utilised areas in our city, including areas where businesses have been made redundant by online platforms, such as closures of retail shops, offices and warehouse spaces.

There are two key considerations when identifying a space for cloud kitchens and cloud stores. The first is the location of the space. It has to be near to consumers to facilitate on-demand delivery, often within minutes of the consumer, while being removed distant enough to accommodate high volumes of vehicle traffic by delivery vehicles. The second is the internal configurability of the space. It has to be able to accommodate the configuration of physical layouts for precise and logical workflows to optimise operations while also being easily reconfigurable as business demands evolve with consumer trends. Both considerations for identifying optimal locations follow the pragmatics of scale and efficiency and are different from traditional restaurants and stores. The key differences are summarised in Table 7.5 below.

This makes the fringe locations around neighbourhoods in Singapore, as with most cities, ideal locations. In particular, industrial spaces in neighbourhood fringes meet these considerations very well with their location, relatively lower rents, and ease of configuring the internal space. Hence, for operators of cloud kitchens and cloud stores to succeed, they need to be in the real estate business as much as they are in the food and grocery delivery business. And in Singapore, large aggregator platforms such as Grab, foodpanda, and Deliveroo have opened their own cloud kitchens, leasing out industrial kitchen space to restaurant partners, consulting on branding and digital marketing, and providing exclusive analytics. Grab and foodpanda operate a chain of cloud stores too. Venturing into cloud kitchen and cloud store operations expands the business and ecosystem of on-demand services offered by these aggregator platforms while tapping into the existing delivery rider and driver pools.

SOCIO-SPATIAL IMPLICATIONS FOR THE CITY

The rapid ascension of cloud kitchens and cloud stores in Singapore is facilitated by the promise that they are creating value in the city by rendering the urban built environment platform-ready (Helmond 2015). The spaces occupied by these cloud businesses have been highly configured to the infrastructural demands of achieving the fulfilment of deliveries as a commodity. Hence, these cloud businesses cognise urban space and infrastructure through the discourse of software and platform economies (Shapiro 2023), configuring and reconfiguring their spaces in response to the evolving consumer, as tracked by the data collected by these aggregators and digital platforms. This is a form of pop-up urbanism in the logistical-urban frontier. This fundamental logic of cloud businesses valorises the flexibility in optimising and programming spaces in our cities. This comes with implications.

The Emerging Socio-Spatial Implications of Cloud Kitchens and Cloud Stores

Table 7.5: Summary of key differences in the comparison of the considerations when setting up cloud kitchen and cloud stores

	Comparison of the considerations when setting up cloud kitchen and cloud stores			
	Traditional stores	Cloud store	Traditional restaurants	Cloud kitchen
Location considerations	Consumer accessibility Density of social flows and interactions Spatial differentiation	Last-mile efficiency for delivery	Lower rent for a smaller space that fits the scale of operation that is equipped with commercial-grade kitchen equipment	Last-mile efficiency for delivery
Internal configuration	In-store experience	Fulfilment hubs prioritising efficiency in back-of-house operations	Ambience Service quality Social conductivity	Economies of scale and speed in meal production, assembly, and delivery

Source: Author 2023

The integration of cloud kitchens and cloud stores in Singapore and its neighbourhood fabric signals a new alignment between the platformisation of urban transactions and the urbanisation of supply chain capitalism (Barns 2019). Unbeknown to residents in Singapore, the cyberspace has converged upon their cityscape (Sadowski 2020). This platform urbanisation goes beyond simple digitisation and digitalisation of urban transactions (Richardson 2018). It is accelerating the evolution in getting residents in Singapore to access resources, services, infrastructure, and utilities via technological networks and intermediaries. However, a cloud store is not the same as a physical supermarket or minimart, and a cloud kitchen is not the same as a restaurant or hawker centre. The social and physical interactions that take place in supermarkets, minimarts, restaurants, and hawker centres are no less integral to commodity exchange than the price and quality of goods and services themselves. As retailers, restaurateurs and hawkers move into cloud operations, the sociability and physical interactions are disposed of.

At this time, however, there is no indication suggesting that cloud kitchens and cloud stores have impacted their brick-and-mortar equivalents. The number of licensed food establishments in Singapore has been growing steadily since 2010 (Figure 7.4). The greatest

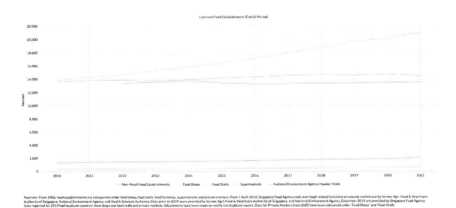

Figure 7.4: Licensed food establishments in Singapore from 2010 to 2021 (*Source*: Singapore Food Agency 2023)

growth is in the number of food shops, which include coffeeshops, restaurants, eateries, food catering businesses, and private markets, growing about 50% from about 14,000 in 2010 to about 21,000 in 2021 (Singapore Food Agency 2023). The number of brick-and-mortar food stalls, hawker stalls, and supermarkets has also grown modestly in the same period. Furthermore, even though the proportion of online transactions for food and beverage services has increased significantly since 2019, each time pandemic-related restrictions were eased in the last three years, we saw a rebound in offline transactions for food and beverage services. This suggests that the social and physical interactions and experiences afforded by in-person consumption when dining out and shopping remain valued.

With the continued rise of the sharing and digital economy, the industry of on-demand cloud services, be it for food, grocery, or other products, is just getting started in Singapore and similar cities. With major global players having announced expansion plans in cloud kitchens and cloud stores, we can expect to see more of them in our city. For instance, foodpanda and Rebel Foods have launched Asia's largest cloud kitchen partnership, targeting 2,000 outlets within Asia in an initial five-year partnership (foodpanda 2021b). In order to support these ambitions, these technology companies will have to expand beyond digital infrastructure into the real estate business as they source, set up, operate, and rent out space in cloud kitchens and cloud stores. In particular, logistical and warehousing spaces and retail and food preparation spaces in the fringes of neighbourhoods would appeal to cloud kitchen and cloud store operations. This will also help wrest logistical value from under-utilised spaces in these locations. To pursue their path to success, they would also harness the use of technology to predict and adapt to evolving consumer demands and to further optimise their operations through automating production and delivery and use their financial strength to market and entice customers to adopt their services. To further reduce costs, companies like foodpanda have started trials with delivery robots and drones in Singapore (foodpanda 2021a; Ng 2022).

In the near future, these cloud services give consumers greater shopping and food variety and options, and the convenience could free up precious time for other activities. This might lead to a more permanent and pervasive reorganisation of how our daily activities are conducted in the city, which may also have downsides to it. Social interaction will be greatly reduced, particularly if these cloud-based delivery services are also fulfilled by robots and drones. Social interaction is critical for our mental well-being (Sun, Harris, and Vazire 2020), and in the context of a rapidly digitalising city, it is then even more important than ever that we preserve and protect the interactions we have in our daily lives. Even the short, opportunistic interactions we have on the way to the supermarket, with the cashier or on the bus are worth saving. Moreover, there are physical and mental health benefits to getting people out of their couches to incorporate small amounts of physical activities and exercises while they are out and about their activities. Grocery runs to the supermarket are still an important activity for the family and, for many, are a destination and activity that engages both the young and old. The experience and quality time afforded by a visit to the brick-and-mortar supermarket is difficult, if at all possible, to replicate in cloud stores. Dining out and doing so with friends and family is also an important aspect of the culture in Singapore. In fact, the tradition of eating out in hawker centres has been recognised by the United Nations for its importance to Singaporean culture (UNESCO n.d.).

On a more macro level, the charm and vibrancy of neighbourhoods that contribute towards the hustle and bustle that define cities might be greatly diminished if much of retail and food moves to cloud operations. That means fewer restaurants, hawkers, and shops, and fewer people and activities on the street. This has been observed in cities in North America and Europe, where shops on high streets and town centres are replaced by cloud kitchens and cloud stores. Leo Cassarani, a councillor in Camden, Britain explained that the hyper-optimised and more lucrative cloud kitchens and stores directly competed with local eateries and shops, by offering consumers the convenience of having food and grocery delivered to their doorstep using an app (Noone 2021). This impacted businesses and the vibrancy of the high street. Further, non-descript cloud kitchens near residential areas in Camden led to disamenities that affect the liveability of neighbourhoods as they can produce large amounts of food odour and local traffic because it acts as a local hub for delivery riders and drivers. While new economic opportunities and lifestyles arise from the appearance of cloud kitchens and cloud stores in this sharing and digital economy, where these operations are located within the city will matter if we seek to preserve the charm and vibrancy characteristic of different neighbourhood centres in Singapore. Certainly, Singaporeans will value having a thriving town centre with interesting eateries and shops where you can go for a meal or shopping.

CONCLUSION

Cloud kitchens and cloud stores are a new phenomenon in the city that is rapidly changing how we consume in the city. They mark the digitalisation and evolution of consumer behaviour in the sharing and digital economy but their implications on our city are yet to fully unfold.

Nevertheless, the "pop-up logistics" of cloud kitchens and cloud stores provide an early glimpse into a future where the logistical-urban frontier is brought much closer to where people live and play. As this concept is finessed, we could expect it to be experimented with beyond the food and beverage, grocery, and retail sectors. While there are more unknowns at this nascent stage, there are early indications that cloud kitchens and cloud stores are not the same as brick-and-mortar restaurants, eateries, and supermarkets. Crucially, because of their unique operational model, one cannot expect them to be concerned with issues such as sense of place and identity formation (see Chapters 6 and 10). On the hope of maintaining a vibrant and thriving neighbourhood and city, we should therefore be mindful of where they site and the role they play within our city.

REFERENCES

Acumen Research and Consulting. 2022. "Cloud Kitchen Market Size — Global Industry, Share, Analysis, Trends, and Forecast 2022–2030."

Acumen Research and Consulting. https://www.acumenresearchandconsulting.com/cloud-kitchen-market.

Alimahomed-Wilson, Jake, and Ellen Reese, eds. 2020. *The Cost of Free Shipping: Amazon in the Global Economy*. Wildcat : Workers' Movements and Global Capitalism. London: Pluto Press.

Altenried, Moritz. 2019. "On the Last Mile: Logistical Urbanism and the Transformation of Labour." *Work Organisation, Labour & Globalisation* 13 (1), 114–129. https://doi.org/10.13169/workorgalaboglob.13.1.0114.

Barns, Sarah. 2019. "Negotiating the Platform Pivot: From Participatory Digital Ecosystems to Infrastructures of Everyday Life." *Geography Compass* 13 (9), e12464. https://doi.org/10.1111/gec3.12464.

Chua, Charmaine, Martin Danyluk, Deborah Cowen, and Laleh Khalili. 2018. "Introduction: Turbulent Circulation: Building a Critical Engagement with Logistics." *Environment and Planning D: Society and Space* 36 (4): 617–629. https://doi.org/10.1177/0263775818783101.

Delfanti, Alessandro. 2021. "Machinic Dispossession and Augmented Despotism: Digital Work in an Amazon Warehouse." *New Media & Society* 23 (1): 39–55. https://doi.org/10.1177/1461444819891613.

foodpanda. 2021a. "Foodpanda Advances Future of Delivery With Autonomous Delivery Partnerships." Foodpanda. June 10, 2021. https://www.foodpanda.com/newsroom/foodpanda-advances-future-of-delivery-with-autonomous-delivery-partnerships/.

foodpanda. 2021b. "Foodpanda and Rebel Foods Launch Asia's Largest Virtual Brands Partnership." foodpanda. October 21, 2021. https://www.foodpanda.com/newsroom/foodpanda-and-rebel-foods-launch-asias-largest-virtual-brands-partnership/.

Hamari, Juho, Mimmi Sjöklint, and Antti Ukkonen. 2016. "The Sharing Economy: Why People Participate in Collaborative Consumption." *Journal of the Association for Information Science and Technology* 67 (9): 2047–2059. https://doi.org/10.1002/asi.23552.

Helmond, Anne. 2015. "The Platformization of the Web: Making Web Data Platform Ready." *Social Media + Society* 1 (2): 205630511560308. https://doi.org/10.1177/2056305115603080.

Hill, David W. 2020. "The Injuries of Platform Logistics." *Media, Culture & Society* 42 (4): 521–536. https://doi.org/10.1177/0163443719861840.

Jo Bakes. n.d. "Jo Bakes." Facebook. Accessed June 30, 2023. https://www.facebook.com/jobakes.sg/.

National Environment Agency. 2021. "Hawkers Get More Help to Go Digital." National Environment Agency. September 23, 2021. https://www.nea.gov.sg/media/news/news/index/hawkers-get-more-help-to-go-digital.

Ng, Keng Gene. 2022. "Drone Whisks Food Orders from Sentosa to St John's Island in Delivery Trial." *The Straits Times*, March 23, 2022. https://www.straitstimes.com/singapore/consumer/drone-whisks-food-orders-from-sentosa-to-st-johns-island-in-delivery-trial.

Noone, Greg. 2021. "The Slow and Silent Rise of Dark Kitchens." Tech Monitor. October 18, 2021. https://techmonitor.ai/leadership/digital-transformation/slow-and-silent-rise-of-dark-kitchens.

Reddy, Geetha, and Rob M. van Dam. 2020. "Food, Culture, and Identity in Multicultural Societies: Insights from Singapore." *Appetite* 149 (June): 104633. https://doi.org/10.1016/j.appet.2020.104633.

Richardson, Lizzie. 2018. "Platforms and the Publicness of Urban Markets." *Mediapolis: A Journal of Cities and Culture*, Roundtables, 3 (4). https://www.mediapolisjournal.com/2018/10/platforms-and-the-publicness-of-urban-markets/.

Rinaldi, Chiara, Marlene D'Aguilar, and Matt Egan. 2022. "Understanding the Online Environment for the Delivery of Food, Alcohol and Tobacco: An Exploratory Analysis of 'Dark Kitchens' and Rapid Grocery Delivery Services." *International Journal of Environmental Research and Public Health* 19 (9): 5523. https://doi.org/10.3390/ijerph19095523.

Rout, Arun, Milind Dawande, and Ganesh Janakiraman. 2021. "Cloud-Kitchens in High-Density Cities: Economies of Scale Through Co-Location." *SSRN Electronic Journal*, August. https://doi.org/10.2139/ssrn.3914446.

Sadowski, Jathan. 2020. "Cyberspace and Cityscapes: On the Emergence of Platform Urbanism." *Urban Geography* 41 (3): 448–452. https://doi.org/10.1080/02723638.2020.1721055.

Shapiro, Aaron. 2023. "Platform Urbanism in a Pandemic: Dark Stores, Ghost Kitchens, and the Logistical-Urban Frontier." *Journal of Consumer Culture* 23 (1): 168–187. https://doi.org/10.1177/14695405211069983.

Singapore Department of Statistics. 2023a. "Online Food & Beverage Sales Proportion." Table. https://tablebuilder.singstat.gov.sg/table/TS/M602001.

Singapore Department of Statistics. 2023b. "Online Retail Sales Proportion (Out of the Respective Industry's Total Sales)." Table. https://tablebuilder.singstat.gov.sg/table/TS/M601861.

Singapore Food Agency. 2023. "Licensed Food Establishments (End of Period)." Department of Statistics Singapore. https://tablebuilder.singstat.gov.sg/table/TS/M890531.

Singh, Sarwant. 2019. "The Soon to Be $200B Online Food Delivery is Rapidly Changing the Global Food Industry." *Forbes.* September 9, 2019. https://www.forbes.com/sites/sarwantsingh/2019/09/09/the-soon-to-be-200b-online-food-delivery-is-rapidly-changing-the-global-food-industry/.

Smart City Kitchens. 2023. "Cloud Kitchens vs Traditional Restaurants — Which Is Better?" Smart City Kitchens. February 22, 2023. https://smartcitykitchens.com/blog/cloud-kitchens-vs-traditional-restaurants/.

Song, Tricia, and Nathan Nguyen. 2019. "Robust Growth of Food Factories." Colliers International. https://www.reitas.sg/wp-content/uploads/2019/07/ColliersFlash-20190529-Food-Factories_RR.pdf.

Statista Research Department. 2022. "Cloud Kitchen Market Size Worldwide 2021." Statista. https://www.statista.com/statistics/1078732/cloud-kitchen-market-size-us/.

Statista Research Department. 2023. "The 100 Largest Companies in the World by Market Capitalization in 2023." https://www.statista.com/statistics/263264/top-companies-in-the-world-by-market-capitalization/.

Suliman, Adela. 2019. "Feature — New on the Menu: Could 'Dark Kitchens' Gobble up Britain's High Street Restaurants?" *Reuters.* October 8, 2019. https://www.reuters.com/article/britain-cities-foodidAFL5N26G43S.

Sun, Jessie, Kelci Harris, and Simine Vazire. 2020. "Is Well-Being Associated With the Quantity and Quality of Social Interactions?" *Journal of Personality and Social Psychology* 119 (6): 1478–1496. https://doi.org/10.1037/pspp0000272.

Swee Choon. n.d. "Swee Choon." Swee Choon. Accessed June 30, 2023. https://www.sweechoon.com/.

TiffinLabs. n.d. "TiffinLabs." TiffinLabs. Accessed June 30, 2023. https://www.tiffinlabs.com.

UNESCO. n.d. "Hawker Culture in Singapore, Community Dining and Culinary Practices in a Multicultural Urban Context." UNESCO. Accessed July 1, 2023. https://ich.unesco.org/en/RL/hawker-culture-in-singapore-community-dining-and-culinary-practices-in-a-multicultural-urban-context-01568.

Sustaining the Magic of the City

© 2024 World Scientific Publishing Company
https://doi.org/10.1142/9789811287848_0008

Through the Looking Glass
Everyday Urbanism in a Pandemic City
2020–2022

Felicity HH Chan, Yunkyung Choi,
Emma En-Ya Goh, Bayi Li[1]

The pandemic, with all its concomitant pandemonium and disruption, also brought with it an uncanny sense of lull and an uneasy silence in the city. The daily rhythms of life were thrown into disarray; the past felt hazily distant and the future felt remotely obscure. We found ourselves in a state of liminality, at the intersection of transient and conflicting events and identities, clumsily navigating the topographies of everyday life.

Fast forward to the present day easing of lockdown restrictions and the gradual reinstatement of normalcy, it feels as though an era has passed and so little of a bygone era remains. Yet, memories of this fever dream of a pandemic have continued to punctuate our consciousness, prompting us to wonder if there perhaps might be some element of permanence to the evanescence of displacement and disruption.

Hence, this chapter presents our attempt to capture a visual assemblage of transitional places, temporalities, objects, and bodies, borne from a city in flux. This is echoed through our title "Through the Looking Glass", a metaphor for any time the world appears

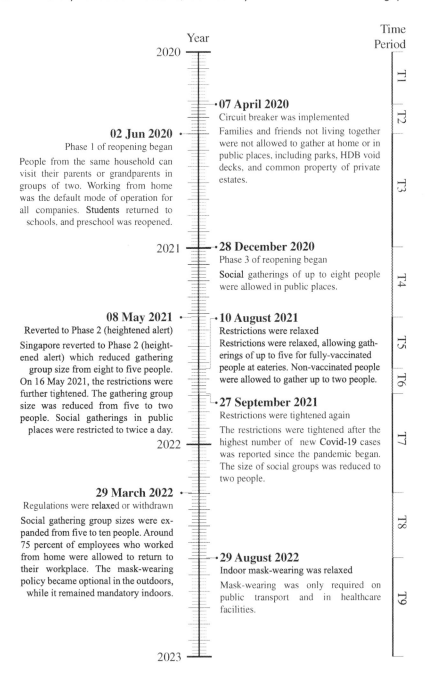

Through the Looking Glass: Everyday Urbanism in a Pandemic City 2020–2022

suddenly unfamiliar, as if turned upside-down. The phrase was coined by Lewis Carroll for the well-loved classic Alice in Wonderland.

Through the lens of everyday urbanism, an approach introduced by Crawford, Chase, and Kaliski,[1] we seek to imbue meaning into the everyday as we elevate unassuming, quotidian sights into still-life pieces. We organised these vignettes of everyday urbanism into different periods of Singapore's COVID-19 restrictions; the restrictions perhaps being the only stalwarts of chronology we could turn to when time seemed to have been suspended. This is represented through the recurring ruler motif that lends some semblance of chronological coherence to the photos presented.

Gathering these fragmented snapshots of everyday life between 2020 and 2022, we sorted them into five themes that composed urban life in Singapore during the pandemic as we saw it. We recognise that this is only one way of lending coherence to life in the city, among many. For this reason, our aim through this photo essay is guided by Mies van der Rohe's famous dictum, "Less is More," giving space to readers to interpret and make sense of their take on everyday life in this period, albeit through our looking glass. A short text introduces each of the five subsequent sections and captions are kept to a minimum. For each piece, we have included the date, location, and time as basic references, in a season of otherwise ambivalence.

CONTROL

With rules and regulations slapped onto almost every sphere of our lives during the pandemic, we could not help but wonder if this marked the dawning of an Orwellian future of personal surveillance. In this section, we depict how our lives had to be recalibrated around measures of control. In doing so, we also ask our readers to consider what forces lie beneath this veneer of law and order.

216 *The City Rebooted: Networks, Connectivity and Place Identities in Singapore*

Figure 8.1: Generation COVID at our socially-distanced university graduation ceremony (*Source*: Jiaxuan Wang, T7: October 2, 2021)

Through the Looking Glass Everyday Urbanism in a Pandemic City 2020–2022 217

Figure 8.2: (Top) An other-than-human's response to social distancing measures (*Source*: Emma Goh, T1: January 1, 2020)

Figure 8.3: (Bottom) Preschools adjusting for COVID (*Source*: Dinithi Jayasekara, T4: March 1, 2021)

218 The City Rebooted: Networks, Connectivity and Place Identities in Singapore

Figure 8.4: (Top) One of the many unsuccessful illogical barricades to redirect habitual foot traffic (*Source*: Felicity HH Chan, T2: August 25, 2020)

Figure 8.5: (Bottom) A COVID Hopscotch? queueing at Burger King along Bukit Timah road (*Source*: Felicity HH Chan, T1: May 14, 2020)

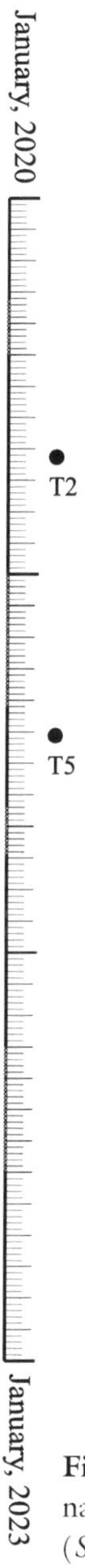

Through the Looking Glass—Everyday Urbanism in a Pandemic City 2020–2022 219

Figure 8.6: (Top) The 30-minutes wait after my first dose of COVID vaccination in a community centre turned into an emergency vaccination hall (*Source*: Felicity HH Chan, T5: June 4, 2021)

Figure 8.7: (Bottom) Domestic travel experience: crossing new border control at Jurong East mall (*Source*: Felicity HH Chan, T2: September 8, 2020)

Figure 8.8: An article in *The Straits Times* on the outbreak of coronavirus in foreign worker dormitories (*Source*: *The Straits Times*, T2: April 14, 2020)

Through the Looking GlassEveryday Urbanism in a Pandemic City 2020–2022   221

JIAK!

A colloquial term, Jiak is a common greeting used before meals to urge each other to tuck in before the food gets cold. In this section, we explore what happens when restrictions encroach upon our dining spaces and how eating — a communal and convivial activity — was re-appropriated during the pandemic.

Figure 8.9: No more loud and convivial Chinese dinners, please! (*Source*: Felicity HH Chan, T2: August 22, 2020)

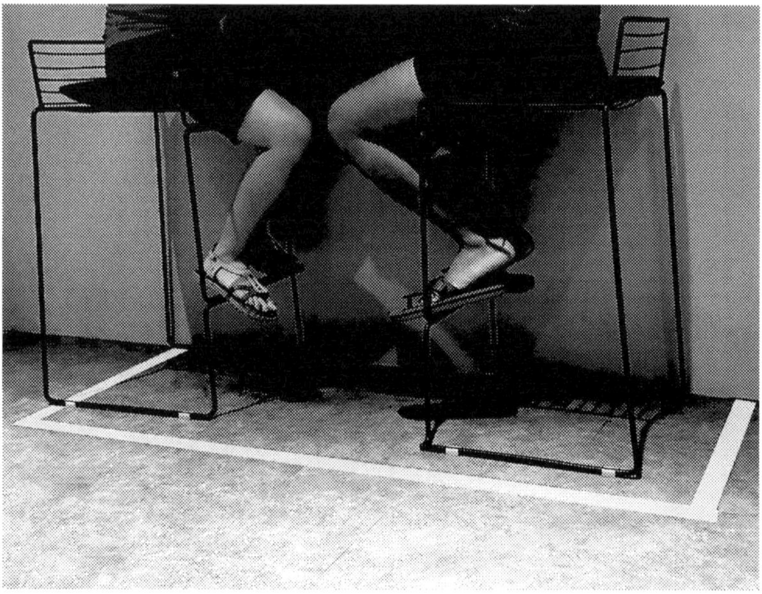

Figure 8.10: (Top) Ice-cream date in a two-by-two box at salted caramel along Lorong Kilat near Beauty World Metro Station (*Source*: Felicity HH Chan, T3: December 2, 2020)

Figure 8.11: (Bottom) All masked up and waiting at the door for customers to return during a peak dinner hour in Kovan neighborhood (*Source*: Felicity HH Chan, T3: March 5, 2021)

Through the Looking Glass—Everyday Urbanism in a Pandemic City 2020–2022 223

Figure 8.12: (Top) The rise of the lockdown Circuit Breaker Bento Sets to minimise food sharing in groups and make the lunch hour while working from home easy (*Source*: Felicity HH Chan, T2: June 13, 2020)

Figure 8.13: (Bottom) No dining in, takeout only at the local Burger King joint (*Source*: Felicity HH Chan, T5: May 19, 2021)

Figure 8.14: Hygiene dividers separate each seat in a school canteen from the front and sides (*Source*: Emma Goh, T4: March 10, 2021)

Through the Looking Glass—Everyday Urbanism in a Pandemic City 2020–2022 225

Figure 8.15: No group seating allowed — lunching alone at a table for six at Bendemeer Market and Food Centre (*Source*: Felicity HH Chan, T5: June 29, 2021)

Figure 8.16: A taste of normalcy — satay at Lau Pa Sat after the easing of restrictions (*Source*: Yunkyung Choi, T8: June 25, 2022)

WORK

Home and hybrid working arrangements became the new normal for many during the pandemic. Yet, this was just a fraction of the story. In this section, we explore work arrangements during the pandemic across a spectrum of class and race.

Figure 8.17: "How home-based learning shows up inequality in Singapore — a look at three homes" (*Source: The Straits Times*, T2: April 18, 2020)

Through the Looking GlassEveryday Urbanism in a Pandemic City 2020–2022 227

Figure 8.18: An empty Central Business District during COVID-19 (*Source*: Brigid Trenerry, T2: April 10, 2020)

228   The City Rebooted: Networks, Connectivity and Place Identities in Singapore

Figure 8.19: The impossible juggle: Parenting and working from home during COVID-19 (*Source*: Brigid Trenerry, T5: July 29, 2021)

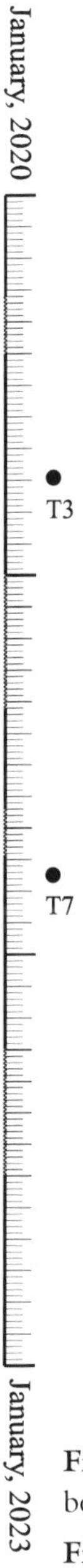

Through the Looking Glass—Everyday Urbanism in a Pandemic City 2020–2022 229

Figure 8.20: (Top) Working from home right after maternity leave without being able to hire a helper (*Source*: Xin Yang, T3: September 29, 2020)

Figure 8.21: (Bottom) Home office for a couple (*Source*: Qian (Cathy) Huang, T7: October 13, 2021)

Figure 8.22: (Top) Working hard to make iconic Fullerton Bay Singapore beautiful (*Source*: Felicity HH Chan, T5: July 14, 2021)

Figure 8.23: (Bottom) Workers waiting to be picked up by the company bus after work in Upper Bukit Timah (*Source*: Felicity HH Chan, T6: September 14, 2021)

Through the Looking GlassEveryday Urbanism in a Pandemic City 2020–2022 231

THE OUTDOORS

Lockdown restrictions undeniably left us with a heightened reliance on urban green spaces. Our engagement with these green spaces provided us with much needed reprieve from the narrow confines of our homes, and was even vital to maintaining sanity for some. In this section, we look at how green oases were re-experienced during the pandemic.

Figure 8.24: Staying Sane: Neighbourhood walks and Community gardening during COVID-19 (*Source*: Brigid Trenerry, T4: December 29, 2020)

Figure 8.25: (Top) Mask-up! then play, a child catching frogs at a farm in Yio Chu Kang (*Source*: Jiaxuan Wang, T6: August 21, 2021)

Figure 8.26: (Bottom) About a month before the lockdown ... picnicking outside Somerset Metro Station on a late Sunday afternoon (*Source*: Felicity HH Chan, T1: March 1, 2020)

Through the Looking Glass—Everyday Urbanism in a Pandemic City 2020–2022   233

Figure 8.27: (Top) Solitude in the city at the Guoco Tower in Tanjong Pagar (*Source*: Felicity HH Chan, T4: April 27, 2021)

Figure 8.28: (Bottom) Social distancing Yoga at Capitol Theatre plaza in Downtown Singapore on a weekday night (*Source*: Felicity HH Chan, T7: November 17, 2021)

Figure 8.29: A collage of safe-distancing signs from Singapore Botanic Gardens and Bukit Timah Nature Reserve created by Bayi Li (*Source*: Qian (Cathy) Huang, T7: December 4, 2021)

Through the Looking Glass Everyday Urbanism in a Pandemic City 2020–2022 235

Figure 8.30. Christmas Wonderland at Gardens by the Bay after the lifting of restrictions (*Source*: Yunkyung Choi, T9: December 31, 2022)

THE TOURIST GAZE

In this section, we present an alternate way of visually experiencing the city — from outside in, as observed from the gaze of a tourist doing staycations and in quarantine.

Figure 8.31: Scenes of the Flower Dome in Gardens by the Bay Across the Pandemic. The Flower Dome was almost empty when regulations were tightened, but experienced a surge in attendance once the regulations were relaxed, then people freely walking around without any restrictions during the post-pandemic period. (*Source*: Yunkyung Choi, T7: November 2, 2021 (left), T8: June 27, 2022 (middle); Bayi Li, T9+: March 3, 2023 (right))

Through the Looking Glass Everyday Urbanism in a Pandemic City 2020–2022   237

Figure 8.32: Silence in the gallery (*Source*: Jiaxuan Wang, T3: December 1, 2020)

Figure 8.33: My first visit to Singapore started with a 14-day quarantine at a hotel, where I could view the empty streets (*Source*: Yunkyung Choi, T6: August 10, 2021)

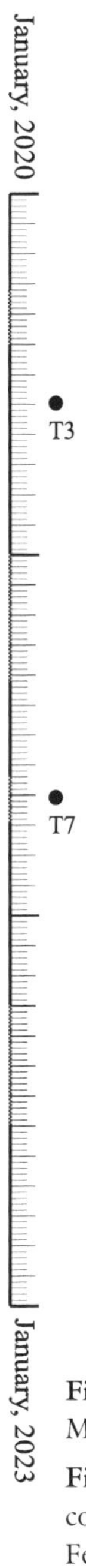

Through the Looking Glass Everyday Urbanism in a Pandemic City 2020–2022   239

Figure 8.34: (Top) Great to see the iconic symbol without tourists in Merlion Park (*Source*: Yunkyung Choi, T7: September 2, 2021)

Figure 8.35: (Bottom) A surreal city of dreams and stark realities colliding — a view from a cable car from Sentosa to Mount Faber (*Source*: Felicity HH Chan, T3: July 30, 2020)

Figure 8.36: My daughter was amazed by one of the exhibitions at Marina Bay Sands (*Source*: Yunkyung Choi, T9: April 14, 2022)

ENDNOTES

1. Author credits: the order of the authors follows the alphabetical order of their last names. Content curation: All authors; Chapter conceptualisation: Felicity HH Chan; Essay: Emma EY Goh and Felicity HH Chan; Timeline Creation: Yunkyung Choi; Design Graphics: Bayi Li; Photo captions: Photographers.
2. Chase, J., Crawford, M., Kaliski, J. (1999). Everyday Urbanism. The Monacelli Press.

© 2024 World Scientific Publishing Company
https://doi.org/10.1142/9789811287848_0009

The Magic of Modernity

Chan Heng Chee, Winston Yap & Sara Ann Nicholas

According to Liu Thai Ker, the renowned Singapore architect and urban planner, foreign visitors to Singapore always say to him, "I love visiting Singapore." He would ask them, "Why?" "Because everything works here," was the invariable reply (Chan 2021). The reaction of the visitors sums up the appeal and success of Singapore as a global city and a liveable city.

During the COVID-19 pandemic, as with all cities globally, the city state largely fell silent. Visitor arrivals fell sharply, circuit breakers or lockdowns put a halt to movement in and out of the city centre. A dramatic illustration of this city silence was the unprecedented fall in the population of Singapore. Pre-COVID in 2019, the population of Singapore was 5.7 million. In 2021, the population of Singapore was reported to be 5.45 million (Singapore Department of Statistics 2023). In two years, the population had reduced by more than 200,000 due to departures and border restrictions to entry. As people worked from home, new patterns of travel emerged and the rise of the neighbourhood was reported. Seeing the trends and following the discussions of urbanologists and architects in the West, government leaders, business executives, real estate investors, office workers, and urban planners wondered about the possible hollowing out of the city centre in Singapore.

The key question, asked with some sense of urgency in the early months of the pandemic, was whether cities would lose their prominent role and ways of life. City life would be totally reset and remodelled, experts predicted. Some spoke of sweeping radical makeovers (Florida *et al.* 2020).

Some of us did not think so (Institute of Policy Studies 2020). Sociologists have argued that we should not underestimate the human tendency to revert to norm. There would not be fundamental transformation post-COVID, but the use of technology has changed patterns of work, education and shopping, moving activities online at a much faster pace. What would cities look like? Batty (2021) experimented with hypothetical simulations and came up with the conclusion that "it is unlikely that cities will explode at their edges after the pandemic ends for it will be impossible to ignore the layers and layers of history which have built the central city historically. There may be some increase in decentralised living and there is certain to be a new kind of mobility with respect to living and working remotely" (Batty 2021, 4).

Richard Florida, Andres Rodriguez-Pose, and Micheal Storper on examining the immediate and long-term effects of the pandemic on cities and on economic geographies argue that the duration of the pandemic and when vaccination was introduced matters. Even if cities do not lose their prominent roles, they will be changed and transformed in the short term. They added that what they observed was more relevant for Western Europe and the US, but understood that some cities, especially those not part of Western industrialised economies, may have different outcomes (Florida, Rodríguez-Pose, and Storper 2023).

Florida, Rodríguez-Pose, and Storper (2023) concluded that firstly, there will be a long-lasting transformation of work and shopping, with knock-on effects because the pandemic forced people to adjust to working at home or working a few days a week. This acceleration of online shopping will threaten the survival of high street unless there is government intervention. This development will also exacerbate the inequality between the high-knowledge, high-skill worker and the low-skill worker and service staff who work in high touch jobs. The trend of less work in the office and the growing online shopping trend could affect real estate values in a major way.

Secondly, the importance of cities will not be affected but the functions of cites might change to more of a cultural and civic gathering place, presumably from its role as an energetic economic centre. More activities will be outdoors, and city centres are likely to be turned into pedestrian centres and bike ways. They envisage a change in the population from the older rich who might leave for the suburbs and younger, creative people coming in to take their place.

Finally, they note that one result of the "winner take all" effect of economic geography will continue to prevail post pandemic. New York and London will survive as will other special cities such as Shanghai, Singapore, Tokyo, or Paris. Medium-sized cities and rural areas will lose out. This last point is borne out by Joel Kotkin's study of American cities which he argues are going through an existential crisis worsened by the pandemic (Kotkin 2021).

THE CASE OF SINGAPORE

Singapore is always an interesting and different case. We are a city and a city state. Unlike many cities in the industrialised world, Singapore is a city without many options. Its land area is 728.3 km² or 278 square miles. The land area is about 0.9 times the size of New York City. Hong Kong, by comparison, is 1,104 km² or 428 square miles. The city centre population cannot and does not flee to live in the suburbs or to cities in the region. It does not make sense as distances are not meaningful. The impact of the COVID-19 pandemic has led Singaporeans to appreciate the urban design and planning of their city state. The planners, grasping early that different aspects of the city works as a system with functions interlinked with each other, juxtaposed housing near amenities, transport, recreational parks, and green spaces that cities seek now in a post-pandemic redesign. For the city it was adding on, upgrading, and tweaking what it had been implementing as design for a liveable and sustainable city.

This propitious circumstance was not an accident. It grew from a strategic decision made by Prime Minister Lee Kuan Yew at independence in 1965. Faced with the prospect of making a city state work as a country, Lee Kuan Yew concluded that the economic strategy for

Singapore was twofold — firstly, to leapfrog the region and link up with the developed world, with Japan, the United States, and Europe, to attract their industries to Singapore and secondly, to create a First World oasis in a Third World region (Lee 2000).

In 1972, S. Rajaratnam, the first Foreign Minister of Singapore, fully developed the idea that Singapore should become a global city, hurdle the immediate region which was hostile to economic cooperation given that the three countries, Singapore, Malaysia, and Indonesia had just ended tension and a bitter conflict with each other. Singapore promoted its place as a vision of a global city before the word entered the economist's or sociologist's vocabulary (Chan, and ul Haq 2007).

MODERNITY AT ITS CORE

Singapore set out to implement a first world modernity and embraced modernity as its identity. This modernity was and is expressed in its infrastructure building and communications — the hardware, as well as in an invisible modernity in the attitudes and the management of policy processes — the software. In combination, these qualities have become the distinctive characteristics of Singapore.

People come to Singapore to do business, set up factories, get an education, receive healthcare, and as tourists because they are drawn by the functioning convenient modernity of the global city. In Singapore, things are perceived to "work like magic", and the modernity expressed through efficiency, the sense of agency, and the solutioning of problems prevalent throughout the country became a magical attraction. It is thus not far-fetched to suggest that it is the magic of its modernity that has contributed to Singapore's reputation as a thriving centre and hub in the region. Some of the greatest cities in the world, London, New York, Paris, Tokyo, and Shanghai have pulled people to their cities partly because of the magical attraction of the modernity of the city, the opportunities, and the buzz.

Though Singapore has done well in the competitive globalised world undergoing geopolitical and technological paradigm shifts, the city state must adjust to the changing context and keep maintaining and improving its game. What new considerations should be added to redesign a resilient, liveable city in the post-pandemic era?

There is a long tradition of debating and defining the concept and meaning of modernity in social sciences and other disciplines. Without wishing to be caught up in the discourse of critical theory and urban theory, we will use a working definition of modernity in this essay. Modernity here refers to the application of science and technology to ways of doing things and finding solutions with the purpose of improving lives and the environment (Hamel 1993; Dennis 2008).

In the 1950s, squatter colonies and ramshackled huts were common sights in Singapore. The People's Action Party ran on a platform in the 1959 General Elections, promising to solve unemployment and the acute housing crisis. In 1960, the Housing and Development Board (HDB) was established and tasked to construct low-cost housing. HDB's first Five-Year Building Programme was to build 52,842 flats at an estimated cost of S$230 million, about 10,000 units a year. By 1969, HDB had built its first 100,000 units and by 1989, 88% of Singapore's population were living in HDB flats. With the majority of the city state population living in clean, good quality housing, the emergence of well-planned and designed housing estates swiftly lent Singapore the image and the physical reality of a modern city (Housing and Development Board 2020).

When people were relocated and moved in massive numbers into public housing estates, the planners were aware they had to reduce and sub-divide the city into smaller urban cells, precincts, and neighbourhoods to create an urban high-rise village and a sense of community. Creating this sense of community in public housing estates is still the goal and a work in progress.

The housing crisis was not the only critical issue. The urgency to deal with unemployment became acute after 1965, when Singapore became independent unexpectedly, and within a couple of years, the British announced its military pull-out east of Suez which meant the British bases in Singapore would be closed. The base contributed 20% of the Gross Domestic Product (GDP) and employed 25,000 workers, a large number at that time considering the population was 2 million. The Singapore government decided that to bring investment and business to Singapore, they would build a Central Business

District (CBD) to boost business, commercial, and financial activity (Ho 2016).

Expanding public housing and building the CBD required urban renewal but land was in short supply in the city, occupied by existing shophouses. The PAP government exercised political will to pass the Land Acquisition Act in 1966 which enabled the government to acquire land legally and to compensate the landowners at near market price. This crucial piece of legislation has been the secret to Singapore's rapid physical transformation. The ability to settle land rights and access to land facilitated the shaping of the built environment. Lee Kuan Yew and his government were keen to move Singapore into a different league of cities, towards a first world environment which would be attractive to business and visitors to Singapore, turning it into a hub for the region.

Singapore prioritises keeping the city state clean, building good roads, reducing flooding and pollution, cleaning up the dirty waterways, and most importantly, the polluted Singapore River. Special attention was invested in seeding a garden city. In June 1963, Lee Kuan Yew planted a pink mempat tree to mark the commencement of the Garden City Campaign. In hindsight, it was a most significant and defining act which underscored the city's pursuit of clean and green. Today, Singapore sees itself as a City in the Garden. According to Tan Wee Kiat, the CEO of Gardens by the Bay and former CEO of National Parks Board, it was not an easy decision. Initially, officials were not convinced of spending valuable resources on plants and flowers. The competition between land for economic use and land for parks saw strong pushback in favour of the former. But Lee Kuan Yew, as the strongest advocate of greening the city, helped, and attitudes have changed overtime, especially when it was demonstrated that trees and greenery in Singapore reduced the heat island effect by 2 degrees (Tan 2016). Today, the government fully supports creating a gracious living environment with tree-lined streets linking parks and gardens throughout the city. The national budget set aside to expand and enhance parks, the park connector network and recreational cycling routes in 2021 amidst the pandemic was $315 million (Ng 2021). The greenness of Singapore has surprised many who come to the city for the first time.

In Europe and the United States, one of the first moves in redesigning cities post pandemic was to expand the bicycle lanes and sprouting parks for wellness enhancement. In Singapore, it was an ongoing project to green the city, and parks were created near the public housing neighbourhoods and all over the island. Bicycling has developed as a hobby and as an environmentally friendly mode of transport. But in the short term, COVID-19 seems to have increased the awareness of people about the benefits of being around nature. As the circuit breakers permitted people to go out of their homes for exercise, the National Parks Board noted that there was a significant increase of visitors to parks, gardens, and nature reserves (Lee 2022).

Singapore draws wonderment too from visitors because of the absence of gridlock traffic congestion found in many Asian cities and Western cities. This is due to a carefully balanced structure of disincentives and incentives. Car ownership is costly, intentionally to nudge the population towards a car-lite society, backed by a good public transportation system and electronic road pricing. We will return to discuss transport in Singapore in a later section on Sustainability.

THE CHANGING IDEA OF MODERNITY

We have given a quick description of the components of modernity and how Singapore was imagined, and the ideas implemented. It was physical modernity clearly in the early phase of post-war and independent Singapore's development from 1960 to the 1990s. In 1998, Singapore was counted in the grouping of world cities. From 2000, when it was the trend to rank cities in indexes, a way of branding cities driven by competitiveness in the rapid globalisation of the world, Singapore was constantly named in the major indexes of Global Cities (Lohr *et al.* 2021; Kearney 2022; Institute for Urban Strategies 2022; Schroders 2023), Global Smart Cities (Kaur, Low, and Dujacquier 2021; Berrone and Ricart 2022), and Alpha Cities (GaWC 2020). Singapore began its development identifying and implementing policies in a virtuous circle. This has endowed it with advantages.

This position must be constantly maintained, and there is a need to refresh and rethink the concept of a modern functioning city. In the first phase, modernity was defined and measured globally by the improvements of the physical infrastructure of the city. In the later 1980s, it became evident with the pressures of climate change and environmental degradation that modern cities must embrace the concept of sustainability and introduce policies and measures to promote sustainable living. So, the eco city, the green city and the sustainable city entered our discussions seriously. Furthermore, "modern", which implies applying science and technology for solutions, would incorporate "smart" in the management of the city. Modernity, if it is to keep its magical attraction in the 21st century, must fulfil and advance the dimensions of sustainable and smart, and even grapple with what the metaverse city presents.

A NEW SUSTAINABILITY

Singapore, as a resource-challenged country, inherently understood the existential prerequisite of sustainable development and sustainability. This thinking came before the Brundtland Report, also known as *Our Common Future,* in 1987, which set off the global discussion on development, climate, and environment. There are many areas where Singapore became the first mover to experiment with and implement the most radical and sustainable practices and innovative solutions to deal with issues. This is very clear from the water resource management, urban transport management, enhancement of energy efficiency, and ensuring of food security, to name a few of the pressing urban challenges. The UN Agenda for Sustainable Development, which spelt out the 17 Sustainable Development Goals (SDGs), and the UN climate conferences have increased the pressure on countries to reach higher ambitions for fulfilling their UN climate pledges.

In this section, three areas will be discussed — water, transport and food security, which highlight the ingenuity, modernity, and innovation applied to effective outcomes.

WATER

The search for water independence came on the first day of nationhood as Singapore relied totally on Malaysia for its water. As Lee Kuan Yew said, "I knew if I did not become less dependent — at that time I did not believe I could be totally independent, but less dependent on Malaysian supplies (of water), I would always be a satellite." (Khoo 2016, 92).

Singapore pioneered urban water harvesting on a large scale not found in any other city or country. Singapore meets two thirds of its needs from water catchment areas from 17 reservoirs and about 8,000 km of waterways — rivers, canals, and drains created throughout the island. The includes the Marina Reservoir, which collects water from the Kallang and Singapore Rivers in the central business district (Khoo 2016). Collecting urban water needed an integrated approach of government agencies, land-use planning, and environmental management to ensure clean catchment and the ability to separate storm water from sewerage water. But even this coordination would have limited impact but for the application of new technologies. Singapore harnessed technology to create the infrastructure to collect water. Technologies such as desalinisation made possible the conversion of sea water to potable water and membrane technology made possible the conversion of wastewater into recycled pure water. This is done through three stages: (1) microfiltration/ultrafiltration to filter out microscopic particles and bacteria, (2) reverse osmosis where a semi-permeable membrane only allows water molecules to pass through, (3) ultraviolet disinfection which kills all bacteria and viruses (Ho 2016). This water has been labelled NEWater and is a key innovation in Singapore to build its water supply resilience. There are now five NEWater plants in Singapore. The bulk of NEWater is used for industrial purposes. It is so pure it is used in wafer fabrication plants. Paradoxically, Singapore from its beginnings as a water-challenged country, is now a water technologies and systems exporter, as well as a small exporter of water to some regional countries.

The city state's water conservancy has been woven into the urban landscape. In every HDB housing estate, there are neighbourhood parks and gardens, and many will feature a lake, which can serve as a mini reservoir in times of water crises. Punggol 21 Plus, the latest new town, incorporates a man-made waterway, a key green blue feature, which transforms Punggol into a sustainable waterfront housing project. It has recreational facilities, bicycling lanes, and a jogging route. Bidadari Housing Estate, launched in 2015, besides having a rich historical heritage, will hold Singapore's first underground service reservoir, which will store drinking water to supply to homes, underneath a community lawn. It will also create the new Alkaff Lake, which residents and families can enjoy strolling around. On rainy days, the lake will double up as a storm water retention pond to slow down and reduce peak storm water from running into public drainage, reducing the risk of floods (Housing and Development Board 2020).

URBAN TRANSPORT MANAGEMENT

There is no doubt that sustainability is at the heart of the transport policy. In 1975, Singapore was the first country to use the price stick to discourage car usage. The mechanism, known as the Area Licensing System (ALS), prevented cars from entering the most congested zones during restricted hours without a permit. This led to the Road Pricing System in 1995, which charged motorists for the use of certain roads, encouraging those who did not wish to pay to use alternative roads. In 1998, the Electronic Pricing System (ERP) was introduced, allowing for a flexible system with shoulder-peak charges in accordance with the volume of traffic for each road in the Restricted Zone. There was a noticeable drop in traffic volume after the ERP was introduced, which showed motorists were aware of the true cost of their journeys, and they made travel-related decisions based on cost, necessity of trips, and alternative routes (Figure 9.1).

Besides the ERP system, there is the Vehicle Quota System which places a quota on the number of new vehicles that can be registered in Singapore. A Certificate of Entitlement (COE) must be purchased by the buyer, which entitles him/her the right to own the car. This is a prohibitive tax and is a major disincentive to purchase cars in Singapore.

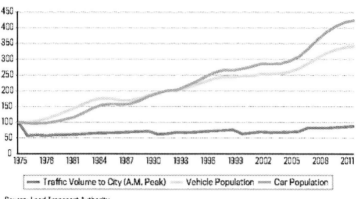

Figure 9.1: Traffic volume into the city (A.M. Peak) with ALS and ERP implementation (*Source*: Centre for Liveable Cities Singapore 2021)

A recent study by the Land Transport Authority (LTA) shows that even with the high disincentives, the younger population in Singapore still aspires to car ownership (Figure 9.2). A very small number say they can live without a car and a large minority indicate they will consider buying an electric vehicle (EV) (Figure 9.3).

According to Senior Minister of Transport and Communications and Information, Dr Janil Puthucheary, the government is pushing ahead with its plans to achieve long-term sustainability for the land transport system. This will entail firstly, making Walk Cycle Ride (WCR) the preferred modes of transport in Singapore, secondly, moving to cleaner and greener vehicles which are energy efficient, which means promoting EVs until other technologies are found for adoption, and thirdly, to optimise the land transport system for the future, experimenting with new technologies, such as Autonomous Vehicles (AVs) (Puthucheary 2020).

With an eye on the climate pledges it has made with other United Nations (UN) members at the climate conferences to avert climate catastrophe, Singapore committed itself to Net Zero emissions by

The Magic of Modernity 253

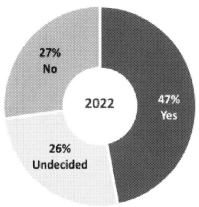

Figure 9.2: Car ownership aspirations among youths (*Source*: Civil Service College 2022)

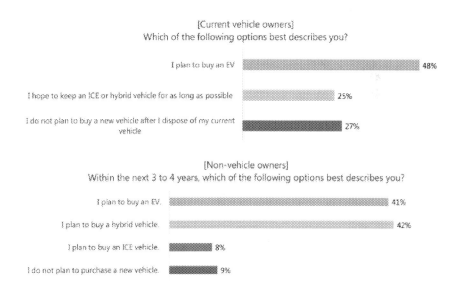

Figure 9.3: EV purchase intentions among vehicle owners and non-vehicle owners (*Source*: Civil Service College 2022)

2050, but the public sector committed to achieving this ambition by 2045. A carbon tax will be raised progressively by 2024 (Wong 2022).

Finally, urban transport management through the Land Transport Master Plan 2040, which is an ambitious document, will have a significant impact in reshaping the city and how people will live. Singapore is envisioned to be a 45-minute city, with 20-minute towns, where all journeys to the nearest neighbourhood centres using WCR modes will take 20 minutes, and 9 in 10 peak hour journeys using WCR will be completed in 45 minutes as commuters will have public, active, and shared modes of transport choices. The pandemic made everyone conscious of the importance of convenience and accessibility, and shorter intimate journeys help promote neighbourliness because of encountering the familiar. It has the added value of reducing the carbon footprint.

FOOD SECURITY AND URBAN FARMING

Faced with severe land constraints, Singapore decided early on not to dedicate land to agriculture. It has been a shrinking sector. Today, the city state imports 90% of its food from overseas. Singapore's push towards food security and urban farming as one aspect of food security is a recent emphasis. There has always been great concern about food security from the health standards aspect and the sourcing of the food, but in 2019, even before the start of the COVID-19 pandemic, the Singapore Food Agency (SFA) advocated a 30 × 30 vision of Singapore, which meant that Singapore should be producing 30% of its food needs by 2030. The disruption in the supply chains, a consequence of the COVID-19 pandemic, strained the flow of imported food to the republic, further accelerating this direction for the policymakers. At the 27th Conference of Parties (COP27), Minister of Sustainability and Environment Grace Fu spoke of the need "to pivot to a resilient and sustainable food production" because of climate change (Tan 2022).

SFA reported that between 2019 and 2021, the number of local farms grew from 221 to 260, producing vegetables, eggs, and seafood for Singapore households (Shafeeq 2022). Local farms now produce

30% of the eggs consumed, 4% of the vegetables, and 8% of the seafood. This is a long shot from the goal of 30 × 30, but Singapore is determined to gain food resilience.

In fact, the confluence of technology, engineering, and design is expected to bring about a transformation for farming in Singapore. The physical boundaries of farming have been redefined. New regulations enable farms to sprout on rooftops, in parks, and in viaducts. This will reimagine the use of space in the city as well as the city centre. Vertical farming has taken on. The most cited example is Sky Greens. Established in 2011, the first low carbon, hydraulic-driven vertical farm with nine-metre-tall towers of green plants which has generated interest from China and the Middle East, and elsewhere. But the most interesting project is the conversion of the former Queenstown Remand Prison, housing 1,000 inmates at its peak, into 8,000 square metres of urban farm, the Edible Garden City. Every HDB rooftop can now be turned into community vegetable and flower gardens, looked after by the residents themselves. The economic functions of urban farms can be integrated with a social space for people and families looking for a recreational and educational visit to the farm. It is a rare opportunity for the totally urbanised Singaporeans to connect back to nature.

Urban farming in Singapore has been fuelled by top down as well as bottom-up initiatives. Singaporeans have embraced urban farming with gusto, especially since the pandemic. Bjorn Leow, the founder of Edible City, said individuals are now producing vegetables in their own flats. Thousands of community gardens are springing up in unutilised spaces like rooftops and several start-ups have tried to produce food using advanced techniques that minimise the use of natural resources. With this new emphasis on food security, it can be anticipated that there will inevitably be a tussle in the allocation for land use as priorities will be viewed differently.

SMART NATION SINGAPORE

At the launch of Singapore's Smart Nation initiative in 2014, Prime Minister Lee Hsien Loong remarked: "50 years ago, we built a modern city. Today, we have a metropolis. 10 years from now, let's have a smart nation!" (Lee 2014). As we find ourselves today in yet another era with its own triumphs and tribulations, "modern" takes on a different meaning. More than being a city where "everything works", things must work well. Significant innovation is required for cities to remain modern in a knowledge-based and globally competitive world.

As we write, the COVID-19 pandemic continues to unleash profound changes on our societies and economies — changing urban mobility patterns, accelerating digital adoption, and disrupting global value chains. Aside from work, many essential services such as education, healthcare, and social support had to be shifted online. Initially, these changes posed deep technical challenges for governments as many lacked the tools and infrastructure to operate services digitally. As cities began recovering from the pandemic, many had to re-look and re-evaluate their planning approach — rethinking a balance between efficiency (just-in-time) and contingency (just-in-case). As a country with no natural resources, Singapore is no stranger to just-in-case planning. Singapore started building its digital capacities before COVID-19 struck its shores. By design, the Singapore government has been a key architect of national digitisation efforts since the early 1980s. The pandemic only served as a catalyst to accelerate Singapore's digital push.

Singapore's decade long commitment to smart nation planning came through in its rapid digital response to COVID-19. Throughout the pandemic, smart solutions kept up dynamically with emerging needs, playing a pivotal role in Singapore's public health response. For example, a novel Q&A chatbot catering to COVID-19-specific questions was developed within two weeks of the first confirmed case in Singapore (Chan 2020). The Singapore government's use of technology in their pandemic response has garnered the country global praise, with TIME and Bloomberg hailing Singapore as a "winner" for its pandemic response and "the world's best place to be during Covid" (Bremmer 2021; Hong 2021). Among global cities, Singapore also ranks among the top in the most recent Institute for Management Development — Singapore University of Technology and Design

(IMD-SUTD) Smart City Index for its prompt and coordinated COVID-19 health response. "Singapore had a clear roadmap that it followed but remained flexible. The citizens were kept informed and therefore onboard with the decisions and the loss of freedom that these entailed," said Professor Arturo Bris, who is the director at the IMD World Competitiveness Centre. A recent survey of citizen sentiments further espouses these sentiments where 88% of Singaporeans believe that their country has done a good job dealing with the pandemic (Silver and Connaughton 2022). Singapore's success highlights the importance of: (1) prudent forward planning to identify emergent needs, and (2) building the execution ability and institutions to carry out tasks.

Clearly, how smart a city is perceived to be is increasingly intertwined with its ability to respond effectively to complex urban challenges. In this vein, we begin with a brief discussion on Singapore's Smart Nation journey and its relation to the ongoing pandemic. We highlight innovations from the smart manufacturing sector given recent implications on global supply chain disruptions. Against the backdrop of systemic trends of innovation, we evaluate how the unfolding of the COVID-19 pandemic has challenged and enriched Singapore's smart city paradigm.

SINGAPORE'S SMART JOURNEY AND COVID-19

Singapore's smart city journey depicts a progressive and persistent race with modernity. Recognising that human capital was (and is) our most valuable resource, early plans in the 1980s and 1990s focused on developing a smart and technologically equipped civil sector. Plans such as the National Computerisation Plan (1980–1985) and the National IT Plan (1986–1991) saw the widespread implementation and adoption of novel systems such as TradeNet for trading operations, Medinet for healthcare, and the Integrated Land Use System (ILUS) for urban and road planning. As technology usage became normalised and productivity gains from using technology became more apparent, the intuitive next step was to include the rest of the population in the ongoing tech revolution. Subsequent plans such as IT2000 (1992–2000), E-government (2000 onwards), and Infocom 21 (2000–2003) established much of the groundwork for nationwide broadband, multimedia, and telecommunication networks, helping to connect society at large. By 2016, Singapore had one of the highest smart phone penetration rates (85%) in the world and a national broadband coverage of approximately 90% of the population (Chan 2016). Despite these successes, Singapore could not rest on its laurels as a new era of modernity with its contemporary set of challenges was unfolding. Up till then, the global climate of competition for capital had never been stronger. Many cities, including Singapore, had to push full steam ahead to maintain their relevance in the new digital economy.

Towards developing a competitive edge, Singapore launched its Smart Nation initiative in 2014, with the hopes of improving the lives of its people and businesses through technology. Projects under the initiative are organised under three key pillars — Digital Economy, Digital Government, and Digital Society, helping to propel transformations across health, transport, urban living, government services, and business sectors. Forward planning allowed Singapore to build a robust digital infrastructure ecosystem before the COVID-19 pandemic hit its shores. As the pandemic progressed, the importance of digital solutions for pandemic resilience only became clearer. In response, the Singapore government doubled down on efforts to adopt smart solutions, putting forth an enhanced budget of SGD 3.8 billion for 2022 (compared to SGD 2.7 billion in 2019) for information and communications technology (ICT) spending.

MANUFACTURING

Manufacturing has played a key role in Singapore's growth and modern transformation into a global hub over the decades. The early 1960s to late 1980s saw the transformation from an import-substitution approach to an export-led industrialisation model with an explicit focus on knowledge-based industries. While early initiatives helped Singapore to develop a robust economic base and move up the global value chain, economic growth was soon challenged by diminishing returns to investment and the 1985 financial recession. Faced with a narrowing cost advantage in the region, the economic planners knew the economy needed to pivot towards higher value goods and services. Towards this objective, the Singapore government pursued a twin-engine of growth model, where advanced manufacturing coupled with the pursuit of modern financial and business services. The 1991 National Technology Plan and subsequent plans focused on research and development to promote adoption of advanced manufacturing and engineering technologies in high-value areas, such as the pharmaceutical, tech, and medical industry. As manufacturing in high-value areas thrived, emphasis was then shifted to local enterprises, which forms the majority of Singapore's enterprise count. In 2017, the Committee on the Future Economy (CFE), established by the Ministry of Trade and Industry Singapore, identified smart manufacturing as a key driver and support mechanism for local businesses.

Across various planning scales, we observe a systemic shift towards the development of flexible and adaptable manufacturing spaces. At the district level, Jurong Town Council (JTC) is building Singapore's leading Industry 4.0 manufacturing hub with its Jurong Innovation District (JID) (Figure 9.4). Unlike previous manufacturing districts which focused primarily on production, JID adopts an integrated planning approach which recognises the close relationship between research, innovation, and production. An attractive and clean-living environment will be achieved through sustainable and smart urban design, helping to bring together factories of the future, research institutions, and urban communities.

At the local scale, companies in Singapore are also adopting automated solutions to build dense and resilient production systems. For example, Tee Yih Jia Food Manufacturing has built Asia's largest fully automated cold storage facility, which employs state-of-the-art storage solutions to allow high density storage and help reduce human touch points throughout the manufacturing process (Figure 9.5). Smart manufacturing solutions help to reduce over-reliance on labour and create safer and cleaner production environments.

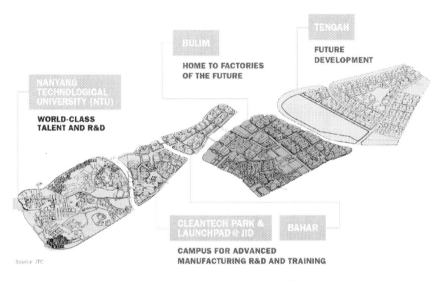

Figure 9.4: Jurong innovation district.
It covers 620 hectares and comprises five unique districts. The district features ample parks and green spaces and will form a creative and liveable manufacturing cluster. The first phase of the district is expected to be completed by around 2022, creating over 95,000 new jobs (*Source*: K 2022)

Figure 9.5: Rack clad high bay warehouse provides optimal factory space utilisation and goods retrieval from vertical storage locations (*Source*: SSI Schafer n.d.).

Digital solutions have ameliorated many challenges and helped Singaporeans to emerge stronger from the pandemic. The pandemic has also manifested palpable implications for smart city planning — accentuating the importance of health and resilience as fundamental components of smart urban systems. More specifically, we observe three interconnected, ongoing trends: (1) the importance of developing robust and self-sufficient in-house, local technical expertise; (2) a greater emphasis on digital inclusivity; and (3) recognising the significance of regional (especially cross-border) digital ties.

In-house capabilities played a crucial role in ensuring that digital services could be developed and delivered in a timely manner. As mentioned by Chan Cheow Hoe, Government Chief Digital Technology Officer and Deputy Chief Executive of GovTech, "Having the capabilities within GovTech means that we can build and make changes on the fly." Aside from technical expertise, development of in-house capabilities warrants building inclusive Artificial Intelligence (AI) governance frameworks to support an increasingly pervasive AI ecosystem. New technologies such as AI introduce various ethical, legal, and governance challenges. Robust and comprehensive AI governance frameworks are required to ensure mutually beneficial multi-stakeholder relationships between users, tech companies, and public administrators. Since 2018, Singapore's Advisory Council of the Ethical Use of AI has been set up to provide guidance to the Singapore government on the responsible development and deployment of AI. Building on these initiatives, Singapore also released its 2020 Model AI Governance Framework (2nd edition) to provide clearer guidance of responsible use of AI technologies. These collective efforts will help to form the basis for a more transparent, accountable AI ecosystem that can benefit all parties.

Digital inclusivity in a post-pandemic world includes not only a competent public and tech sector, but also greater involvement with citizens. Despite digital prevalence, digital exclusion remains an issue which affects a significant subset of the population. As part of the 2021 Smart Nation and Digital Government Group's (SNDGG) Emerging Stronger Conversations, conversations with more than 400 Smart Nation Ambassadors identified community digital learning opportunities as key to supporting Singapore's recovery from COVID-19. To promote digital literacy among older adults, SG Digital Office (SDO) implemented its flagship "Seniors Go Digital" and "Hawkers Go Digital" programme, providing personalised digital support for more than 100,000 senior citizens and 18,000 stallholders respectively. Such initiatives are important in helping older adults and stallholders to obtain essential skillsets and gain the confidence to navigate their lives in a rapidly changing urban landscape.

Last but not least, the disruption of global value chains underscores the importance of building robust, resilient digital regional and international communication channels. In a post-COVID world, it is crucial that countries do not turn inwards, and instead be more proactive in pursuing win-win collaborations with each other. Based on Asian Development Bank estimates, a $459 billion annual economic infrastructure investment gap continues to exist between cities in Asia and the Pacific (Ra and Li 2018). On this front, Singapore has begun several initiatives such as the ASEAN Smart Cities Network (ASCN), Infrastructure Asia, and Digital Economy Agreements (DEAs) to address regional infrastructure gaps and augment digital communicative channels in Asia and beyond. ASCN is a communicative platform that promotes economic integration and sharing of ICT best practices among ASEAN states. Till date, Singapore has concluded negotiations on four DEAs — Chile and New Zealand, Australia, United Kingdom, and South Korea. Moving forward, it will be critical for countries to keep global supply and communication channels open while strengthening digital connectivity.

Towards this end, the metaverse has emerged as the next evolution of the internet. While the smart city focuses largely on the optimisation of separate, strategic urban components, the metaverse city looks to develop a multifunctional and integrated virtual environment. It is this emphasis of a holistic and integrated environment that qualitatively distinguishes the metaverse city from previous planning concepts. For example, instead of multiple digital applications, a single metaverse environment can be used to promote digital exchange, collaboration, and capability building. Amidst what appears to be a metaverse revolution, several cities such as Seoul, Shanghai, and

Dubai have laid out ambitious plans to achieve the metaverse city. Yet, it is not entirely clear how the metaverse will look or function as different cities have vastly varied approaches and conceptualisations of the metaverse. While some leaders view the metaverse as a just-in-case space for emergencies, others envision the metaverse as replacement for physical planning. In the next section, we take a closer look at the metaverse city and its implications for planning and modernity.

THE METAVERSE CITY

As social interactions moved online, many soon realised that virtual meetings provided a poor replacement for in-person interaction. In particular, Zoom or Microsoft Teams meetings could not convey the same sense of immediate social presence and intimacy characterised by face-to-face meetings. Simultaneously, evidence began surfacing on the negative psychological effects of long-term and continuous virtual interaction. As the pandemic wore on, phenomena such as "Zoom fatigue" and "virtual burnout" emerged as unintended built-in features of the WFH experience (Kretchmer 2020).

Towards this dilemma, leading companies and governments have taken to the "metaverse" as a solution. At its simplest, the metaverse promises a fully dynamic and immersive experience that will change the way people interact virtually. For instance, Meta's "Horizon Workrooms" is an application that aims to promote collaboration among remote workers. The application allows users to enjoy a proximate spatial environment, brainstorm and interact on a common whiteboard, and even import physical objects (such as personal devices and tools) into virtual reality. Another similar application is Microsoft's Mesh, which additionally features holographic projections of a person's self-image in real-time. These formative examples indicate the expansive potential of how the metaverse will change the way that people communicate and connect with one another in a virtual age. In Bill Gates' words, "People shouldn't assume that the quality of the software that lets you have virtual experiences will stay the same. The acceleration of innovation is just starting." Many experts already view the metaverse as the future of digital business and collaboration.

As cities continue to negotiate their participation in the metaverse, it will be important to examine their wider implications for society. City policymakers and planners need to start thinking about what these technologies will mean for cities as they plan for the next phase of development. In the next section, we briefly define the metaverse and provide some explanation for its recent popularity.

WHAT IS THE METAVERSE?

Metaverses (or Web 3.0) are shared online spaces that aim to enhance social interaction through the assimilation of virtual and physical interfaces. Technologies such as 3D graphics, virtual reality, 5G/6G cellular technology, digital twins, and blockchain technology are fundamental building blocks of the metaverse. The idea was initially mooted by science fiction author Neal Stephenson in his 1992 novel *Snow Crash*. Stephenson's metaverse, aptly named "Street", features a massive virtual urban strip where users can interact with one another via digital avatars. Since then, numerous iterations of the metaverse have manifested in a mixture of sci-fi (The Matrix, Ready Player One) and real-time (Minecraft, Second Life, Fortnite) examples.

While uptake was initially slow, the metaverse industry has since seen rapid development and is estimated to be worth US$800 billion by 2024 (Bloomberg Intelligence 2021). For example, Meta (formerly Facebook) has invested up to US$10 billion in their Reality Lab Division to support metaverse development. Similarly, Microsoft plans to acquire Fortune 500 video game giant Activision Blizzard for US$68.7 billion by 2023. Outside of the United States, China's Tencent Holdings purchased Black Shark Gaming (previously owned by Xiaomi Corporation) for US$470 million and is reportedly poised to be the region's leading metaverse developer (Boghani 2022).

Aside from private organisations, city governments have also looked to apply the metaverse in the planning and design of cities. At the recent MIT Future Compute Conference, the Seoul Metropolitan Government announced the five-year "Metaverse Seoul" project which will provide Seoul residents unparalleled access to all areas of municipal administration (e.g., traffic enforcement, tax payment, tourism) through the metaverse. By 2023, Seoul residents will be able to visit a virtually staffed "Metaverse 120 Centre" to obtain municipal services from the comforts of their home. As a more palpable example, Santa Monica, California implemented a metaverse of their downtown district to promote footfall in the area. Users can move around a digital city and collect digital tokens, which can be redeemed for physical items at on-site retailers. As part of a wider SingaporeVerse, Singapore has also begun early experimentations with metaverses under initiatives by the Development Bank of Singapore (DBS). DBS BetterWorld is a human-centric metaverse platform to further environmental social governance (ESG) goals. Early initiatives involve using the metaverse to profile social entrepreneurs in Asia who have been driving positive ESG impact through innovative business models. According to Forbes, 30% of organisations in the world will have metaverse-ready products and services by 2026 (Ravinutala 2022). Many business experts view the metaverse as the future of digital business, citing it as a way to create a competitive advantage in a new digital economy (Minevich 2022).

What makes the metaverse so attractive and how did it get so popular? Ongoing discourse identify many factors which we broadly classify into two main themes: (1) the state of technology, and (2) the socio-economic potential of the metaverse. As a technical construct, the metaverse is dependent on several critical technologies. Until just a decade ago, the massive computational resources that was required to construct nontrivial computer graphics was inaccessible to the population at large. Recent advancements in both software and hardware have progressed to such a level that users of handheld devices are able to have practical virtual experiences. To put things into perspective, pocket smartphones today have more computing power than the supercomputer onboard NASA's Perseverance Mars rover. Aside from technological drivers, the metaverse is distinct among virtual environments in promoting a viable virtual economy. This is made possible through unique digital identifiers which enable users to be consumers, producers, and even owners of creative content. For example, non-fungible tokens (NFTs) have taken the art industry by storm. Since 2021, NFT auctions by auction house Sotheby's has accrued more than US$130 million in value (Sotheby's 2022). These developments have prompted the world's largest broker of fine arts to build an entire digital replica of its London galleries.

As we write, the metaverse remains a concept in flux and continues to be iteratively defined. Visions and implementations of the metaverse are rapidly emerging across various industries — business, art, social media, healthcare, and education. Gartner estimates that the metaverse will not be fully mature before 2030, however, leaders need to start evaluating opportunities now (Nguyen, Lee, and Verma 2022).

IMPLICATIONS FOR CITIES

Sometime in August last year, millions of netizens attended Ariana Grande's concert through their digital avatars. Fast forward to this year, amidst an Omicron wave, moviegoers were treated to a metaverse rendition of the Sundance Film Festival (Zeitchik 2022). These developments indicate the profound changes that the metaverse will have on our relationship with urban spaces and simultaneously raises key questions about cities. For example, how should city leaders plan for the future in anticipation of emergent technologies such as the metaverse? As with our experiences with previous innovations (e.g., Web 1.0 and 2.0), it is clear that it will take substantial effort to align the developments of Web 3.0 with the emancipatory goals of planning — equality, inclusivity, sustainability, and accountability. As aptly mentioned by Nick Clegg, President of Global Affairs at Meta, "We can have the ethical, moral, societal, regulatory debates now rather than bolting them on as an afterthought, which is what we've done, if you like, with the first kind of wave of the internet." As our societies become increasingly digitally embedded, it is timely to consider how the metaverse will change our urban fabric. We highlight ongoing discourse on what the metaverse means for cities and what opportunities and challenges loom on the horizon.

Central among concerns is how the metaverse will contribute to the existential digital divide. As the COVID-19 pandemic has exposed, almost half of the world's population has no access to the internet (Broom 2020). In particular, women and older adults remain under-represented on digital platforms. Aside from individuals, the metaverse is also expected to exacerbate the digital divide between companies. Metaverse initiatives requires sizable resources and hardware, which limits the participation extent for nonprofit sectors. Indeed, many of the first-movers in the metaverse are commercial companies (Ouyang 2022). Yet, nonprofit organisations play a fundamental role in creating more equitable and liveable communities. For example, nonprofit entities provide the means to draw public attention to important social issues, helping to fill gaps and identify critical needs in our societies. These developments accentuate the need and opportunity to develop early regulatory frameworks. As history has often shown, such frameworks are rarely realised through free market forces. Towards the realisation of an equitable and sustainable metaverse, early governance and pragmatic planning will be an indispensable ingredient.

Another emergent concern is the juxtaposition of virtual and physical spaces. While the decline of brick-and-mortar establishments is an age-old concern, a metaverse perspective warrants additional considerations: (1) a change to city planning approaches; and (2) the increasing fragility of urban landscapes. The extension of urban activities into the digital realm would likely lessen the need for travel and warrant a relook of city planning and design. For example, urban amenities such as car parks and roads could see a dramatic reduction and instead be replaced by parks or recreational facilities. The metaverse also presents opportunities to develop just-in-case digital spaces that could help cities to respond more resiliently to emergent threats (e.g., a global health pandemic). With the option to visit any attraction virtually, it is likely that the conscientious trade-off between the physical and virtual experience would become more mundane and explicit. These changes bring significant place-making opportunities to improve the experiential and symbolic dimensions of physical spaces. Another more explicit concern relates to the fragility of urban landscapes associated with newfound dynamism and immediacy of information flows. As a landmark example, New York City witnessed a dangerous stampede in July 2016 as hundreds of "Pokemon Go" players raced across the city to catch a "rare" Pokemon (Price 2016). Such events underline both the fragility of urban space and how digital information can manifest phenomena in the real world. Against this backdrop, metaverse systems might exacerbate this effect as users are now not only exposed to more digital information, but also have more of their personal information collected, which make them more vulnerable to manipulation. For instance, metaverse headsets with live microphones and cameras can collect sensitive information such as voice, conversations, and videos of private spaces which poses issues for user privacy. These issues would have to be resolved if we are to reap the full benefits promised by the metaverse.

Amid our gradual transition into the metaverse, it is increasingly clear that the metaverse will have a profound effect on cities. The last decade has seen metaverses transforming consumer experiences, sustaining vital human connections, and revolutionising business models across multiple industries. Notwithstanding its enormous potential, the metaverse as it stands remains an unviable solution for our existential urban problems. Towards realising a sustainable and inclusive vision for the modern city, it is important that city leaders are part of the conversation and play an active role in shaping the urban metaverse of the future.

Engagement in the metaverse is in an early stage in Singapore. Without doubt the uses, development, and potential will be closely monitored and embraced in the coming years as a usable virtual hybrid space.

CONCLUSION

There is no doubt that cities are getting more competitive as they face an increasing volatile and disrupted world. Some cities are still grappling with getting its population back to the city centre and city because work regimes have been changed and working from home looks to be a more permanent aspect of urban economic life. Cities want to maintain their position as a thriving global or important international city in spite of the paradigm shifts associated with work and the rerouting of economic geography because of the reconfiguring of supply chains. This chapter has focused on the modernity that made Singapore relevant over the years. It argues that it is the magic of the modernity that explains Singapore's success. But the benchmark of modernity evolves; understanding that fact and knowing what and when to move on to new benchmarks are key to ensuring Singapore's relevance and attraction.

REFERENCES

Batty, Michael. 2021. "What Will the Post-Pandemic City Look Like?" *Findings*, June. https://doi.org/10.32866/001c.23581.

Berrone, Pascual, and Joan Enric Ricart. 2022. "IESE Cities in Motion Index 2022." ST-633-E. IESE Business School, University of Navarra.

Bloomberg Intelligence. 2021. "Metaverse May Be $800 Billion Market, Next Tech Platform." *Bloomberg Professional Services*, December 1, 2021, sec. Research and Analysis. https://www.bloomberg.com/professional/blog/metaverse-may-be-800-billion-market-next-tech-platform/.

Boghani, Priyanka. 2022. "Tencent Poised to Lead China's Charge into the Metaverse." S&P Global. March 17, 2022. https://www.spglobal.com/marketintelligence/en/news-insights/latest-news-headlines/tencent-poised-to-lead-china-s-charge-into-the-metaverse-69311462.

Bremmer, Ian. 2021. "The Best Global Responses to COVID-19 Pandemic, 1 Year Later." *Time*. February 23, 2021. https://time.com/5851633/best-global-responses-covid-19/.

Broom, Douglas. 2020. "Coronavirus Has Exposed the Digital Divide Like Never Before." World Economic Forum. April 22, 2020. https://www.weforum.org/agenda/2020/04/coronavirus-covid-19-pandemic-digital-divide-internet-data-broadband-mobbile/.

Centre for Liveable Cities Singapore. 2021. *Transport: Overcoming Constraints, Sustaining Mobility* (2nd ed.). Urban Systems Studies. https://www.clc.gov.sg/docs/default-source/urban-systems-studies/uss-transport-revised.pdf.

Chan, Cheow Hoe. 2020. "Behind the Scenes — Leading the Digital Response Against COVID-19." Singapore Computer Society. 2020. https://www.scs.org.sg/articles/behind-the-scenes-leading-the-digital-response-against-covid-19.

Chan, Heng Chee. 2016. *The Making of a Smart Nation*, Lecture delivered at the Smart Cities Dialogue Platform, Berlin on 12 Dec 2016." Lee

Kuan Yew Centre for Innovative Cities. December 22, 2016. https://lkycic.sutd.edu.sg/publications/paper-making-smart-nation-professor-chan-heng-chee-delivered-smart-cities-dialogue-platform-berlin-12-dec-2016/.

Chan Heng Chee and Obaid ul Haq. 2007. *S. Rajaratnam: The Prophetic and the Political* (2nd ed.). Institute of Southeast Asian Studies: Graham Brash.

Civil Service College. 2022. "Ethos." Issue 24. https://file.go.gov.sg/ethos-issue-24.pdf.

Dennis, Richard. 2008. *Cities in Modernity: Representations and Productions of Metropolitan Space, 1840–1930.* Cambridge Studies in Historical Geography 40. Cambridge University Press.

Florida, Richard, Edward Glaeser, Maimunah Mohd Sharif, Kiran Bedi, Thomas J. Campanella, Heng Chee Chan, Dan Doctoroff, et al. 2020. "How Life in Our Cities Will Look After the Coronavirus Pandemic." Foreign Policy. May 1, 2020. https://foreignpolicy.com/2020/05/01/future-of-cities-urban-life-after-coronavirus-pandemic/.

Florida, Richard, Andrés Rodríguez-Pose, and Michael Storper. 2023. "Critical Commentary: Cities in a Post-COVID World." *Urban Studies* 60 (8): 1509–1531. https://doi.org/10.1177/00420980211018072.

GaWC. 2020. "The World According to GaWC 2020." GaWC. August 21, 2020. https://www.lboro.ac.uk/microsites/geography/gawc/world2020t.html.

Hamel, Pierre. 1993. "City, Modernity and Postmodernity: The Crisis of Urban Planning." *Canadian Journal of Urban Research* 2 (1): 16–29.

Ho, Peter. 2016. *A Chance of a Lifetime: Lee Kuan Yew and the Physical Transformation of Singapore,* ed. Centre for Liveables Cities, Lee Kuan Yew Centre for Innovative Cities.

Hong, Jinshan. 2021. "Singapore is Now the World's Best Place to Be During Covid." *Bloomberg,* April 27, 2021. https://www.bloomberg.com/news/newsletters/2021-04-27/singapore-is-now-the-world-s-best-place-to-be-during-covid.

Housing and Development Board. 2020. *Home, Truly: Building Dreams, Housing Hopes.* World Scientific Publishing Co. Pte. Ltd.

Institute for Urban Strategies. 2022. "Global Power City Index 2022." Institute for Urban Strategies, The Mori Memorial Foundation. https://www.mori-m-foundation.or.jp/english/ius2/gpci2/index.shtml.

Institute of Policy Studies. 2022. *Pre-conference Session: Cities, Civilisations and Geopolitics: In Conversation with George Yeo and Liu Thai Ker.* Singapore Perspectives 2022. https://youtu.be/UkjCV7-ybH8

K, Matt. 2022. "Parc Oasis Review: Convenience, Views and Facilities in Jurong at an Affordable Price." *AsiaOne.* March 13, 2022. https://www.asiaone.com/money/parc-oasis-review-convenience-views-and-facilities-jurong-affordable-price.

Kaur, Sulina, John Low, and Damien Dujacquier. 2021. "Bridging the Digital Divide." Roland Berger. February 8, 2021. https://www.rolandberger.com/en/Insights/Publications/Bridging-the-digital-divide.html.

Kearney. 2022. "Readiness for the Storm: The 2022 Global Cities Report." https://www.kearney.com/documents/291362523/293469161/Readiness+for+the+storm%E2%80%93the+2022+Global+Cities+Report.pdf/4d8684c4-3c33-d90e-3a76-40eb03f31a67?t=1666554433000.

Khoo, Teng Chye. 2016. "Harvesting Every Drop : The Singapore Water Story." In *A Chance of a Lifetime: Lee Kuan Yew and the Physical Transformation of Singapore*, by Peter Ho, ed. Centre for Liveables Cities, Lee Kuan Yew Centre for Innovative Cities.

Kotkin, Joel. 2021. "The Battle for Cities." Tablet Magazine. August 2, 2021. https://www.tabletmag.com/sections/news/articles/battle-cities-joel-kotkin.

Kretchmer, Harry. 2020. "Why 'Video Call Fatigue' Might Be Making You Tired During Lockdown — and How to Beat It." World Economic Forum. May 6, 2020. https://www.weforum.org/agenda/2020/05/zoom-fatigue-video-conferencing-coronavirus/.

Lee, Hsien Loong. 2014. "Transcript of Prime Minister Lee Hsien Loong's Speech at Smart Nation Launch on 24 November." GovTech Singapore. November 24, 2014. https://www.tech.gov.sg/media/speeches/transcript-of-prime-minister-lee-hsien-loong-speech-at-smart-nation-launch-on-24-november.

Lee, Kuan Yew. 2000. *From Third World to First: The Singapore Story, 1965–2000* (1st ed). HarperCollins Publishers.

Lee, Loraine. 2022. "The Big Read: Post-Pandemic, Life Isn't as Different as Predicted but Some Changes — Big and Small — Have Stuck." *Channel News Asia.* November 21, 2022. https://www.channelnewsasia.com/singapore/big-read-post-covid-19-pandemic-life-changes-remote-working-masks-e-commerce-3086086.

Lohr, Armin, Vladislav Boutenko, Marcos Aguiar, Thilo Zelt, Nikolaus Lang, and Joel Hazan. 2021. "Cities of Choice: Global City Ranking." Boston Consulting Group. https://media-publications.bcg.com/bcg-cities-of-choice-june-2021-v5.pdf.

Minevich, Mark. 2022. "The Metaverse and Web3 Creating Value in the Future Digital Economy." *Forbes.* June 17, 2022. https://www.forbes.com/sites/markminevich/2022/06/17/the-metaverse-and-web3-creating-value-in-the-future-digital-economy/.

Ng, Keng Gene. 2021. "Budget Debate: $315m to Expand and Enhance Parks, Park Connector Network and Recreational Routes." *The Straits Times.* March 5, 2021. https://www.straitstimes.com/singapore/315m-to-expand-and-enhance-parks-park-connector-network-and-recreational-routes.

Nguyen, Tuong, Adrian Lee, and Anushree Verma. 2022. "Metaverse Opportunities for Tech Product Leaders." Gartner. April 8, 2022. https://www.gartner.com/en/articles/metaverse-evolution-will-be-phased-here-s-what-it-means-for-tech-product-strategy.

Ouyang, Iris. 2022. "Metaverse and NFTs: From Gucci to Starbucks, Luxury and Consumer Brands Rush Into the Virtual World for Their Pots of Gold." *South China Morning Post.* March 12, 2022. https://www.scmp.com/business/companies/article/3170110/metaverse-and-nfts-gucci-starbucks-luxury-and-consumer-brands.

Price, R. Darren. 2016. "Rare Pokemon Sparks Stampede in Central Park." NBC4 New York. July 18, 2016. https://www.nbcnewyork.com/news/local/pokemon-go-players-stampede-new-york-central-park/642115/.

Puthucheary, Janil. 2020. "Speech by Dr Janil Puthucheary, Senior Minister of State for Transport and Communications and Information at The Ministry of Transport's Committee of Supply Debate 2020 on Towards A Future-Ready Land Transport System." Ministry of Transport. March 5, 2020. http://www.mot.gov.sg/news/speeches/Details/speech-by-dr-janil-puthucheary-senior-minister-of-state-for-transport-and-communications-and-information-at-the-ministry-of-transport-s-committee-of-supply-debate-2020-on-towards-a-future-ready-land-transport-system.

Ra, Sungsup, and Zhigang Li. 2018. "Closing the Financing Gap in Asian Infrastructure." ADB South Asia Working Paper Series. ADB South Asia Working Paper Series. Asian Development Bank. https://doi.org/10.22617/WPS189402-2.

Ravinutala, Raghu. 2022. "Into the Metaverse: The Future of Virtual Interactions." *Forbes.* July 11, 2022. https://www.forbes.com/sites/forbestechcouncil/2022/07/11/into-the-metaverse-the-future-of-virtual-interactions/.

Schroders. 2023. "Schroders Global Cities Index." Schroders. February 2023. https://www.schroders.com/en-gb/uk/intermediary/spotlight/global-cities/global-cities-index/.

Shafeeq, Syarafana. 2022. "Number of S'pore Farms Grows Over Past 3 Years, Contributing 1 in 3 Eggs Eaten Here." *The Straits Times*, April 8, 2022. https://www.straitstimes.com/singapore/number-of-spore-farms-grows-over-past-3-years-contributing-1-in-3-eggs-eaten-here.

Silver, Laura, and Aidan Connaughton. 2022. "Partisanship Colors Views of COVID-19 Handling Across Advanced Economies." Pew Research Center. https://www.pewresearch.org/global/2022/08/11/partisanship-colors-views-of-covid-19-handling-across-advanced-economies/.

Singapore Department of Statistics. 2023. "Indicators On Population." Table. https://tablebuilder.singstat.gov.sg/table/TS/M810001.

Sotheby's. 2022. "Sotheby's to Present Landmark Live Evening Auction for Single Lot of 104 CryptoPunk NFTs." Sotheby's. February 8, 2022. https://www.sothebys.com/en/press/sothebys-to-present-landmark-live-evening-auction-for-single-lot-of-104-cryptopunk-nfts.

SSI Schafer. n.d. "SSI Exyz Storage-Retrieval Machine." SSI Schafer. Accessed June 28, 2023. https://www.ssi-schaefer.com/en-th/products/storage/pallet-rack-systems/exyz-storage-retrieval-machine-82532.

Tan, Cheryl. 2022. "Climate Change Impacts Add Urgency to Boosting Food Security, Innovation: Grace Fu." *The Straits Times*, November 13, 2022. https://www.straitstimes.com/singapore/climate-change-impacts-add-urgency-to-boosting-food-security-innovation-grace-fu.

Tan, Wee Kiat. 2016. "Greening Singapore: Imagining and Seeding the Garden City." In *A Chance of a Lifetime: Lee Kuan Yew and the Physical Transformation of Singapore*, by Peter Ho, ed. Centre for Liveables Cities, Lee Kuan Yew Centre for Innovative Cities.

Wong, Lawrence. 2022. "Minister for Finance, Mr Lawrence Wong, Delivered Singapore's FY2022 Budget Statement on 18 Feb 2022." Ministry of Finance. February 18, 2022. https://www.mof.gov.sg/docs/librariesprovider3/budget2022/download/pdf/fy2022_budget_statement.pdf.

Zeitchik, Steven. 2022. "This is What it Feels Like to Attend a Film Festival in the Metaverse." The *Washington Post*. February 4, 2022. https://www.washingtonpost.com/technology/2022/02/04/sundance-metaverse-quest-virtual-reality/.

© 2024 World Scientific Publishing Company
https://doi.org/10.1142/9789811287848_0010

Cultivating Magic: The Discreet Charm of the City Centre

Rafael Martinez, Sara Ann Nicholas & Špela Močnik

CITY CENTRES' PURPOSE, PITFALLS, AND PROSPECTS

Often lauded as the heart and soul of a country, the appeal of the city core has traditionally relied on its provision of a panoply of functions — the palpable dense network of office buildings, for instance, has long-serving market and administrative functions (Hohenberg and Lees 1985; Kotkin 2005). In recent decades, the draw of the city centre has broadened to include socio-cultural amenities ranging from public institutions, transport infrastructures, entertainment and recreational facilities, retail stores, and food and beverage (F&B) outlets. Indeed, the "constant bundle of urban amenities" (Glaeser and Gottlieb 2006, 1288) offered by the city centre has become one of its defining features (Clark *et al.* 2002; Florida 2014; Moos, Pfeiffer, and Vinodrai 2018). Furthermore, planners have increasingly emphasised the use of modern and aesthetically pleasing architecture — sometimes *starchitecture* — to create an iconic image of the city centre as a distinctive and desirable place one should aspire to visit, live, or work in (Godfrey and Gretzel 2016; Speake and Kennedy 2022). The dual features of diverse amenities and attractive architecture have most recently been reiterated by Garvin (2019) as characteristics of vibrant 21st century American downtowns.

Scholars and planners therefore seem to focus on *hardware* — functional elements of the built environment such as amenities and architecture — to explain the allure of the city centre. Yet, city centres across the world have been suffering from a persistent emotional deficit "crisis" where denizens feel disconnected and bereft of meaningful experiences — all despite living in the urban nucleus, the purported heart and soul of a country (Sim 2021). Arguably, the decentralisation of retail, office, and leisure functions over the past decades has contributed greatly to the socio-economic decline of city centres across the world (Thomas and Bromley 2000; Balsas 2007). Thus, many city centres have tried to reinvent themselves and diversify their functions to attract more people, businesses, and tourists. The city centre revitalisation strategies at the end of the 20th century and the beginning of the 21st century aimed to expand the functions beyond the nine-to-five paradigm, with some arguing for the concept of a "24-hour city" which encouraged mixed-uses, the consumption of the evening economy, and a round-the-clock lively atmosphere (Heath 1997), or a more radical approach to transforming the city into a playground (Glaeser and Ratti 2023). Hence, focusing on the intangible and affective — *software* — dimensions of the city centre has gained some traction in city centre planning over the years.

THE PANDEMIC CITY

Fast forward to today, cities have been stricken with yet another crisis: a global pandemic. Because of it, the way we do work has fundamentally, and perhaps permanently, changed. Around half (50.2%) of our survey participants preferred to work from home.[1] The top three reasons they cited were time savings (84.3%), money savings (69.5%), and greater flexibility in terms of organising their work (54.4%). Due to safe-distancing measures, we have spent more time at home and in our immediate neighbourhoods, changed the way we behave as consumers, and engaged with the hospitality industry less than ever before. City centres seem to no longer adequately support the way we live our lives in the post-pandemic world, and vice versa — the way we live our lives can no longer sustain city centres' economies. So, if pre-COVID-19 city centres were already bereft of allure for many of its users, how does the pandemic play into this crisis? It could either worsen it or, as we will argue, provide an opportunity to reimagine and revive our city centres in ways that were unimaginable before.

In the post-COVID-19 world, we will have to envisage more sustainable city centres that offer not only economic incentives, but meaningful experiences, i.e., "more survivable, liveable and enjoyable way(s) of urban or semi-urban life" (Cooke 2021, 11) that will attract a variety of users. Rather than just shopping destinations, office hubs, or recreational hubs (Glaeser and Ratti 2023), they may become cultural and civic gathering places (Florida, Rodríguez-Pose, and Storper 2021). New land uses in the repurposed city centres may include new residential conversions and family-focused attractions (Cooke 2021). The old emphasis on urban-scape (the physical environment) that has been at the heart of the development of city centres, will need to give space to "human-scape" for city centres to remain attractive (Cilliers et al. 2021). "Human-scape" emphasises the human dimension of cities, i.e., cultural and social systems. The post-pandemic urban identity of cities and urban development will be driven by human capital, social issues, and liveability considerations (Cilliers et al. 2021). Human capital represents the human needs that will shape cities in the future instead of the usual economic, technical, and other imperatives that dictated urban development up until now. Now, perhaps more than ever, city dwellers crave meaning and social experiences that can elevate their quality of life in a post-pandemic urban setting. The urban identity of places becomes important as it can provide opportunities for creating meaning and unique experiences, and not just ephemeral leisure activities — gone swiftly without leaving a trace in the landscape of the cities. The reconfigured post-pandemic city centres with strong urban identities that place human capital at their heart can enhance urban living by providing social experiences, spaces to support physical and mental health, and flexible transport modes, among others (Cilliers et al. 2021). In short, future city centres will be shaped by "high-value connection spaces (that) embrace quality of life, deep connections, cultural recharge, and sanctuary" (Cilliers et al. 2021, 8–9).

Evidently, as a result of the pandemic, old wounds of city centres pending irrelevance have deepened, while the importance of paying greater heed to *software* qualities of the city centre has also resurfaced. Such is discernible in Singapore too: Low (2021) believes that in order to safeguard Singapore's Central Business District (CBD) post-pandemic future, the country needs to inject the "density and 24/7 buzz" that places like Kendall Square in Cambridge, Massachusetts have. Echoing these sentiments are views from Singapore's C-Suite executives, who suggest that planners must cultivate exciting and versatile (in)tangible spaces in the CBD to ensure its vibrancy post-pandemic (Wong 2021). Beyond a vibrant city centre, many have also raised exigencies for more human-scaled cities that pay heed to people's experiences, emotions, and attachments to place (Sim 2021; Stott 2021). Moreover, in the Lee Kuan Yew Centre for Innovative Cities (LKYCIC) survey conducted in 2021 titled *Survey on Citizens and the City: Changing Perceptions of Singaporeans* (LKYCIC 2021, see Annex below), it was found that the top four reasons that attract people to Singapore's city centre are leisure and culture (71.7% of participants agreed or strongly agreed with leisure and culture being the reason for attraction), followed by location and accessibility (67.4% of participants agreed or strongly agreed with this reason), ambience (64.5% of participants agreed or strongly agreed with this reason), and the buzz (61.4% of participants agreed or strongly agreed with this reason) (Table 10.1). It becomes apparent then, that focusing solely on the *hardware* of city centres is inadequate to save them, and their *software* needs to be activated. At this point, it is pertinent to emphasise Singapore's ongoing placemaking efforts, which have been taking place in the past few decades (Urban Redevelopment Authority 2021). However, the pandemic has profoundly changed our lives and deepened some pain points existing in the downtown areas. Cities all around the world, including Singapore, have acknowledged the need for bold, innovative solutions to recover from COVID-19 and ensure the city centre's prosperity. This global conversation recognised that the cities would need to adapt in unprecedented and creative ways (Fulton 2021; Hadden Loh and Kim 2021). In cities like Singapore, such adaptation has started to yield favourable results. People are returning to office life while the buzz of streets and public places is gradually coming back.

Table 10.1: Survey on citizens and the city: Changing perceptions of 2000 Singaporeans (2021)

	Strongly agree	Agree	Neutral	Disagree	Strongly disagree
Working	197 (9.8%)	772 (38.6%)	795 (39.8%)	168 (8.4%)	68 (3.4%)
Doing business	226 (11.3%)	772 (38.6%)	690 (34.5%)	234 (11.7%)	78 (3.9%)
Shopping	239 (11.9%)	771 (38.5%)	705 (35.2%)	223 (11.2%)	62 (3.1%)
Ambience	285 (14.2%)	1,006 (50.3%)	551 (27.6%)	114 (5.7%)	44 (2.2%)
Leisure and culture	379 (18.9%)	1,056 (52.8%)	463 (23.1%)	67 (3.4%)	35 (1.8%)
Social	239 (11.9%)	867 (43.4%)	675 (33.8%)	170 (8.5%)	49 (2.4%)
Food	241 (12.1%)	813 (40.6%)	701 (35.0%)	185 (9.2%)	60 (3.0%)
Buzzing	268 (13.4%)	961 (48.0%)	624 (31.2%)	101 (5.0%)	46 (2.3%)
Location and accessibility	310 (15.5%)	1,037 (51.9%)	531 (26.6%)	86 (4.3%)	36 (1.8%)

Source: Authors 2021

Towards these ends, this chapter adopts a software approach to examining Singapore's city centre. By software, we refer to the intangible, affective, and elusive — in contrast with hardware, which comprises the rational and quantifiable built environment features, such as amenities and architecture. Specifically, we explore software through the lens of *magic* to suggest how planners can reconfigure Singapore's city centre post-COVID-19. While city centres have not been strangers to forces and historical changes that have negatively impacted their vibrancy and viability, COVID-19, with its peculiarities and demands, offers an avenue to rethink city centres in a way that was never needed before. Moreover, by adopting the lens of magic, we hope to offer a more nuanced understanding of the city centre that goes beyond conventional approaches in urban studies. We believe that incorporating magic in the post-pandemic city centre can help urban planners reconfigure and reinvigorate it as well as build up its urban identity and create meaningful social experiences for visitors.

It is not our aim to imply that software is more important than hardware. Rather, both elements must work in tandem in order for places to be magical. Yet, because the pandemic has shown that more attention needs to be paid to people's experiences and emotions in a place, we emphasise the software dimensions of the city centre. While providing in-depth blueprints of the post-pandemic city centre is beyond the scope of this chapter, we endeavour to show how magic is a viable means of rethinking the city centre. We start by providing our interpretation of magic, and later discuss three case studies which deliver insights on using magic to plan cities. Thereafter, we suggest how planners might incorporate magic in city centre reconfiguration post-COVID-19 and propose novel solutions applicable to Singapore.

MAGIC OF THE CITY CENTRE

While we acknowledge that defining magic is tricky given its subjective and multi-faceted nature, we propose the following definition for the magic of the city centre: its *genius loci* which defies the ordinary and/or instils a sense of belonging. *Genius loci* denotes the prevailing atmosphere or "spirit of place" (Norberg-Schulz 1980, 18), and is ambiguous and never clearly defined. This atmosphere encompasses the interactions between a place and its users, which imbue the place with meanings that shape its distinctive character (Volgger 2019). In other words, the atmosphere impels one to feel, think, or act in a certain way, and transforms a place into a destination or experience. We posit that the magic of the city centre inheres in its *genius loci*, and it is this very atmosphere that draws people to the city centre.

The *genius loci* we speak of has two strands: it can mean something which defies the ordinary, or it can be something that fosters a sense of belonging. In terms of the former, the magic of the city centre resides in its buzz, dynamism, and unfamiliarity. It is in the city centre where one experiences the hustle and bustle of urban life and its protean nature; where one experiences novel encounters that deviate from the quotidian and banal settings of everyday life; where one feels full of vim and vigour. In terms of the latter, the magic of the city centre lies in its ability to instil a sense of belonging for its users.

As Kotkin (2013) opines, "a city exists for its people", and what people need is a city that "raises sentiments and commitment to a place", a city that inculcates a "sense of home" (16–18). The city centre must therefore be a place one can fall in love with and feel proud to be in (Waldie 2013).

One might argue that the concept of magic is elusive given its inherently abstract nature. Yet, it is precisely because of this quality that magic lends itself as a suitable lens to examine the city centre. Magic is able to describe the ineffable, intangible, and affective dimensions of the city centre, which vitally explain why people are drawn to city centres. Put another way, magic has a profoundness to it that captures the essence of city centres. By using magic as a heuristic tool, urban planners will therefore be able to design a post-pandemic city centre that captivates people, and more importantly, that people love.

A TALE OF THREE PLACES

To demonstrate the enchantment of city centres, we delve into three case studies which offer glimpses into how such magic can be (re)produced. We begin by exploring Mexico City's *Pueblos Mágicos* (Magical Towns), followed by *Kota Tua* (Old Town) in Jakarta and *Tiong Bahru* in Singapore. Though influenced by the idiosyncrasies of each country's history and culture, these case studies provide valuable insights on how we can utilise magic to reconfigure Singapore's city centre. While the sites were examined in the pre-pandemic context, we believe that lessons drawn are germane to present and prospective times.

PUEBLOS MÁGICOS, MEXICO CITY

Although Mexico City is blessed with an impressive number of landmarks, a plethora of tourist attractions, and a thriving arts scene, the bulk of international tourists use Mexico's capital as a hub to reach other destinations. Like some other cities in Latin America, Mexico City has achieved notoriety for its crime and violence (Observatorio Nacional Ciudadano 2021). Year after year, travel advisories worldwide warn their citizens to avoid the city, citing petty crime, violent and non-violent delinquency, and kidnapping (U.S. Department of

State 2022). Added to the aforementioned violence and insecurity is the fact that Mexico City is permanently exposed to natural phenomena. Located in a high seismic risk zone, the Mexican capital experiences earthquakes of unpredictable number and magnitude every year (Tourism Review News Desk 2017). Both natural hazards and social issues have taken a toll on Mexico City, which for years has been lagging in attracting visitors in comparison with other destinations within the country. To reverse the trend, the Government of Mexico City, in partnership with the Ministry of Tourism, thus nominated several boroughs as *Pueblos Mágicos* (Figure 10.1). As its name implies, Magical Towns is a programme meant to promote a series of towns offering visitors special experiences because of their natural beauty, cultural richness, traditions, arts, and cuisine (Secretaría de Turismo, 2020). The *Pueblos Mágicos* are defined as places with great symbolism and legends. Their historical importance has been fundamental for the development of history, and they enhance the national identity in each of its spots.

A few years after being launched, notwithstanding the large amounts the city government spent transforming different picturesque neighbourhoods, the success of Magical Towns in Mexico City in attracting foreign visitors has been rather disappointing. Some have

Figure 10.1: Magical town in Mexico (*Source*: Alvarado 2017)

argued that this failure stemmed from the indifference of international tourism agencies in promoting Mexico City's Magical Towns, which originated in what they perceive as staged authenticity (Gross 2011) of these attractions. Nevertheless, the last few years have seen an impressive increase in the number of local visitors to Mexico City's Magical Towns. In a matter of years, like in other parts of the country, Magical Towns have been some of the most popular weekend getaways for city inhabitants, particularly among younger Mexicans, comprising a large chunk of millennials and Gen Z-ers (Perez-Romero et al. 2021). Furthermore, this success has been confirmed — and to a certain extent perpetuated — by the way these destinations have been memorialised and consumed through social media.

Observing the case of Mexico City, Bernkopf and Nixon (2019) have found that user-generated content (UGC) images from Instagram are more effective at improving destination image than the UGC images reposted by a destination-marketing organisation (DMO). A critical aspect of this content has to do with narratives accompanying images. Narratives, in effect, are most important in terms of their contribution to an improvement in overall destination image, presenting a reusable set of visual features for future work on using annotations in the measurement of visual destination image (Bernkopf and Nixon 2019). Hence, like in other cities around the world, the use of social media and new platforms have led Mexico City's authorities to re-evaluate the city's marketing strategy, redefine targets, and update promotional efforts. And perhaps for the first time in decades, too, by adopting the use of new platforms as well as specific social media tactics to promote campaigns, the government has successfully been able to advertise Mexico City as an attractive weekend tourist destination. The revitalisation and resurgence brought about by the socio-physical rebuilding in Mexico City indeed speak to the resilience of its urban context (Chapter 1).

KOTA TUA, JAKARTA

Despite its importance as the most significant economic and political city of the largest nation in maritime Southeast Asia and in the world's largest island country, the landmarks and spots that could make

Indonesia's vibrant capital Jakarta a tourist magnet are very few. Chaotic, polluted, crowded, prone to severe flooding, and immersed in a virtual permanent gridlock, Jakarta attracts only a marginal number of international tourists each year (Central Bureau of Statistics of Indonesia 2023). Looking to attract tourists, the first and foremost complexity the government of Jakarta faced was the need to provide the city with a long-needed landmark. This is why, in 2015, the Jakarta City administration launched an ambitious programme meant to revitalise the picturesque — although decaying — Jakarta's Old Town, or *Kota Tua*.

The 1.3 km² area known as *Kota Tua* stands today as the core of the colonial-era city of Batavia, a roughly square complex located near Sunda Kelapa, Jakarta's old port, and intersected by the Ciliwung River (Abeyasekere 1987). It is a compact architectural enclave that contains a rich variety of heritage places, such as colonial period buildings, houses and temples showing Chinese Indonesian (*Tionghoa*) influence, Arab–Betawi mosques, and post-independence modernist architecture (Padawangi *et al.* 2016). With most of the historical sites in the area deteriorating, the city government strategy was to set in motion several restoration efforts to include *Kota Tua* as Indonesia's ninth site in the United Nations Educational, Scientific, and Cultural Organisation's (UNESCO) World Heritage List (Raditya, 2015).

For more than three years, the city government, in collaboration with private investors, invested trillions of rupiah into the revitalisation of the district. Yet, after the government first submitted the nomination dossier for *Kota Tua* to UNESCO in 2018, the France-based International Council on Monuments and Sites (ICOMOS) reported that *Kota Tua* lacked "integrity and authenticity" as an old town. According to ICOMOS (2018), the many "unsympathetic intrusions" into the area had "irreversibly changed the visual appearance and skyline of *Kota Tua*". Even though it came as a surprise to few, the failure of *Kota Tua* to be recognised as a UNESCO World Heritage site represented a crushing defeat for the city government in its attempt to transform some areas through heritage and sustainable tourism (The Jakarta Post 2018). Yet, against all odds, soon after *Kota Tua*'s failed bid, the area saw a sudden massive influx of local visitors. Attracted perhaps by the sudden media attention, numerous

Figure 10.2: Fatahillah Square in Kota Tua, Jakarta (*Source*: National Geographic Indonesia 2019)

visitors, especially young men and women, started flocking to *Kota Tua* (ibid). As shown by the numerous photographs geotagging their location as *Kota Tua*, Fatahillah Square (Figure 10.2) is the place to be, especially during the weekends, for the Indonesian youth.

In this open space surrounded by colonial and modernist buildings, all of a sudden, visitors found something unusual in Jakarta: a place to simply stroll through, sit casually in the middle of the square, or on the steps of symbolic buildings in this massive outdoor area. Fatahillah Square is nowadays a meeting point for friends to chat, drink, or eat; enjoy outdoor concerts (Figure 10.3) and buskers; as well as a hotspot for lovebirds to take pre-wedding photos. In a way, the unexpected arrival of massive numbers of young visitors recently experienced by *Kota Tua* could be explained by identifying the social fabric to which Fatahillah Square caters. Unlike many public venues that are able to potentially attract young people in Jakarta, Fatahillah Square does not charge visitors to simply stay and enjoy the place. Yet, this cost-free factor may not be the most important motivation driving throngs of Jakartans to *Kota Tua* every weekend. For many, in

Figure 10.3: A Gathering in Kota Tua for a traditional music concert (*Source*: Authors)

fact, the attractiveness of the square is its always-changing entertainment offerings (e.g., concerts, performances, as well as a place to buy trendy and fashionable gadgets at affordable prices). Thus, for many young Jakartans — especially those from lower- and lower-middle class homes — the appeal of Fatahillah Square and *Kota Tua* comes from concentrating the excitement of always new selections of things within a picturesque compact and convenient space. Thus, within a few years, extended areas of *Kota Tua* have not only left behind the ghostly image of urban abandon and neglect, but have also been transformed into a quintessential environment for Jakartan youths, who see this place massively patronised almost every day of the week by local and city visitors alike, as a vibrant and trendy district. It is in *Kota Tua's* ability to regenerate and reinvent itself that we bear witness to its resilience (see Chapter 1).

TIONG BAHRU, SINGAPORE

Developed by the Singapore Improvement Trust (SIT) in 1936 to tackle a shortage of housing, *Tiong Bahru* is a bastion of Singapore's social and architectural heritage and was awarded conservation status by the Urban Redevelopment Authority (URA) in 2003 (National Heritage Board 2013). In the 1980s, revitalisation efforts saw an influx of younger residents and visitors to the estate, which led to the proliferation of upscale businesses such as art galleries, boutiques, and cafes. Today, owing to its eclectic medley of old, new, local, and foreign elements, the neighbourhood is unlike any other in Singapore, making it popular amongst locals and tourists alike. For many, the appeal of *Tiong Bahru* is in its novelty. This is engendered by various features of the estate, ranging from its hipster stores that exude an "aura of Bohemian authenticity" (Chua and Tan 2014, 11), its unique maze-like configuration, the variegated front doors that pepper its street level, and the back alleys that offer intriguing and spontaneous finds (Figure 10.4). All these and more evoke a sense of curiosity, wonder, and excitement in the neighbourhood, and have especially attracted the attention of a large youthful population. Indeed, Gen Zs and millennials taking "Instagrammable" pictures or couples having their pre-wedding photoshoots are common sights in the estate. *Tiong Bahru* thus boasts a strong social media presence and was dubbed by British Vogue as one of the world's coolest and hippest neighbourhoods (Remsen 2014).

At the same time, *Tiong Bahru*'s attractiveness also lies in its rich history. Under the aegis of the URA, austere conservation measures ensure that the estate's identity, charm, and heritage value are protected (Urban Redevelopment Authority 2019). There, conserved low-rise SIT flats with their unique five-foot ways and spiral staircases serve as a "bank of memories" and invoke a sense of nostalgia for residents (To, Chong, and Chong 2014, 62). The estate's quaint features capture the aesthetics of a bygone age, standing in stark contrast to the lofty and modern skyscrapers of the city centre just a stone's throw away (Figure 10.5). Additionally, traditional hawker stalls and mom-and-pop shops continue to serve the sizeable elderly population that resides in the estate. To visitors and younger residents, the older generation of residents and their personal histories "offer (a) comforting sense of connectedness to the past" (Morgan-Owens and Owens 2016, 134). In all, *Tiong Bahru* tenaciously retains its "traditional character" and a "strong sense of place within the collective consciousness of Singaporeans" (Yeoh and Kong 1995, 113).

Figure 10.4: Interesting finds along Tiong Bahru's Back Alleys (Left: wall mural; Right: makeshift shelving) (Source: Authors 2023)

How *Tiong Bahru* is able to remain so fiercely nostalgic amidst constant developmental pressures speaks to the resilience of its community. Apart from the state's efforts to conserve the estate's built heritage, residents, grassroots organisations, and business owners

Cultivating Magic: The Discreet Charm of the City Centre   289

Figure 10.5: Tiong Bahru's low-rise flats in contrast with the nearby city centre (*Source*: Tiong Bahru Estate n.d.)

actively partake in preserving the neighbourhood's social heritage — its strong community spirit. For instance, both public and private groups such as the *Tiong Bahru* Hawker Association, *Tiong Bahru* Youth Network and *Tiong Bahru* Neighbours, to name a few, tend to the functional needs of the community and build rapport amongst its members through daily interactions and events. These impart an endearing sense of community, pride, and ownership in the neighbourhood, and it is precisely this distinctive village or *kampung* quality which sets *Tiong Bahru* apart from other estates and contributes to its allure (Chua and Tan 2014; To, Chong, and Chong 2014; Morgan-Owens and Owens 2016). Here, we hark back to the axioms raised in the opening chapter: the resilience of *Tiong Bahru*'s community not only safeguards its traditional mores, but also ensures that the neighbourhood can accommodate novel cultures and evolve with the times (Chapter 1). The marriage of old and new, local and global makes *Tiong Bahru* a unique, endearing, and magical place for many.

Hence, from the cases of Mexico, Indonesia, and Singapore, we witness how magic is not necessarily found in the built environment of a place per se, but rather in the interplay between the place and its users (Figure 10.6). The everyday interactions between people and

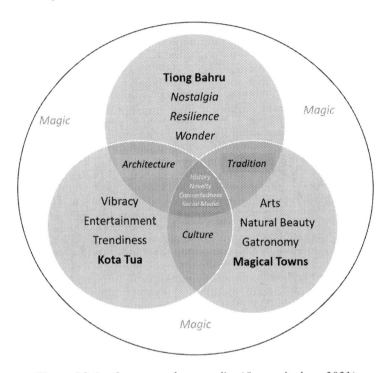

Figure 10.6: Summary of case studies (*Source*: Authors 2021)

people, and between people and place, impart meaning to each place and endow it with a unique *genius loci*. On one hand, this atmosphere offers a deviation from ordinary, everyday life. On the other, it also fosters a sense of attachment and love for the place. It is for these reasons that places like *Pueblos Mágicos*, *Kota Tua*, and *Tiong Bahru* have become destinations that continue to attract visitors. The magic of a place, therefore, relies largely on its *software* rather than (only) *hardware*. Moreover, the case studies have shown that it takes the planned, top-down actions of the state and the organic, bottom-up initiatives driven by the users of a space (Lew 2017) working in tandem to re(produce) magic. How then, can we draw on the lessons offered by the three locales to reconfigure Singapore's city centre through the lens of magic?

PLANNING MAGIC?

As the case studies have shown, the idea of magic, or what could potentially transform a place into something magical, is sometimes difficult to anticipate and hence, to plan for. Even though the motivations of those patronising successful sites could be somewhat different, in the three cases people recognise characteristics that they find inviting and interesting enough to return — those that defy the ordinary and/or instil a sense of belonging. Thus, we contend, magic could be described as an unsuspected potential that places possess, largely derived from an interplay between the place and its users, which creates meanings that shape its distinctive character. Magic in effect refers to an invisible or immaterial form of agency by means of which certain spaces have recognised value through their subjective attributes or legibility. In other words, magically infused spaces do not automatically uplift neighbourhoods as this largely depends on the way the neighbourhood/people interact with it (Jacobs 1992).

One of the most important challenges for cities and decision makers is to secure magic's existence in public spaces. A way to achieve that, we posit, is by ensuring: (1) the ambiguous reading of spaces, and (2) the space's diverse "hinterland" that can support the usage of the space (Jacobs 1992). The magic of the city could draw from individual perceptions, or at times be collectively embraced. In face of this reality, the planners' role is to design spaces, the reading of which is open to multiple interpretations rather than imposing a strict script. Spaces should be designed to accommodate spontaneity and, to a certain extent, unpredictable practices by users. A way to achieve this, we suggest, is by designing or allowing spaces to be used or interpreted as multipurpose. This is precisely why, rather than thinking of creating new spaces, emphasis should be given to highlight existing spaces, meanings, and interpretations of which can be cultivated anew. Such spaces can already contain some inherently or potentially attractive characteristics (e.g., green areas, bodies of water, historical landmarks, or aesthetically unique environments) which can help bring about magicality, but they are not the only prerequisite and cannot guarantee magic in isolation. Spaces' diverse "hinterlands" can importantly contribute to their potential magicality. Namely, spaces tend to garner popularity, usage, and emotional attachment from people if there is enough diversity in the immediate surroundings — economic and social diversity that can supply a constant flow of different users with different schedules (Jacobs 1992) that inject life into the space at any time of the day. Any space that is surrounded with the "functional monotony of surroundings in any form" (Jacobs 1992) will be devoid of users for at least some time in the day, which in turn strips it of life, and thus the potential for magic.

Although magic is something intangible, unpredictable, and ambiguous, and for some even sacred[2], the acknowledgement of it as a potential — and sometimes already ongoing reality — should be considered in the design and planning process of cities, especially after COVID-19. Such acknowledgement will allow spaces to be more relatable and connected with people, while simultaneously working as a spatially imbued rationale meant to restore economic viability to a given area by appealing to emotions or memories. But magic should not be exclusively seen as an instrument to ensure the hustle and bustle of spaces within the city. It should also be connected to peaceful spaces, or perhaps more accurately, oases of silence right in the middle of cities (Chua 2021). During the pandemic, the city centre's user values and needs have been transforming. People's work-life patterns, usage of the built and natural environments, and liveability considerations have changed. The urban space in "ghost towns" (i.e., post-pandemic city centres) will need to be sustainably and innovatively repurposed (Cooke 2021). Magic will play an important role in reinventing and rejuvenating spaces. Where, then, can this magic be cultivated? We propose that the magic of the city centre exists in the everyday, nondescript spaces that are often overlooked. These include micro public spaces (Ng 2021), interstitial spaces (Stott 2021), and what Whyte (2010) terms the "leftovers, niches, odds and ends" that inadvertently come to be good urban spaces. Also pertinent is Kotkin's (2013, 14) notion of sacred spaces, or places that make one feel "an irrational commitment to a place". It is in these spaces, as we shall find out in the next section, that one finds intimacy, wonder, comfort, and respite, in brief, the magic of the city centre.

THE MAGIC OF SPATIAL COMPENSATION

Attempts at identifying and anticipating the magic of spaces are not new in Singapore's CBD. An example of this is the illumination of landmarks with colourful artworks and projections in the "Light to Night Festival" or as part of the National Day celebrations (Ang 2021) (Figure 10.7). As this demonstrates, sustaining the magic of some spaces should also be framed within a pragmatic view — it has to accept the unmodifiable physical reality of terrain (i.e., the design and architectural features as well as the history attached to it). On the other hand, those features also entail acknowledgement of the inherent complexities of these spaces, freeing up potential ambiguous interpretations and unpredictable readings of them. This is confirmed, for instance, by the abundance of surveillance systems, e.g., Closed-Circuit Televisions (CCTVs), as well as a wide range of temporary and permanent hostile architectural interventions and alterations to existing buildings.

In addition to the aforementioned conditions are frameworks and regulations stringently imposed on any intended form of transformation. In Singapore, developers and architects proposing works within conservation areas are required to comply with the conservation guidelines that apply to such areas like the CBD. These guidelines are applied in varying degrees to the different groups of conservation areas, taking into consideration their historical significance, the context of the surrounding developments, and the long-term planning intention for each area. Consequently, any kind of alteration within conservation areas is required to comply with strict planning parameters and restoration guidelines for conserved building typologies, as well as planning parameters and envelope control guidelines for new buildings within conservation areas (Urban Redevelopment Authority 2021). Along these lines, we propose the concept of spatial compensation.

294 The City Rebooted: Networks, Connectivity and Place Identities in Singapore

Figure 10.7: Light to night festival in Singapore (*Source*: Authors; Chan Heng Chee 2022)

In general, spatial compensation works as a mitigation mechanism by which planning- and design-originated miscalculations in public spaces like the above described, could be reduced, or attenuated. But unlike other forms of mitigation[3], spatial compensation does not aim at achieving a permanent transformation of space. In fact, its value resides in the fact that it addresses problems without permanently transforming spaces or places. Based upon the principle of transitoriness, spatial compensation could be found around temporary interventions. In Singapore, for instance, temporary interventions have been meant to attract walkers by transforming and enlivening some streets through highly "Instagrammable" installations (e.g., the Bras Basah–Bugis corridor) (National Heritage Board 2022). Therefore, to pique the sense of magic in space is not simply a matter of providing a place to sit, socialise, or just be idle. To accommodate or boost magic, however, temporary interventions should not only be meant to attract people or passers-by but arouse their surprise and sense of rediscovered attachment to a particular place.

Magic's unique, inviting, and emotionally relatable nature arises largely from people's ability to find the unexpected, counterbalancing daily life's predictability with an element of randomness. Temporary interventions like pop-up parks can restore a sense of surprise and unpredictability to rigidly planned areas (Andres *et al.* 2021; Martinez Almoyna Gual 2021). Simple, cost-effective, and relatively easy to implement, these interventions are an attractive solution for any unutilised, or underused plots of land, such as parking lots or vacant lands, both private- and state-owned, in this premium land area. Made with planter boxes and movable furniture, pop-up parks represent an alternative for areas where urban growth leaves little room for conventional green spaces and even oases of silence within bustling urban areas. Placing such parks into areas that are surrounded with rich "hinterlands" will allow for a constant flow of visitors at any time of the day, who would make the park lively and inviting. Furthermore, people will be attracted to use the park if they interpret it as multipurpose and able to accommodate their various activities. These temporary venues, too, constitute one possible means to help meet the demands of urbanites for more opportunities to connect with nature otherwise only available in their neighbourhoods (Ecological Society of America 2019). In addition, small green spaces like temporary parks and impromptu or planned community gatherings (e.g., farmers' markets) confer a wide variety of social benefits. Some studies, for example, have found that these spaces bring opportunities for social interactions which, in turn, result in physical and psychological restoration, reductions in computer, cell phone, and television "screen time", and more overall time spent outdoors (Mata *et al.* 2019).

Increasingly, researchers demonstrate that spaces, places, and landscapes are the outcome of numerous social activities. The production of these spaces is dynamic and highly challenged as well as permeated by cultural beliefs while being marked by social differences. As scholars have argued, "… in the course of generating new meanings and decoding existing ones, people construct spaces, places, landscapes, regions, and environments … they construct geographies" (Anderson and Gale 1992, 4). A way in which geographies can be constructed is through social media. Like in the cases of Mexico City, Jakarta, and Singapore, social media helps to produce and endlessly curate the narratives granting or withdrawing the halo of magic, before taking it to another place. In recent years, social media and influencers have been a driving force, finding "magic" in different places. This has been achieved, first, by using different spaces as idyllic backgrounds for the reproduction of standardised photographic poses and almost ritualised actions; and second, by transforming such actions into arguably mandatory performances. Failure to do so will result in, quoting social media lingo, individuals falling into a potential Fear of Missing Out (FOMO) situation. Hence, as the case studies show, urban youths play an instrumental role in the production of magic — however fleetingly it might be — through social media. Through these platforms, young people manage to supplement and embellish narratives describing spaces, sometimes randomly chosen, with curated images capable of arousing interest, emotions, and even marvel.

As we have shown, magic's *genius loci* denotes the spirit of the place, which is the result of interactions between people and people,

people and spaces, as well as spaces and spaces. By the latter, we mean connections or networks between different streets and spaces that together form the fabric of the city centre. Just like "no man is an island", spaces can rarely exist or succeed on their own either. The city centre's streets and spaces must become like microscale neighbourhoods without well-defined boundaries that overlap and interweave, to form the visual, economic, and social variety for users to enjoy (Jacobs 1992). Post-pandemic city centres should strive to reconfigure their existing spaces and streets into such a fabric, where users with various interests and different backgrounds can always find something for themselves. Spaces that offer different experiences or invoke different feelings each time one visits them hold the promise of possibilities. The possibility defies the ordinary and invokes magicality.

CONCLUSION

It is pertinent to ask whether magic in a space could expire. Magic, we contend, is not permanent. Magic of spaces is not immune to changes in the surrounding environment or the city. Also, it will not escape unscathed by fads or generational changes. By constantly adopting new practices and forms of spatial interaction, new generations do not only put under stress the magic of spaces. They also lead planners to revisit Whyte's (2010) and others', for decades, unmovable principles in the design of public spaces. Spaces, including potentially magical ones, are increasingly competing with new forms of socialisation with virtual spaces that different technologies make increasingly real. Hence, a crucial way to sustain magic is by acknowledging the importance of young people.

Acknowledging the role of young people entails recognising magic as a dynamic force capable of transforming, sometimes ephemerally, spaces a priori innocuous. Put differently, magic might not necessarily be static; it could be transient or mobile. Such mobile character is largely enabled by different technologies, including social media. These platforms can transform spaces into abodes of magic overnight. In other words, social media can act as a catalyst to help intertwine *hardware* and *software* and, as a result, liberate the discreet charm of magic in city centres.

Overall, this chapter has elucidated how magic can be used to reconfigure Singapore's city centre post-pandemic. If the pandemic has taught us anything, it is that the human-scape is indispensable to how we live and where we live. Now, more than ever, there is a need to emphasise the software of city centres — their abilities to captivate users and foster love for place — rather than solely looking at built and functional elements. Notwithstanding the destruction it has brought in its wake, the pandemic has afforded us a fighting chance to rebuild our city centres better. Quoting Jacobs (1992), "Dull, inert cities, it is true, do contain the seeds of their own destruction and little else. But lively, diverse, intense cities contain the seeds of their own regeneration, with energy enough to carry over for problems and needs outside themselves." By cultivating magic in our city centres, we can put them on the mend — it is as simple and as hard as it sounds.

Annex

LKYCIC conducted a survey in February 2021, with the aims of understanding how work, play, and life are changing in Singapore as a result of the COVID-19 pandemic. The survey was developed by the LKYCIC research team and run by online survey platform Rakuten Insight.

The survey was conducted online in English with 2,000 adults aged 18 years and older living in Singapore (Table A). Respondents comprised primarily of Singapore Citizens/Permanent Residents (97%) working in various industries. Other respondents included S Pass/Work Permit holders (2%) and Employment Pass holders (1%). The bulk of respondents worked in the services industry (75%), followed by manufacturing (13%), construction (12%), and others (1%).

The first portion of the survey comprised questions related to perceptions of COVID-related risks in public spaces (the workplace, food and shopping spaces, and public transport). Respondents were asked about their comfort levels, concerns, and opinions on countermeasures in these spaces. The second segment focused on the workplace. Questions asked related to commuting behaviours, accessibility to offices, and work preferences (e.g., working from home or working from the office). Subsequently, respondents were asked about their shopping and leisure behaviours, and questions covered the same categories — commuting behaviours, accessibility, and preferences (e.g., online shopping or physical shopping; outdoor leisure activities or ICT-based leisure activities). In the penultimate section, respondents were asked about their perceptions of Singapore's city centre, as well as what attracts them to the city centre. Finally, questions on well-being were included to assess the respondents' leisure, job, and life satisfaction.

Table 10.2: Demographic table
Survey on Citizens and the City: Changing Perceptions by Singaporeans (2021)

	Frequency	Percentage (nearest %)
Gender		
Female	1000	50
Male	1000	50
Age		
18–24 yo	143	7
25–34 yo	518	26
35–44 yo	491	25
45–54 yo	478	24
55–65 yo	327	16
66 yo and above	43	2
Resident Status		
Singapore Citizen/PR	1930	97
Employment Pass	31	2
S Pass/Work Permit	36	2
Others	3	0
Employment		
Full-time	1,881	94
Part-time	119	6
Job Industry		
Manufacturing	260	13
Construction	170	9
Services	1,498	75
Others	72	4
Monthly Household Income		
No income–<$5,000	592	30
$5,000–$9,999	724	36
$10,000–$14,999	396	20
$15,000 and above	288	14

(*Continued*)

Table 10.2: (*Continued*)

	Frequency	Percentage (nearest %)
Education		
No formal schooling	4	0
Primary school	4	0
Secondary school	156	8
Post-secondary school (non-tertiary)	119	6
Polytechnic diploma	360	18
Professional qualification and other diploma	280	14
Bachelor's and above	1,077	54

Source: Authors 2023

ENDNOTES

1. Refer to the Annex for survey details and methodology.
2. Offering comfort and respite, the magic that some find in oases of silence in busy and noisy districts could be compared to what others identify with sacredness. Hence, like magic, the production of sacred space has been connected with narratives (Schääuble 2011) or the embedment of different ideological narratives (Feldman 2008).
3. Mitigation is commonly used as a tactic to address environmental problems. In the context of climate change, for instance, mitigation has been an effective tool as it helps to address issues that cannot be solved by making them less severe or reducing further damage (Klein, Schipper, and Desai 2005).

REFERENCES

Abeyasekere, Susan. 1987. *Jakarta: A History*. Oxford University Press, 1987.

Alvarado, Luis. *Street of Tlaquepaque*. 2017. Photograph. https://www.shutterstock.com/image-photo/guadalajara-jalisco-mexico-november-23-2017-772099840?irclickid=y2O09DxnRxyPTlzygDUDWXhtUkF2yYXaW153zg0&irgwc=1.

Anderson, Kay, and Fay Gale, eds. 1992. *Inventing Places: Studies in Cultural Geography*. Longman Cheshire; Wiley, Halsted Press.

Andres, Lauren, John R. Bryson, and Paul Moawad. 2021. "Temporary Urbanisms as Policy Alternatives to Enhance Health and Well-Being in the Post-Pandemic City." *Current Environmental Health Reports* 8 (2): 167–176. https://doi.org/10.1007/s40572-021-00314-8.

Ang, Qing. 2021. "7 Landmarks in Bras Basah–Bugis Turn Red and White for National Day." *The Straits Times.* August 1, 2021. https://www.straitstimes.com/singapore/7-landmarks-in-bras-basah-bugis-turn-red-and-white-for-national-day.

Balsas, Carlos J. L. 2007. "City Centre Revitalization in Portugal: A Study of Lisbon and Porto." *Journal of Urban Design* 12 (2): 231–259. https://doi.org/10.1080/13574800701306328.

Badan Pusat Statistik Provinsi DKI Jakarta. 2020. "Kunjungan Wisatawan Mancanegara Yang Datang Ke DKI Jakarta Dan Indonesia 2020-2022." Badan Pusat Statistik Republik Indonesia. 2023. https://jakarta.bps.go.id/indicator/16/241/1/kunjungan-wisatawan-mancanegara-yang-datang-ke-dki-jakarta-dan-indonesia.html.

Bernkopf, Denis, and Lyndon Nixon. 2019. "The Impact of Visual Social Media on the Projected Image of a Destination: The Case of Mexico City on Instagram." In *Information and Communication Technologies in Tourism 2019*, Juho Pesonen and Julia Neidhardt, eds., 145–157. Cham: Springer International Publishing, 2019. https://doi.org/10.1007/978-3-030-05940-8_12.

Chua, Mui Hoong. 2021. "Quiet Zones Will Make Singapore a More Appealing Global City." *The Straits Times.* July 23, 2021. https://www.straitstimes.com/opinion/quiet-zones-will-make-singapore-a-more-appealing-global-city.

Chua Yi, Jonathan, and Sherman Tan. 2014. "The Rise of 'Hipster' Culture in Singapore: Spatial Transformation in Tiong Bahru." National University of Singapore (NUS): Migration Cluster, Asia Research Institute (ARI) & Faculty of Arts and Social Sciences (FASS). 2014.

Cilliers, Elizelle Juanee, Shankar Sankaran, Gillian Armstrong, Sandeep Mathur, and Mano Nugapitiya. 2021. "From Urban-Scape to Human-Scape: COVID-19 Trends That Will Shape Future City Centres." *Land* 10 (10): 1038. https://doi.org/10.3390/land10101038.

Clark, Terry Nichols, Richard Lloyd, Kenneth K. Wong, and Pushpam Jain. "Amenities Drive Urban Growth." *Journal of Urban Affairs* 24 (5): 493–515. https://doi.org/10.1111/1467-9906.00134.

Cooke, Philip. 2021. "After the Contagion. Ghost City Centres: Closed 'Smart' or Open Greener?" *Sustainability* 13 (6): 3071. https://doi.org/10.3390/su13063071.

Ecological Society of America. 2019. "Pop-up Parks Deliver Big Benefits in Small Spaces." ScienceDaily, June 3, 2019. https://www.sciencedaily.com/releases/2019/06/190603124547.htm.

Feldman, Allen. 2008. *Formations of Violence: The Narrative of the Body and Political Terror in Northern Ireland*. University of Chicago Press.

Florida, Richard. 2014. "The Creative Class and Economic Development." *Economic Development Quarterly* 28 (3): 196–205. https://doi.org/10.1177/0891242414541693.

Florida, Richard, Andrés Rodríguez-Pose, and Michael Storper. 2021. "Critical Commentary: Cities in a Post-COVID World." *Urban Studies* 60 (8): 1509–1531. https://doi.org/10.1177/00420980211018072.

Fulton, William. 2021. "6 Post-Pandemic Predictions About How Cities Will Be Different Going Forward." Rice University, Kinder Institute for Urban Research. March 14, 2021. https://kinder.rice.edu/urbanedge/6-post-pandemic-predictions-about-how-cities-will-be-different-going-forward.

Garvin, Alexander. 2019. *The Heart of the City: Creating Vibrant Downtowns for a New Century*. Island Press.

Glaeser, Edward L., and Joshua D. Gottlieb. 2006. "Urban Resurgence and the Consumer City." *Urban Studies* 43 (8): 1275–1299. https://doi.org/10.1080/00420980600775683.

Glaeser, Edward L., and Carlo Ratti. 2023. "Opinion | 26 Empire State Buildings Could Fit Into New York's Empty Office Space. That's a Sign." *The New York Times*, May 10, 2023, sec. Opinion. https://www.nytimes.com/interactive/2023/05/10/opinion/nyc-office-vacancy-playground-city.html.

Godfrey, Andria, and Ulrike Gretzel. 2016. "The Use of Modern Architecture in City Marketing." *Travel and Tourism Research Association: Advancing Tourism Research Globally*. August 8, 2016. https://scholarworks.umass.edu/ttra/2010/Visual/33.

Gross, Toomas. 2011. "Divided Over Tourism: Zapotec Responses to Mexico's 'Magical Villages Program'." *Anthropological Notebooks* 17 (3): 51–71.

Hadden Loh, Tracy, and Joanne Kim. 2021. "To Recover from COVID-19, Downtowns Must Adapt." Brookings. 2021. https://www.brookings.edu/articles/to-recover-from-covid-19-downtowns-must-adapt/.

Heath, Tim. 1997. "The Twenty-Four Hour City Concept — A Review of Initiatives in British Cities." *Journal of Urban Design* 2 (2): 193–204. https://doi.org/10.1080/13574809708724404.

Hohenberg, Paul M., and Lynn Hollen Lees. 1985. *The Making of Urban Europe, 1000–1950*. Harvard Studies in Urban History Harvard University Press.

ICOMOS. 2018. "Evaluations of Nominations of Cultural and Mixed Properties." ICOMOS Report for the World Heritage Committee. UNESCO, June 24, 2018. https://www.icomos.org/images/DOCUMENTS/World_Heritage/Volumes_Evaluation/ICOMOS_Evalauation_Volume_WHList_2018_EN.pdf.

Jacobs, Jane. 1992. *The Death and Life of Great American Cities.* Vintage Books ed. Vintage Books.

Klein, Richard J.T., E. Lisa F. Schipper, and Suraje Dessai. 2005. "Integrating Mitigation and Adaptation into Climate and Development Policy: Three Research Questions." *Environmental Science & Policy* 8 (6): 579–588. https://doi.org/10.1016/j.envsci.2005.06.010.

Kotkin, Joel. 2005. *The City: A Global History.* Modern Library Chronicles Modern Library.

Kotkin, Joel. 2013. "What is a City For?" Working Paper. Working Paper Series No. 1. Lee Kuan Yew Centre for Innovative Cities.

Lew, Alan A. 2017. "Tourism Planning and Place Making: Place-Making or Placemaking?" *Tourism Geographies* 19 (3): 448–466. https://doi.org/10.1080/14616688.2017.1282007.

LKYCIC. 2021. *Survey on Citizens and the City: Changing Perceptions of Singaporeans.* Lee Kuan Yew Centre for Innovative Cities.

Low, Jeng-tek. 2021. "How Gen Z Can Save the CBD and Business Parks." *The Straits Times.* September 6, 2021. https://www.straitstimes.com/opinion/how-gen-z-can-save-the-cbd-and-business-parks.

Martinez Almoyna Gual, Carlos. 2021. "Appropriation, Interaction and Conflict in Temporary Public Space." Te Herenga Waka-Victoria University of Wellington. Conference contribution. https://doi.org/10.25455/wgtn.15185865.v2, https://doi.org/10.25455/WGTN.15185865.V2.

Mata, Luis, Georgia E Garrard, Fiona Fidler, Christopher D Ives, Cecily Maller, Joab Wilson, Freya Thomas, and Sarah A Bekessy. 2019. "Punching Above Their Weight: The Ecological and Social Benefits of Pop-up Parks." *Frontiers in Ecology and the Environment* 17 (6): 341–347. https://doi.org/10.1002/fee.2060.

Moos, Markus, Deirdre Pfeiffer, and Tara Vinodrai, eds. *The Millennial City: Trends, Implications, and Prospects for Urban Planning and Policy.* Global Urban Studies. Abingdon, Oxon: Routledge, 2018.

Morgan-Owens, Jessie, and James Owens. 2016. "'Neighbors': A Tiong Bahru Series." In *Contemporary Arts as Political Practice in Singapore*, by Wernmei Yong Ade and Lim Lee Ching, eds. Palgrave Macmillan. https://doi.org/10.1057/978-1-137-57344-5.

National Geographic Indonesia. 2019. "Bingung Tujuan Liburan di Jakarta, Coba Yuk Berkunjung ke Kota Tua Saat Malam Hari. Dijamin Bikin Ketagihan!" *National Geographic*. 2019. https://nationalgeographic.grid.id/read/131774665/bingung-tujuan-liburan-di-jakarta-coba-yuk-berkunjung-ke-kota-tua-saat-malam-hari-dijamin-bikin-ketagihan.

National Heritage Board. 2013. "Tiong Bahru Heritage Trail." National Heritage Board. 2013. https://www.nhb.gov.sg/~/media/nhb/files/places/trails/tiong%20bahru/tiongbahru%20(1).pdf.

National Heritage Board. 2022. "Welcome to Bras Basah.Bugis." National Heritage Board. 2022. https://www.nhb.gov.sg/brasbasahbugis/who-we-are/welcome-to-bras-basah-bugis.

Ng, Michelle. 2021. "Time to Rethink City Planning as S'pore Prepares to Live with COVID-19." *The Straits Times*. July 19, 2021. https://www.straitstimes.com/opinion/time-to-rethink-city-planning-as-spore-prepares-to-live-with-covid-19.

Norberg-Schulz, Christian. 1980. *Genius Loci: Towards a Phenomenology of Architecture*. Rizzoli, 1980.

Observatorio Nacional Ciudadano. 2021. "Reporte Trimestral Sobre Incidencia Delictiva En El Estado de México Primer Semestre de 2021." Observatorio Nacional Ciudadano. 2021. https://onc.org.mx/public/rednacionaldeobservatorios/public/onc_site/uploads/ReporteEdomex1s2021.pdf.

Padawangi, Rita, Miya Irawati, Titin Fatimah, and Theresia Budi. 2016. "Vernacular City Kota Tua: Cultural Identity in Everyday Urban Heritage: Final Report." UNESCO Jakarta. February 2016. https://unesdoc.unesco.org/ark:/48223/pf0000247906.

Raditya, Margi. 2015. "What to Know About UNESCO Heritage Sites in Indonesia." *The Jakarta Post*. July 4, 2015. https://www.thejakartapost.com/news/2015/07/04/what-know-about-unesco-heritage-sites-indonesia.html.

Remsen, Nick. 2014. "Global Street Style Report: Mapping Out the 15 Coolest Neighborhoods in the World." *Vogue*. September 5, 2014. https://www.vogue.com/slideshow/fifteen-coolest-street-style-neighborhoods.

Schäauble. 2011. "How History Takes Place: Sacralized Landscapes in the Croatian-Bosnian Border Region." *History and Memory* 23 (1): 23. https://doi.org/10.2979/histmemo.23.1.23.

ScienceDaily. "Pop-up Parks Deliver Big Benefits in Small Spaces." Accessed June 28, 2023. https://www.sciencedaily.com/releases/2019/06/190603124547.htm.

Secretaría de Turismo. 2020. "Pueblos Mágicos de México." 2020. http://www.gob.mx/sectur/articulos/pueblos-magicos-206528.

Sim, Joshua. 2021. "Sensing the City." 2021. https://www.ura.gov.sg/Corporate/Resources/Ideas-and-Trends/Sensing-the-City.

Speake, Janet, and Victoria Kennedy. 2022. "Changing Aesthetics and the Affluent Elite in Urban Tourism Place Making." *Tourism Geographies*, 24 (6–7): 1197–1218. https://doi.org/10.1080/14616688.2019.1674368.

Stott, Michael. 2021. "The Role of Placemaking and Tactical Urbanism in the Post-COVID City." Urban Redevelopment Authority. June 4, 2021. https://www.ura.gov.sg/Corporate/Resources/Ideas-and-Trends/Role-of-placemaking-tactical-urbanism.

The Jakarta Post. 2015. "Puppeteers Strive to Attract Youth." *The Jakarta Post*. September 13, 2015. https://www.thejakartapost.com/news/2015/09/13/puppeteers-strive-attract-youth.html.

The Jakarta Post. 2018. "Kota Tua: Slowly Lost in Time." *The Jakarta Post*. 2018. https://www.thejakartapost.com/academia/2018/07/07/slowly-lost-in-time.html.

Thomas, Colin J., and Rosemary D. F. Bromley. 2000. "City-Centre Revitalisation: Problems of Fragmentation and Fear in the Evening and Night-Time City." *Urban Studies* 37 (8): 1403–1429. https://doi.org/10.1080/00420980020080181.

To, Kien, Zhuo Wen Chong, and Keng Hua Chong. 2014. "Identity of a Conserved Housing Estate: The Case of Tiong Bahru, Singapore." *International Association for the Study of Traditional Environments Traditional Dwellings and Settlements Working Paper Series, IASTE Working Paper Series* 254 (2014): 50–72. https://www.academia.edu/23753060/Identity_of_a_Conserved_Housing_Estate_The_Case_of_Tiong_Bahru_Singapore.

Tourism Review News Desk. 2017. "Tourism in Mexican States Harmed by Earthquakes." *Tourism Review News*. October 30, 2017. https://www.tourism-review.com/earthquake-in-mexican-states-destroyed-tourism-news10352.

Urban Redevelopment Authority. 2019. "Tiong Bahru: Do It Right. A Quick Guide on Works to Conserved Tiong Bahru Pre-War Units." Urban Redevelopment Authority. 2019. https://www.ura.gov.sg/-/media/User%20Defined/Conservation%20Portal/Guidelines/Pre-war-SIT-Flats-in-Tiong-Bahru-Conservation-Area.pdf?la=en.

———. 2021. "Evolution of URA's Placemaking Journey." Urban Redevelopment Authority. 2021. https://www.ura.gov.sg/Corporate/

Get-Involved/Shape-A-Distinctive-City/Placemaking-and-Partnership/Evolution-placemaking-journey.

U.S. Department of State. 2022. "Mexico Travel Advisory." U.S. Department of State. 2022. https://travel.state.gov/content/travel/en/travel advisories/traveladvisories/mexico-travel-advisory.html.

Volgger, Michael. 2019. "Staging Genius Loci: Atmospheric Interventions in Tourism Destinations." In *Atmospheric Turn in Culture and Tourism: Place, Design and Process Impacts on Customer Behaviour, Marketing and Branding*, by Volgger Michael and Dieter Pfister, eds. Vol. 16. Emerald Publishing Limited, 2019.

Waldie, Donald J. 2013. "Falling in Love With Where You Are." Newgeography. 2013. https://www.newgeography.com/content/003763-falling-in-love-with-where-you-are.

Whyte, William Hollingsworth. 2010. *The Social Life of Small Urban Spaces*. 7. print. Project for Public Spaces.

Wong, Valerie. 2021. "CBD Reimagined and Repurposed." *The Business Times*. July 26, 2021. https://www.businesstimes.com.sg/views-from-the-top/cbd-reimagined-and-repurposed.

Yeoh, Brenda, and Lily Kong. 1995. "Place-Making: Collective Representations of Social Life and the Built-Environment in Tiong Bahru." In *Portraits of Places: History, Community and Identity in Singapore*, by Brenda Yeoh and Lily Kong, eds., 88–115. Singapore: Times Editions, 1995.

© 2024 World Scientific Publishing Company
https://doi.org/10.1142/9789811287848_bmatter

Epilogue

Chan Heng Chee & Rafael Martinez

This collection of essays on the socio-spatial reconfiguration of the city is timely to address some long-standing questions about how to make cities work efficiently and more meaningfully for the people, and to address future challenges. Our team of writers came together at a time when urban leaders and urban scholars everywhere were spurred to rethink the city after the pandemic struck, inspired by their contagious energy. There was an urgency in the air. Clearly, there is a need to respond and improve the urban structures from a health and economic perspective, but it is also a great opportunity to rethink, transform, and redesign the urban project.

Singapore is widely recognised as a well-designed city, a pacesetter in recognising and finding solutions to new emerging issues in urbanisation. We were early in the game to come to grips with the issue of inclusion and equity in urban housing, tackling climate change in a resource-poor environment, managing mobility and congestion, greening the city and yet developing a lively buzzy urban core. Solutions can always be improved and must be refurbished to keep up with technology change and changing demands and expectations of the population.

What we tried to do in the essays was to examine what was done in the past to address specific enduring questions but also to look ahead and address contemporary and future issues. Chan Heng Chee and Špela Močnik launched the discussion on the theme by examining cities that responded to crises, both health and terrorism crises, and the road to recovery they took to jumpstart the economy, crucial questions confronting every country today. But this is now a more complex time because of geopolitical tensions piling on climate and environmental concerns and inflation. Senior Minister Tharman Shanmugaratnam coined the moniker "The Perfect Long Storm" which we should bear in mind in thinking of the future.

Winston Yap and Sara Ann Nicholas questioned if the city centre was hollowing out but concluded that it was not, but the character of the city was changing. The digital economy was taking over. The Digital Economy by Dinithi Jayasekara and Fredrik Hansson examine what an ecosystem for the digital economy means and some urban design considerations that would appeal to these young innovators. Sam Conrad Joyce and Nazim Ibrahim examined the push to rethink the future of the office and addressed future hybrid formats. Harvey Neo and Li Bayi reinvestigated the old question of whether polycentres work in Singapore, and how to think about polycentres, while Samuel Chng analysed the new phenomenon of cloud kitchens that have sprung up, strengthened by the pandemic, which clearly have implications for urban design in considering hospitality and retail.

The section on Sustaining the Magic of the City contains three essays which consider the age-old question about cities, if cities are losing their appeal, how to sustain the magic of the city, and how to make the city centre more loveable and liveable. How do city nooks and corners and structures become adopted as "sacred spaces" by the people? The photo essay by Felicity Chan, Emma Goh, Li Bayi and Joy Choi provides a poignant snapshot of a moment in time, a shared memory by everyone in the city of Singapore during the COVID-19 lockdown. It is an interlude to remind us of why we are rethinking our city. The Magic of Modernity points to the old formula of modernity that Singapore pursued, focusing on building good infrastructure and making things work. It highlights what the Singapore government got right and what it is trying now to push as modernity today must embrace sustainability and smart. The essay peeks into what the metaverse could mean for the city state. Finally, in redesigning the city centre, Rafael Martinez, Sara Ann Nicholas and Špela Močnik examine small intimate spaces, small interventions which are people-centric, and open spaces, pop-up spaces instantly designed by people, that "cultivate magic" and are critically important for successful placemaking.

A common touch point of these essays is the need to enhance social capital insofar as it is either an enabler of, or a virtuous outcome of, urban developmental processes. Social capital is a term identified most with Roger Putnam and James Coleman, but increasingly the French sociologist Pierre Bourdieu is mentioned along with the two names. Francis Fukuyama and his concept of trust as social capital has been widely adopted too. Urbanologists and urban planners will remember that in the 1960s, Jane Jacobs extolled the importance of designing for neighbourliness in the big, modern city to differentiate safe neighbourhoods from unsafe ones. Putnam acknowledges Jacobs as "one of the inventors" of the concept.

With social capital's frequent usage, there are many definitions, and they are sometimes seemingly contradictory. Social capital is viewed as a multidimensional phenomenon encompassing a stock of shared norms, values, trust, obligations, relationships, and interactions that facilitate cooperation and collective action for mutual and community benefit. It is about building social connections and social networks. Social capital is considered an asset in building communities and nations, and is as important as physical capital. In fact, it is argued by Putnam, Fukuyama, and Bourdieu that social capital explains strong economies and competitiveness. For Fukuyama, the economic function of social capital is to reduce the transaction costs associated with formal mechanisms such as contracts, hierarchies, and rules. Beyond the economic realm, social capital is also imperative in forging a sustained sense of identity and building trust that lasts in communities.

Singapore political leaders emphasise trust and social cohesion as important elements to build a functioning society. It is often said Singapore must not lose its social cohesion if it is to do well. And more recently, MIT computer scientist Alex Pentland's research empirically confirmed the value of social interactions and social capital in generating ideas and innovation.

Social capital is well valued and the need to create social capital, design for social capital is sought after by social scientists, policymakers, and planners. It has to be pointed out that the understanding of social capital is quite sophisticated. Everyone is aware of the dark side of social capital, which can create hostility and alienation, and too much in-group thinking. Finding the balance is crucial.

Since Putnam, Coleman, Bourdieu, and Fukuyama's books and papers have been published, behaviour has further changed with new technology. Pentland takes this into account. Social capital is typically understood as a resource that emerges from social connections, relationships, and networks. However, in increasingly individualistic societies, like those of which will soon be led by Generation Z (hereafter referred to as Gen Z), social relations could also be based on loose arrangements emerging from benefits and advantages envisaged by individuals rather than groups.

Gen Z refers to the cohort of individuals who have grown up at a time characterised by rapid technological advancements, increased access to information, and significant shifts in social values. While it is important to note that individuals within Gen Z can exhibit diverse characteristics and values, some trends can be observed in relation to individualism and its impact on this generation. These aspects include:

- Tech-savvy: Gen Z has grown up in a highly connected world, surrounded by social media platforms, smartphones, and instant access to information. This digital fluency has fostered individualistic tendencies as people curate their online personas, engage in self-expression through various digital platforms, and prioritise personal online interactions.
- Embracing individuality: Gen Z tends to place strong emphasis on personal identity, self-expression, and individuality. They often seek to define themselves based on their unique qualities and interests. This can be seen in their fashion choices, online presence, and the desire to stand out from the crowd.

Although individualism is prevalent among Gen Z, it doesn't necessarily mean collective values or community-oriented behaviours are completely rejected. Many individuals within this generation recognise the importance of collaboration, teamwork, and collective efforts to bring about positive change. However, unlike relations framed perhaps within traditional views, social capital for Gen Z — and perhaps future generations — could also be seen from the point of view of individuals who, seeking leverage for personal gain, could transform this form of capital into opportunistic ventures. That might be done by establishing transient social capital relations.

First and foremost, different people might use transient social capital relations as an instrument to address, supplement, or complement deficiencies in their daily lives. Thus, transient relations would be the outcome of tactical and strategic decisions made by people not necessarily permanently connected to each other. Transient social relations are in effect commonly based on multiple collaborations among unrelated people. Rather than being oriented towards a common good, these collaborations originate in application of opportunistically driven decisions developed within the framework of politics of individual benefit. Hence, the emergence of transient relations or expressions of quasi social capital will always depend on the extent to which the value of the collaborators enacting them remains.

Transient social capital draws from an individual agenda or the affiliation of numerous individual agendas. This results in ad hoc social capital relations. Ad hoc social relations work as spaces of permanent experimentation and negotiations which, based upon a trial-and-error approach and the calculated management of risks, guarantees opportunities and benefits to those involved. Consequently, transient social capital relations aim at compensating for or offsetting the risks and other negative outcomes of precarious or uncertain conditions faced by people, always safeguarding their most precious attribute and strategic resource, i.e., their individuality.

It is clear that transient social capital is a new developing phenomenon but also another way to look at social capital. In the established usage, social capital is there as a stock. We can talk of differentiation, but this differentiation which we have identified is real and important. The question is whether transient social capital is illusory or substantive and a basis to build on and harnessed for good or positive outcomes. Does this transient social capital or connections disappear like smoke, filling the room then clearing out? How is transient social capital absorbed into the larger stock of social capital, or is it an increasingly significant element to be reckoned with and understood for its effects? Does it necessarily mean that transient social capital, unlike conventional social capital, cannot forge a sustained sense of identity? That is the subject of another study, and we invite other social scientists interested in this concept. to research and investigate further.

Our essays seek to relate their inquiry and analyses to the theme of creating social capital, remembering in the last few years due to the pandemic lockdown that social capital could be lost or depleted. There are some recommendations modestly put forward. In any case, to help generate and stimulate the growth of social capital by people's interactions with urban design or with our urban assets is the unspoken mission of all planners and architects and the political leaders who develop the city and country. The allegiance to place, the emotional attachment to the place, is the best appreciation citizens can return to the city.

© 2024 World Scientific Publishing Company
https://doi.org/10.1142/9789811287848_bmatter

Index

7/7 bombings, 15
9/11 attack, 13
24-hour city, 276
1991 Master Plan, 166

A

activity-based work (ABW) model, 134–135
agent-based model, 140–142
alternative workplace models, 134–135
Amazon, 200–201
antifragile work, 115–120
application programming interface (API), 41
area licensing system (ALS), 251
artificial intelligence (AI), 71, 261
ASEAN Smart Cities Network (ASCN), 262
Asian Development Bank, 262
autonomous vehicles (AVs), 252

B

Basar, Shumon, 107
Batty, Michael, 243
Bidadari Housing Estate, 251
bid-rent model, 43
Bris, Arturo, 257
build-to-order (BTO), 58, 74

Bureau of Foreign Trade, 12
business recovery grants (BRG), 14
business-to-business (B2B), 93

C

Campanella, Thomas J., 6
Carroll, Lewis, 215
Cassarani, Leo, 206
cathode-ray tube (CRT), 114
Central Business District (CBD), 23, 36, 58, 246–247, 278
Chan Cheow Hoe, 261
Chase, J., 215
China–United States, 66
Christaller's Central Place Theory, 163
cities post-crisis, 7–8
city centres, 36–37, 55–57, 275–301
Civic District, 36
Clegg, Nick, 267
closed-circuit televisions (CCTVs), 293
cloud kitchens, 185–207
CloudKitchens, 186
cloud stores, 185–207
Clubhouse model, 134
clustering, 148–149
clustering coefficient, 137

315

committee on the future economy (CFE), 259
communication, 131–133
communication methods, 123–126
connectivity, 167–177
coronavirus, 220
Coupland, Douglas, 107
COVID-19, 3, 5, 19–22, 44–45, 54–55, 66, 107–109, 115–118, 132–134, 164, 227–228, 231, 256–258, 267, 278
Crawford, M., 215
cross-border privacy rules (CBPR) system, 89

D
dark grocers, 198
dark kitchens, 185
dark stores, 198
data embassy, 90
data localisation, 89
data protectionism, 89
degree centrality, 137–138
destination-marketing organisation (DMO), 283
Development Bank of Singapore (DBS), 265
digital economic partnership agreement (DEPA), 70
digital economy, 66–71, 258
digital economy agreements (DEAs), 70, 91, 262
digital economy and society index (DESI), 75
digital economy framework for action, 66
digital ecosystem, 81–87
digital government, 258
digital inclusivity, 95–96, 261

digital leadership, 82
digital mailbox, 77
digital society, 258
digital solutions, 261
digital transformation, 71–75
diversity ratio, 147–148
donut effect, 35
Draft New Official Plan, 178

E
earthquake, 107–108
e-commerce, 201
economic structure of city centre, 39
e-Estonia, 78–81
electronic pricing system (ERP), 251
e-lobby concept, 74
engineered obscurity, 200
environmental social governance (ESG), 265

F
fear of missing out (FOMO), 296
five-year building programme, 246
fixed seating, 146
Florida, Richard, 4, 84, 243
food aggregators, 187
food and grocery delivery, 186–188
foodpanda, 205
food security, 254–255

G
Gates, Bill, 264
Generation Z, 84, 312–313
genius loci, 280, 290, 296
Geographic Information Sciences (GIS), 40

Index 317

ghost kitchens, 185
gig economy, 91
Glaeser, Edward, 4
global innovation index, 72
global knowledge economy, 38–39
global supply chains, 92–94
"Go Digital" programme, 74
"goldilocks" solutions, 134–135
GrabKitchen, 195
great resignation, 110, 120
gross domestic product (GDP), 246

H
Hall, Edward T., 140
Hidalgo, Anne, 4
Horizon Workrooms, 263–264
Housing Development Board (HDB), 58, 73, 85, 246
hub-and-spoke model, 134, 194
human-scape, 277
hybrid working, 140–144

I
individual planning areas, 45
industrialisation, 119
industry composition, 50–54, 56–57
inflow and outflow of firms, 54–55
Infocomm Media Development Authority (IMDA), 66
information and communications technology (ICT) industry, 67
Infrastructure Asia, 262
Inland Revenue Authority of Singapore (IRAS), 77
Institute for Management Development-Singapore University of Technology and Design (IMD-SUTD) Smart City Index, 256–257
integrated land use system (ILUS), 257
international communication campaign, 10–11
International Council on Monuments and Sites (ICOMOS), 284
International Monetary Fund (IMF), 66
International Tax Competitive Index, 80
Internet of Things (IoT), 71
intra-team engagement, 154

J
Jacobs, Jane, 298
Jiak, 221–225
Jobs, Steve, 132
Jones Lang LaSalle (JLL), 56
Jurong Innovation District (JID), 259
Jurong Town Council (JTC), 259

K
Kaliski, J., 215
Katz, Bruce, 4
kill zone, 91
K-Nearest-Neighbour-30 (KNN-30) algorithm, 42
Kota Tua, 283–286

L
Land Acquisition Act, 247
Land Transport Authority (LTA), 252
Land Transport Master Plan 2040, 254

Lee Kuan Yew, 38, 85, 244, 247
Lee Kuan Yew Centre for Innovative Cities (LKYCIC), 56, 278, 299–301
Liu Thai Ker, 242
local area network (LAN), 114
logistical space, 201–202
logistical-urban frontier, 200
London, 15
London Bombings Relief Charitable Fund (LBRCF), 16

M
manufacturing, 258–263
MapBox, 41
metaverse city, 263–264
metaverses, 264–266
Microsoft's Mesh, 264
Ministry of Economic Affairs (MOEA), 12
Mitchell, William, 108
modernity, 242–269
Moreno, Carlos, 4
multinational corporations (MNCs), 36

N
National Centre for Infectious Diseases, 9
National Computerisation Plan, 257
National IT Plan, 257
National Parks Board, 248
Net Zero emissions, 252
NEWater, 250
"New Normal" office, 115–118
New York City, 13
non-fungible tokens (NFTs), 266

O
Obrist, Hans Ulrich, 107
office networks, 136–140
office rentals, 47–48
office transactions, 48–50
once-only principle, 79
online food delivery services, 187–188
Organisation for Economic Co-operation and Development (OECD), 67

P
pandemic city, 276–280
Paris, 16–17
Park Connector Network (PCN), 86
PayNow, 65
People's Action Party, 246
physical office, 55–56
polycentricity, 163–182
Port of Singapore Authority (PSA), 93
Prime Location Public Housing (PLH) scheme, 58
Propst, Robert, 113
Pueblos Mágicos, 281–283

R
Real Estate Information System (REALIS), 397
Rebel Foods, 205
regional centres, 164–181
regionalism, 25
remote working, 130
rentals, 46–47
residential recovering grants (RRG), 14
Rodriguez-Pose, Andres, 243

S

SAIC Motor, 92
Sassen, Saskia, 40
severe acute respiratory syndrome (SARS), 8–10
shortest path length, 137
Singapore, 7–10, 22, 35, 65, 72–75, 165–166, 189–194, 244–245
Singapore Food Agency (SFA), 254
Singapore Improvement Trust (SIT), 286
Singapore Personal Access, 70
Sky Greens, 255
small and medium enterprises (SMEs), 188
small businesses, 19
Smart City Kitchens, 196
Smart City Observatory, 84
Smart Nation and Digital Government Group's (SNDGG), 261
Smart Nation initiative, 65
Smart Nation Singapore, 66, 255–257
social capital, 311
social deficit, 24
social distancing, 223
social interactions, 131–134
social networks, 136–140
spatial compensation, 293–297
"spatially sticky" concept, 179
standardised epidemic control system, 11–13
Storper, Micheal, 243
strategic development incentive (SDI), 58
sustainability, 249
sustainability-green digital infrastructure, 94–95
sustainable development goals (SDGs), 249
Swedish digital economy, 75–78

T

Taipei, 11–13
Tan Wee Kiat, 247
Taylorism, 119
Tee Yih Jia Food Manufacturing, 259
TiffinLabs, 191
Tiong Bahru, 286–290
trade-offs, 151–154
transient social capital, 313
transport networks, 167–177
travel patterns, 167–177

U

urban agglomeration economies and clusters, 39–40
urban disasters, 20
urban farming, 254–255
urbanism, 213–240
urban land markets, 43–45
Urban Redevelopment Authority (URA) 1991 Concept Plan, 166, 180–181, 397
urban resilience, 6
urban spatial structure, 39, 41–42
urban transport management, 251–254
user-generated content (UGC), 283

V

vacancy rates, 45–46
vaccination, 219

Vale, Lawrence J., 6
vehicle quota system, 251
venture-backed start-ups, 87–88
very high-capacity network (VHCN), 75
"virtual" tools, 108
von Thünen's Ring Theory, 163

W
walk cycle ride (WCR), 252

water, 250–251
WeWork, 117
Whyte, William Hollingsworth, 113, 297
work-from-office (WFO), 134
working from home (WFH), 23, 109, 120, 125–126, 156

Z
Zoom, 108, 123–124

Index 319

S
SAIC Motor, 92
Sassen, Saskia, 40
severe acute respiratory syndrome (SARS), 8–10
shortest path length, 137
Singapore, 7–10, 22, 35, 65, 72–75, 165–166, 189–194, 244–245
Singapore Food Agency (SFA), 254
Singapore Improvement Trust (SIT), 286
Singapore Personal Access, 70
Sky Greens, 255
small and medium enterprises (SMEs), 188
small businesses, 19
Smart City Kitchens, 196
Smart City Observatory, 84
Smart Nation and Digital Government Group's (SNDGG), 261
Smart Nation initiative, 65
Smart Nation Singapore, 66, 255–257
social capital, 311
social deficit, 24
social distancing, 223
social interactions, 131–134
social networks, 136–140
spatial compensation, 293–297
"spatially sticky" concept, 179
standardised epidemic control system, 11–13
Storper, Micheal, 243
strategic development incentive (SDI), 58
sustainability, 249
sustainability-green digital infrastructure, 94–95
sustainable development goals (SDGs), 249
Swedish digital economy, 75–78

T
Taipei, 11–13
Tan Wee Kiat, 247
Taylorism, 119
Tee Yih Jia Food Manufacturing, 259
TiffinLabs, 191
Tiong Bahru, 286–290
trade-offs, 151–154
transient social capital, 313
transport networks, 167–177
travel patterns, 167–177

U
urban agglomeration economies and clusters, 39–40
urban disasters, 20
urban farming, 254–255
urbanism, 213–240
urban land markets, 43–45
Urban Redevelopment Authority (URA) 1991 Concept Plan, 166, 180–181, 397
urban resilience, 6
urban spatial structure, 39, 41–42
urban transport management, 251–254
user-generated content (UGC), 283

V
vacancy rates, 45–46
vaccination, 219

Vale, Lawrence J., 6
vehicle quota system, 251
venture-backed start-ups, 87–88
very high-capacity network (VHCN), 75
"virtual" tools, 108
von Thünen's Ring Theory, 163

W
walk cycle ride (WCR), 252

water, 250–251
WeWork, 117
Whyte, William Hollingsworth, 113, 297
work-from-office (WFO), 134
working from home (WFH), 23, 109, 120, 125–126, 156

Z
Zoom, 108, 123–124

Printed in the United States
by Baker & Taylor Publisher Services